The American Presidency
Under Siege

SUNY Series on the Presidency:
Contemporary Issues

John Kenneth White, Editor

The American Presidency Under Siege

Gary L. Rose

State University of New York Press

Cover design by Melanie Macquarrie

Published by
State University of New York Press, Albany

© 1997 State University of New York

All rights reserved

Printed in the United States of America

For information, address State University of New York Press, State University Plaza, Albany, N.Y. 12246

Production by Diane Ganeles
Marketing by Nancy Farrell

Library of Congress Cataloging-in-Publication Data

Rose, Gary L., 1951–
      The American presidency under siege / Gary L. Rose.
          p.   cm.   —   (SUNY series on the presidency)
      Includes bibliographical references and index.
      ISBN 0-7914-3337-4.   —   ISBN 0-7914-3338-2 (pbk.)
      1. Presidents—United States.   2. Political leadership—United
States.   I. Series: SUNY series in the presidency.
JK516.R497   1997
352.23′0973—dc21   96-48608
                                                                CIP

10   9   8   7   6   5   4   3   2   1

For Laurie, Garrison, and Meredith

Contents

Acknowledgments

For permission to reprint material from their publications, I am grateful to the following publishers and authors:

Benjamin I. Page and Mark P. Petracca, *The American Presidency* (New York: McGraw Hill, 1983), concentric circle model of presidential/bureaucratic relations, p. 205.

Center for the Study of the Presidency, publisher of *Presidential Studies Quarterly,* for permission to reprint Table 1 from Leon Halpert, "Presidential Leadership in Congress: Evaluating President Reagan's Success in the House of Representatives," *Presidential Studies Quarterly* 21, fall 1991, p. 722.

The Brookings Institution and Joel D. Aberbach for permission to reprint the table documenting the rise of congressional oversight in Joel D. Aberbach, *Keeping a Watchful Eye* (Washington, D.C.: The Brookings Institution, 1990), p. 35. Copyright © 1990 by the Brookings Institution.

W. W. Norton & Company, for permission to reprint material from Theodore J. Lowi and Benjamin Ginsberg, *American Government: Freedom and Power* (New York: W. W. Norton & Company, 1990), p. 552.

The Center for Responsive Politics, for permission to reprint the bar graph documenting the rise of PAC money from Larry Makinson, *The Price of Admission: Campaign Spending in the 1992 Elections* (Washington, D.C.: Center for Responsive Politics, 1993), p. 14.

Preface

My father died in the winter of 1988. In the early spring, my brother and I began the task of cleaning out the basement of my parents' home where now only my mother lives. Our first major chore was to disassemble a very old and somewhat dilapidated workbench that had been constructed from scrap lumber. I started the job by firmly swinging a large sledge hammer onto one section of the bench, hoping to break the lumber into transportable pieces. After a few hard blows, a section of the bench collapsed onto the concrete floor.

We could not help but notice a rectangular piece of plywood with lettering on one side that tumbled onto the pile. Apparently this piece of wood had been nailed to the underside of the bench as a supportive crosspiece. I picked up the piece of plywood and turned it to read the colored lettering. There, in faded colors, were the words "Vote For Kennedy."

I was astonished, for this was a sign that I had designed during the 1960 presidential campaign. I was in fourth grade then, and I had nailed the sign to a large oak tree in our front yard. I had become a Kennedy supporter after traveling to the New Haven Town Green in a Democratic Party motorcade to see JFK during one of his campaign stops on his way to the presidency. I was no more than thirty feet from the speaker's platform, and I will never forget how radiant and dynamic Kennedy was. Even as a young boy, I found his words stirring. I couldn't wait to return home and build that sign.

Eight presidential elections have been conducted since 1960. As I drove through my hometown during the 1992 campaign, I could not help but notice the absence of handmade signs on the trees of front lawns. Indeed, I haven't noticed such signs for many years now. It is quite evident that something unfortunate has happened which has drained the spirit from presidential campaigns. A general feeling seems to have emerged among the electorate that presidential campaigns are primarily a routine exercise in politics, rather than a "coming to power" of a new national leader. School children appear less enthusiastic about the prospects of a new president, and the American electorate, as expressed by low voter turnout, seems only remotely interested in the outcome of the presidential contest.

While some might identify the shortcomings of the modern presidential campaign as resulting in an apathetic or even alienated electorate, the root of the problem lies much deeper. It is my contention that the current inability of recent presidential candidates to touch the hearts and souls of the American people, in a fashion similar to that of Jack Kennedy, is due primarily to the dramatic and unfortunate decline in presidential power over the course of the past twenty-five years.

The enthusiasm that the American people exhibited towards campaigns of the past was due in large part to the fact that election outcomes often resulted in meaningful and, at times, profound change in the direction of public policy. Campaign promises were more likely to be fulfilled because the presidency was a more powerful and strategically positioned instrument of government. While a fourth grader's handmade sign nailed to an oak tree might have represented an emotional and unsophisticated attraction to the style and charisma of a dynamic presidential candidate, such youthful enthusiasm, perhaps on a subconscious level, was rooted in the belief that presidents could make a difference for America's future.

Precisely why the modern presidency has evolved into an institution incapable of creative leadership is the focus of this book. It examines what has become a major dilemma for American government—a weak and very constrained American presidency.

Throughout the pages of this work, I depict the modern American presidency as an institution in a state of siege—surrounded, bombarded and blocked by a multitude of unfriendly forces including special interest groups, lobbyists, PACs, iron triangles, issue networks, a viperous mass media, an oversized federal bureaucracy and a reactionary Congress. Such systemic forces, I argue, have combined to undermine, sabotage and thwart creative presidential leadership. It is my position that practically all of our recent presidents, regardless of party affiliation, character or charisma, have been unfairly savaged by the political forces which now control the political process inside the Washington Beltway. This new style of American politics, which inherently impedes national leadership, is largely a post-Watergate phenomenon.

In addition to documenting a besieged presidency, I also explain why the American political system has become so fundamentally hostile and unconducive to creative presidential leadership. Here I identify the decline of the American political party system as the root cause of the problem. I realize this is a very familiar story for political scientists. For many of today's college students, however, the discussion is often revealing and enlightening. As the power and role of political parties have declined within the context of American politics, new forces have emerged which have fundamentally inhibited presidential leadership. In the absence of a powerful party system, the American presidency has become isolated, estranged and vulnerable to defeat—in essence, under siege. The failed Carter presidency, and the governing problems that have been encountered by President Clinton, provide the reader with concrete lessons concerning the deleterious consequences that emerge from a political process marked by weak political parties.

In addition to describing and explaining the besieged state of the presidency, I endorse a series of proposals, offered primarily by political scientists, that are designed to enhance the governing capacity of the presidency. The restoration of powerful parties and specific legal reforms which provide the president more leverage within the governing process are advocated. Although recent research has discovered elements of party resurgence—most notably in the form of party organizational development, and rising party unity in Congress—such developments, in my view, have not resulted in a closer bond between presidents, the American people and the Congress. I argue that broader and more dramatic party reform is required if the presidency is once again to be strategically positioned to direct and influence the course of government.

The work concludes with a review of the contributions of America's best presidents. My intention in this section is to demonstrate how strong presidents, governing within the context of a healthy party system, have served the interests of the American people. Problematic issues that will inevitably face future presidents are also identified.

I have specifically designed this work as a supplement for undergraduate courses on the American presidency, political parties and American government. It is not intended to be a core text for either subject. It is instead a fairly short work with a distinct point of view. It is an argumentative work. My own experience suggests that thematic supplements are particularly useful for the purposes of book reviews and for stimulating classroom debate. After twenty years of classroom teaching and ten years as a collegiate debate coach, I can state with certainty that students truly appreciate the opportunity to evaluate and argue a political point of view. Accordingly, a classroom exercise designed to stimulate debate can be found in the work's appendix.

No work is ever completed without the advice and encouragement of colleagues and friends. Professor John White of Catholic University routinely offered excellent advice from start to finish. John is a perceptive political scientist, a fine colleague, and a competent coordinator of projects. Professor A. James Reichley, offered keen advice regarding aspects of the original manuscript, particularly during the early and critical stages of writing.

My good friend Melanie Macquarrie was extraordinarily helpful with respect to editorial recommendations. I sincerely thank Melanie for the time and energy she devoted to this project. My work-study student, Kimberly Nugent, requires recognition for her tireless and dedicated research efforts. I was fortunate to work with such a responsible student.

My political science colleague at Sacred Heart University, John Kikoski, continues to be a loyal and helpful colleague. My former departmental secretary, Sandy Keeton, ably tended to the technical details associated with the work's final draft.

The staff at SUNY Press proved once again to be highly professional and efficient. I thank Acquisitions Editor Clay Morgan for his confidence in the project and for guiding the work through the various phases of production. I also extend thanks to Production Editor Diane Ganeles for bringing this work to light in a timely manner.

My family, as always, served as a source of love and support throughout the writing of this book.

CHAPTER ONE

The Modern American Presidency

He traveled from Monticello to Capitol Hill, following the same route as that of Thomas Jefferson in 1801. Following his inauguration, he opened the White House to the American public, reflecting the tradition of the nation's first people's president Andrew Jackson in 1829. In much the same style as that of John F. Kennedy in 1961, his inaugural address echoed themes of generational change and service to country:

> From this joyful mountain top of celebration we hear a call to service in the valley. We have heard the trumpets, we have changed the guard. And now each in our own way, and with God's help, we must answer the call.[1]

On January 20, 1993, at forty-six years of age, William Jefferson Clinton, a "New Democrat" and former five-term governor of Arkansas, became the forty-second president of the United States. The inaugural atmosphere in the nation's capital was exceptionally optimistic, hopeful, and festive. According to some observers, approximately 800,000 persons were in town for the inaugural event. Compared to the inaugurations of Presidents Reagan and Bush, the crowd at Clinton's inauguration was markedly younger (perhaps "thirty something"), more ethnically diverse, and certainly more casual in appearance and demeanor.[2]

A generational transfer of political power had clearly occured; a young Democrat, inspired by the great presidents of the past, now occupied the American presidency. He had a vision for America, an unlimited reservoir of energy, and a clear plan of action. The presidential election of 1992 marked the end of the Reagan Revolution and, in the rich tradition of American politics, an orderly and peaceful transfer of political power had taken place. With Democratic majorities in both chambers of Congress and a centrist Democrat now in the White House, one could not help but sense that a dynamic and perhaps even "great" American presidency was about to commence. There was even talk of yet another "first one-hundred days."

President Clinton Out of the Blocks

At the time of this writing, the Clinton presidency is approximately two years old. It would be unwise and premature for any political scientist or presidential observer to pass judgment upon a presidency so recently launched. It is not unreasonable, however, to evaluate the Clinton record to date and to inquire whether the newly inaugurated president had an impressive start. Examining evidence gathered from January 1993 to January 1995, one is faced with the inescapable fact that the nation's forty-second president, despite legislative majorities in the House of Representatives and the Senate, governs only with great difficulty. The Clinton presidency is far from paralyzed, but it is clear that serious problems exist.

While it is unfair to compare the Clinton honeymoon with the legendary "first one-hundred days" of Franklin Delano Roosevelt, it *is* appropriate to expect modern American presidents—particularly those with legislative majorities—to begin their administrations with an impressive burst of policy accomplishments. At the same time, it is reasonable to expect American public opinion and the media to be highly supportive of the president and his governing efforts. Virtually every American president, regardless of personality and party, has enjoyed a honeymoon as part of the American political tradition.[3]

Unfortunately, the Clinton honeymoon was virtually non-existent. Consider the following data regarding public approval ratings of ten American presidents after approximately one hundred days in office.

As the data show, public support for President Clinton was extraordinarily low by the time he completed his first four months in office. In fact, support for Clinton is the lowest of all presidents included in the survey. Even President Ford, who had already issued his highly controversial pardon of former President Nixon, governed with more public support than President Clinton after his first four months in office.

Equally troubling is the extent to which Clinton's support declined over a four-month period. In February of 1993, 67 percent

Table 1
Presidential Public Approval
Ratings After Four Months

President	% Approval
Truman	92%
Johnson	78%
Eisenhower	74%
Kennedy	74%
Carter	64%
Nixon	62%
Bush	62%
Reagan	59%
Ford	42%
Clinton	36%

Source: *Time*, June 7, 1993. 800 adults polled
for Time/CNN by Yankelovich Partners, Inc.

of persons polled believed President Clinton to be a "strong and decisive leader." By May only 38% of those polled expressed this view.[4] Twenty-nine percentage points is a dramatic decline in public support, coming as it did during the most critical stage of a new presidency.

Leading news magazines and political commentators, all of whom were counting to the one-hundred day mark, were quick to offer insight into what, during such an incredibly short period of time, had become a beleaguered American presidency. A May 1993 issue of *Time* described the disturbing transformation in the attitude of the American public toward the Clinton presidency in the following terms: "Perhaps most distressing for the President, for the first time since the euphoria that greeted his election, a large plurality of Americans think the nation is on the 'wrong track.'"[5] Indeed, even President Clinton admitted in an interview with *Time* that the early stages of his presidency had been difficult and rather unpredictable: "There's a lot I have to learn about this town."[6]

Public perception of President Clinton's performance over the course of approximately one year can be further evaluated by examining the results of public opinion polls conducted from January 1993 through February 1994. Throughout this period, major polling organizations asked approximately one thousand American adults: "Do you approve or disapprove of the way Bill Clinton is handling his job as President?" Results are presented in Table 2.

Table 2
Public Approval Ratings of President Clinton
January 1993—February 1994

	ABC News/ Washington Post	CBS News/ New York Times	Gallup Organization
	% Approval	*% Approval*	*% Approval*
1993			
January	—	—	56%
February	59%	58%	55%
March	—	55%	52%
April	59%	—	55%
May	—	43%	44%
June	45%	42%	40%
July	—	—	43%
August	45%	38%	44%
September	51%	43%	50%
October	—	43%	48%
November	49%	46%	48%
December	58%	51%	53%
1994			
January	59%	48%	55%
February	—	—	53%

Source: The Roper Center at the University of Connecticut, Storrs. Approval ratings for ABC News/Washington Post Poll represent collapsed responses for two categories: "approve strongly" and "approve somewhat." In months during which multiple polls were conducted, the author calculated an average percentage. Blank spaces indicate no polling data available.

The data clearly indicate a struggling Clinton presidency; re-gardless of poll, President Clinton's public approval ratings never once exceeded 59 percent. Indeed, during several months the ratings were often below 50 percent, suggesting considerable displeasure with the president's performance among the American public. Aver-age approval ratings for President Clinton from January 1993 to February 1994 are: 53% (ABC News/Washington Post Poll), 47% (CBS/ N.Y. Times Poll) and 50% (Gallup Poll). The data do not reflect a good first year for the "New Democrat."

While several of President Clinton's major legislative initiatives have passed Congress[7] (an accomplishment frequently overlooked by critics), the fact still remains that the governing process has been a painful and excruciating experience despite legislative success. Although a partisan majority in both chambers of Congress does not guarantee robust presidential leadership, it is certainly fair to expect a season of relatively painless, harmonious and positive interaction between the executive and legislative branches of government.

Consider, for example, three of the president's legislative measures: the economic stimulus package, his first federal budget proposal, and the North American Free Trade Agreement. The measures were "successful" in that each eventually passed Congress. However, Clinton's $16.3 billion stimulus package, targeted primarily to depressed urban areas, was drastically reduced to $4 billion as the result of an uncompromising Republican filibuster in the Senate.

The president's federal budget passed the legislature, but by the slimmest of margins. The House vote was 218 in favor and 216 opposed—quite astonishing in light of the fact that the Democrats enjoyed a 259 to 176 seat margin over the Republicans. In the Senate, where the Democrats held a 56–44 seat margin Bob Kerrey, a Democrat from Nebraska, voted to support the president's budget after a long and soul-searching deliberation. With Kerrey's support, the vote was 50 to 50, thereby allowing Vice President Gore the opportunity to cast the tie-breaking vote in favor of the President's budget. It was a grueling and wrenching process that clearly threatened the legitimacy of the Clinton presidency. On June 30, 1993, the nation watched the Senate floor with great apprehension as Kerrey announced his decision at the eleventh hour:

> President Clinton, if you are watching now as I suspect you are, I will tell you this: I could not and should not cast a vote that brings down your Presidency. You have made mistakes and know it far better than I. But you do not deserve, and America cannot afford, to have you spend the next sixty days quibbling over whether or not we should have this cut or this tax increase. America also cannot afford to have you take the low road of the too easy compromise, or the too early collapse. You have gotten where you are today because you are strong, not because you are weak. Get back on the high road, Mr. President, where you are at your best.[8]

At the same time, significant portions of the president's budget were seriously compromised to the point where it appeared that the congressional version of the federal budget—rather than the president's—actually prevailed. In addition to Senator Kerrey, another chief opponent to the president's proposed budget was yet another Democratic senator, David Boren of Oklahoma. Boren's opposition to the energy tax proved a serious hurdle for President Clinton, resulting in considerable compromise on the part of the White House and Democratic moderates. In its description of the politics of the president's federal budget and the Boren "revolt," a June 1993 issue of *Business Week* characterized the Clinton administration as "apoplectic" over the unforeseen resistance and "political treachery" in Congress.[9]

The North American Free Trade Agreement also passed both chambers of Congress. It was quite clear, however, that the highly controversial agreement secured legislative support only after a series of extraordinary deals between the president and federal legislators. According to some observers, the trading of votes in exchange for pork barrel projects reached unprecedented and obscene proportions. *U.S. News and World Report* described the NAFTA vote in these terms:

> White House operatives are dangling goodies in front of wavering legislators as if there were no tomorrow—and no deficit. A trade center in Texas. A North American Development Bank in California. The administration has even begun negotiating separate deals with Mexico to protect U.S. producers of sugar, citrus and other products, thus appearing to violate the spirit of NAFTA itself. And all this effort is in pursuit of about twenty votes, possibly enough to eke out a victory.[10]

In addition, it was interesting to find President Clinton depending more on the support of Republican congressmen to secure passage of the trade agreement than that of his own "fellow Democrats." The NAFTA vote in the House garnered "yes" votes among 102 Democrats and 132 Republicans, and "no" votes from 156 Democrats and 43 Republicans. Clearly, Republican support was central to Clinton's victory in the House. Partisan loyalty appeared to mean very little during passage of this widely debated trade agreement.

The entire second year of the Clinton presidency was also characterized by a struggling chief executive. Public approval ratings as measured through the Gallup poll were unimpressive. In January 1994, 55 percent of persons polled expressed approval towards the President's performance. Throughout the remainder of 1994, public approval declined in a fairly steady fashion: 52 percent in March, 52 percent in May, 46 percent in July, 40 percent in August, 42 percent in October, and 44 percent in December. In January of 1995, President Clinton's public approval ratings were recorded at 40 percent.[11]

A Systemic Explanation

While it is expedient and fashionable to attribute President Clinton's difficulties to his legislative skills (as many political opponents have done), or to the fact that he came to power with only 43 percent of the popular vote (hardly an impressive popular mandate), or what some consider a lack of "moral authority" on the part of the president, a penetrating look at the power of the modern presidency and the political environment in which it functions suggests a broader and more systemic explanation. Indeed, the presidency and, more generally, politics "inside the Beltway" have been so radically transformed in recent decades that virtually any American president—regardless of ideology, party affiliation, and political style—will encounter unimaginable hurdles within the context of the governing process. The problem lies not with the offical occupant of the Oval Office (although one cannot discount personality characteristics, philosophy of power, or legislative ability), but more importantly, with the larger system of politics and governance that has evolved over the course of the past twenty-five years.

Although some may disagree with this perspective, the evidence does not suggest any dearth of talent among individuals who have sought the American presidency, or among those who have been elected to serve as president. In fact, recent American presidents have been men of considerable distinction. Bill Clinton was five-term governor of Arkansas prior to seeking the presidency. He is a Rhodes Scholar rated by his political peers as one of the nation's most creative, intelligent and dynamic state governors. Clinton's political credentials are clearly impressive. Yet he governs the nation with great difficulty.

George Bush became president having what could arguably be called one of the most impressive political resumes in American history. Bush served as vice president for two terms under Ronald Reagan, was former director of the Central Intelligence Agency, ambassador to China, chairman of the Republican National Committee, and a former United States congressman. He had far more national decision-making experience than Franklin D. Roosevelt or Abraham Lincoln prior to being elected president. Yet the Bush presidency, particularly in the realm of domestic policy-making, was for all intents and purposes immobilized. Defeated in his bid for reelection by Bill Clinton, President Bush left office with a mere 39 percent public approval rating despite the collapse of communism during his presidency and the swift and decisive military victory attained in Operation Desert Storm.

Ronald Reagan was a former two-term governor from the state of California, which, with 30 million inhabitants, is the nation's most populated and culturally diverse state. California also has the highest standard of living and the highest level of productivity in the world. (If California was a separate nation, it would rank sixth among all nations with respect to gross domestic product.)[12] In addition to his involvement in California politics, Ronald Reagan served as a principal spokesman for American conservatism throughout the 1960s and ran unsuccessfully for the presidency in 1968 and 1976. Prior to becoming active in politics, he was a moderately known movie actor and narrator for Wagon Train, a popular television western. Ronald Reagan, in other words, was almost a household name. However, despite his extensive political credentials, and despite the fact that he was reelected to a second term by an electoral college landslide over Walter Mondale (525–13), the Reagan agenda (termed "the Reagan Revolution") was never realized. Embraced to a great degree by a significant portion of the American population,[13] it was victimized by a political system which inherently impedes creative and dynamic presidential leadership. In the words of presidential scholar Louis W. Koenig: "Like other change-minded Presidents, Reagan ran afoul of the system's powerful sentinels who monitor and constrain presidential initiatives."[14] In Koenig's view, the Reagan presidency was compromised by a political system and process that thwarts effective presidential leadership.

Consider, for example, the Reagan legislative record in the U.S. House of Representatives during his two terms in office.

As the data indicate, President Reagan's legislative success declined precipitously from 74.6% in 1981 to 32% in 1988. The eight-year average indicates that Reagan lost more legislative initiatives in the House of Representatives than he won. Even in 1985, in the immediate aftermath of his huge reelection landslide, Reagan won only 48.3 percent of his legislative measures. Leon Halpert, the author of this study, concludes: "The modern presidency is marked by a narrow 'window of opportunity' when it comes to experiencing success on roll call voting issues in the House."[15] Halpert's conclusion is certainly quite grim: the governing process has evolved to the point where American presidents have at best a short-lived "window of opportunity" in which to enact their policy agenda. Needless to say, the president needs more time than this.

David Stockman, President Reagan's Director of the Office of Management and Budget, confirmed how rapidly the President's

Table 3
House Support Score for President Reagan by Year

Reagan's Position	1981	1982	1983	1984	Year 1985	1986	1987	1988	Average
Won	74.6	54.9	43.6	45.2	48.3	29.8	34.7	32	44.9
Lost	25.4	45.2	54.8	54.8	51.7	71.2	65.3	68	55.1
Total	100	100	100	100	100	100	100	100	100
N=	(71)	(73)	(56)	(73)	(60)	(57)	(75)	(101)	(566)

Source: Leon Halpert "Presidential Leadership of Congress: Evaluating President Reagan's Success in the House of Representatives" *Presidential Studies Quarterly*, vol. XXI (fall 1991): 722. Reprinted with permission by the Center for the Study of the Presidency

legislative honeymoon disintegrated. Stockman noted: "By October 1981, political reality had nearly overtaken the Reagan Revolution."[16] Stockman, who resigned from the Reagan administration due to disillusionment with the policy-making process and the sacrifice of ideals to raw politics, cynically titled his insightful book *The Triumph of Politics.*

In fact, evidence continues to mount suggesting that even this short-lived "window of opportunity" is dissolving for newly elected presidents. In addition to the governing difficulties encountered by President Clinton during his first year in office, consider the evidence pertaining to the Bush presidency. Among the legislative roll calls conducted in 1989 in which President Bush staked a clear position, the President prevailed only 62.6 percent of the time. This was the lowest level of legislative success for any newly elected American President since 1953, the year in which the legislative success measure was first introduced.[17] Although not as vast as the Reagan landslide in 1984, Bush's victory in the electoral college was decisive, comprising 426 electoral votes to Dukakis' 112.

The decline of presidential leadership in recent years has been the topic of extensive discussion among numerous political scientists, historians, journalists and political practitioners. Rather than describe the American presidency in powerful or "imperial" terms, as Arthur Schlesinger, Jr. did in his classic work *The Imperial Presidency*,[18] writers are now prone to underscoring the weakness of the the presidency as a governing institution. Deep concern over the inability of presidents to effectively wield power is a recurring theme throughout the literature regarding presidential politics. Quite often, writers identify the nature of the political system as the principal factor behind the disturbing pattern of failed presidencies.

Forrest McDonald, one of the nation's preeminent American historians, states: "The presidency is often described as the most powerful office in the world. That is the stuff of nonsense. Power is the capacity to do things, to cause one's will to be transformed into action, and by that criterion the president has precious little power." [19]

Theodore C. Sorensen, a former Special Counsel to President Kennedy and author of several works on the American presidency, describes the troubled state of presidential leadership in these terms: "Each of the new presidents took office in a glow of enthusiasm and with a pledge of new solutions. Both the Congress and the opposition vowed cooperation. But each time, the glow faded, cooperation gave way to confrontation, the new solutions sank into confusion and newly shattered hopes swelled the tide of public cynicism." [20]

Richard E. Neustadt, professor of Government at Harvard University whose seminal work on the American presidency essentially redefined the meaning of presidential power, views presidential authority this way: "Weakness is still what I see: weakness in the sense of a great gap between what is expected of a man (or someday woman) and assured capacity to carry through. Expectations rise and clerkly tasks increase, while prospects for sustained support from any quarter worsen as foreign alliances loosen and political parties wane." [21]

Robert Shogan, a highly regarded Washington correspondent for the *Los Angeles Times*, reflects upon recent and failed presidencies: "Their combined experience suggests that the chronic failings of the presidency overshadow differences in the characteristics of our presidents." [22] According to Shogan, the persistent pattern of presidential failure clearly points to problems rooted deep within the context of the American political system.

Political scientist and presidency scholar, Michael A. Genovese, also attributes the failure of recent presidents to systemic variables: "A variety of built-in roadblocks create an immunity system against leadership in all but the most extraordinary of times (i.e., crisis)." [23]

Indeed, recent developments within this system, rather than the ability or character of the presidential incumbent, seem to be at the heart of presidential failure. Until meaningful reform aimed at the larger system of politics and governance in which presidents must function is accomplished, the country seems destined to witness one failed presidency after another. This is not a Bill Clinton, George Bush or Ronald Reagan phenomenon. Instead, the problem is deeply embedded in the new character of American politics that has emerged over the course of the last twenty-five years.

New developments within the political system have routinely victimized presidencies other than those of Clinton, Bush and Reagan. In 1968, President Lyndon Baines Johnson, a man possessing extraordinary legislative skills and advocating one of the most ambitious domestic agendas in the history of the United States (including the Civil Rights Act of 1964, the Voting Rights Act of 1965 and the War On Poverty), chose not to seek a second term in office.[24] Due largely to Johnson's handling of the Vietnam War, his presidency had been deemed ineffective and untrustworthy by the American people. Johnson was elected in 1964 by amassing an enormous 486 electoral votes to Barry Goldwater's 52.

Following a landslide reelection victory in 1972, the presidency of Richard M. Nixon became embroiled in the Watergate scandal. Despite outstanding foreign policy diplomacy, including the establishment of diplomatic relations with mainland China, and detente with the Soviet Union, as well as several domestic accomplishments, including environmental and occupational safety legislation,[25] President Nixon was forced to resign from office in disgrace—the first president in American history to do so.

Following Gerald Ford's interim presidency, which in many ways was tarnished—perhaps even immobilized—as a result of Ford's connection with Nixon, America experienced yet another failed presidency: that of former Georgia governor Jimmy Carter. Carter, possibly one of the most fair-minded, ethical and decent individuals ever to occupy the Oval Office, was denied reelection as the result of a very weak economy, the Iranian hostage crisis, and, more generally, the perception of the American public that Carter was simply incapable of effective leadership.

The problematic state of presidential leadership has been further documented in the public approval ratings of recent presidents. Ronald Reagan's average public approval rating over the course of two terms was 52 percent, Jimmy Carter's 47 percent, Gerald Ford's 47 percent, Richard Nixon's 49 percent, and Lyndon Johnson's 56 percent. The average public approval rating for American presidents from 1964 to 1988 was an unimpressive 53.7 percent, suggesting considerable displeasure with presidential performance among the American people. When these figures are compared with John F. Kennedy's average public approval rating of 71 percent and Dwight D. Eisenhower's rating of 65 percent, and added to the fact that the average public approval rating from 1953 to 1963 was 68 percent, it becomes apparent that factors intrinsic in the American political system are with disturbing regularity, eroding the ability of our presidents to lead the nation.[26] The problem is systemic rather than personal.

Recent American presidents, by the end of their first term in the White House—sometimes sooner—have been deemed ineffective, incompetent, and unworthy of reelection by a cynical American public. Indeed, it appears that the American political system now produces failed presidencies as the norm rather than the exception. Ronald Reagan is the only president since Dwight D. Eisenhower to serve a full two terms in office.

Rather than blame individual presidents for a lack of leadership (which many have done, and which at times is terribly tempting to do), we must instead direct our energy towards examining and addressing those elements of the political system that have contributed to the impotence of the American presidency. We need to focus on the systemic impediments to presidential leadership in order to more fully understand how the presidency has reached its present state of immobility.

CHAPTER TWO

The Presidency Under Siege

There was a time not that long ago in American history when presidents were able to effectively exercise power. (Granted, since the formation of the American republic, all presidents have faced obstacles in governing the country. Even extraordinary presidents such as Jefferson, Jackson, Lincoln, the two Roosevelts and Truman faced resistance in one form or another. No president has ever governed with ease; presidential leadership has never lacked challenge.) Nevertheless, despite impediments, obstacles, and hurdles, it appears that presidents could, when the need arose, lead the nation.

Thomas Jefferson's historic Louisiana Purchase extended the United States from the Mississippi River to the Rocky Mountains, practically doubling the size of the country. James Polk waged war against Mexico and expanded the country's borders from the Rocky Mountains to the Pacific Ocean. Lincoln effectively fought a Civil War, freed the slaves, and preserved the Union. Teddy Roosevelt, using the American presidency as a bully pulpit, assaulted the power of monopolies and aquired new American territories throughout the western hemisphere. Woodrow Wilson and Franklin D. Roosevelt were each able to harness the powers of the presidency, promote sweeping domestic and foreign policy agendas, and effectively lead the nation.[1] Presidents of the past seemed quite capable of rising to the occasion, offering solutions to complex crises, and delivering on their promises.

While it is true that several of our most respected presidents were extraordinary men (the two Roosevelts and—to the nation's surprise—Harry S. Truman), such men were also fortunate to have been elected to an extraordinary office. The American presidency of the past was not forced to function within the context of a political process that was fundamentally hostile, unreceptive and even unconducive to executive leadership. It was an institution capable of exercising decisive and remarkable power. But due to myriad changes in the character and style of American politics and government over the course of the last two to three decades, the modern American presidency no longer enjoys this crucial advantage.

Indeed, as we approach the twenty-first century, a confluence of new forces in American politics has served to systematically undermine and restrict the capabilities of the president. In fact, it may not be an exaggeration to describe the modern presidency in its current form as an institution under "siege."

According to *The American Heritage Dictionary*, "siege" is defined as "the surrounding and blockading of a town or fortress by an army bent on capturing it." Webster's *New World Dictionary* defines siege as "the encirclement of a fortified place by an opposing armed force intending to take it, usually by blockade and bombardment." *The Random House Dictionary* describes siege as "the act or process of surrounding and attacking a fortified place in such a way as to isolate it from help and supplies, thereby making capture possible." In many ways, this is exactly what has happened to the American presidency. It has become surrounded by hostile forces determined to block the policy-making capacities of presidents to such a degree that imaginative and dynamic leadership is almost impossible. The formal constitutional powers of the presidency located in Article Two of the Constitution have not changed. What *has* changed is the political environment in which the presidency must perform. It is this development which has made the process of governing and effectively exercising presidential power a difficult and seemingly impossible task.

The proliferation of special interest groups, the multitude of lobbyists who routinely work to subvert the president's agenda, a dramatic increase of PAC money, and the deep and practically unshakable tripartite relationship between special interests, congressional committees and administrative agencies, (commonly referred to by political scientists as "iron triangles") have resulted in unfortunate consequences for creative presidential leadership. In addition to such developments, one discovers a monstrous and behemoth-like federal bureaucracy capable of thwarting the implementation of presidential policy, a viperous and tabloid mass media with an insatiable thirst for scandal in the White House, and a Congress still conditioned by the Vietnam War and the Watergate scandal fully determined to constrain the powers of the presidency. These are the armies that currently besiege the American presidency.[2]

To more thoroughly understand why recent presidents have failed with alarming regularity, one must first therefore understand the constraining impact of special interests and lobbyists, PAC money, iron triangles, the power of the federal bureaucracy, the current style of political reporting, and the attitude of Congress towards presidential power. These forces, each of which is integral to presidential leadership, require description and discussion.

Special Interests and Lobbyists

When President Clinton initially introduced his health care reform plan, one of the first pieces of commentary in the press concerned resistance from special interest groups. Special interests, the American people were told, were lining up against the president's plan. According to reports, the American Medical Association, pharmaceutical companies, insurance companies, hospital associations, employers' organizations, and other special interests were mobilizing their memberships and mapping legislative strategies designed to dissuade congressional support for the president's controversial proposal. It quickly became evident that President Clinton was about to do battle with entrenched and powerful special interest groups.

Special interest activity in the nation's capital is certainly nothing new. Well organized and highly financed, it has been a permanent component of the American political scene for a good part of the twentieth century. What *is* new, however, is the dramatic proliferation of special interests that systematically impact on the policy process. Special interest groups, along with the lobbyists they employ (to whom some pejoratively refer as "hired guns") have increased in staggering numbers over the course of the last several decades.

In 1961, only 365 lobbyists were registered with the United States Congress in accordance with the Federal Regulation of Lobbying Act of 1946.[3] By 1984, this figure had risen to 6,736. In 1994, records reveal 11,438 individuals formally registered as Capitol lobbyists.[4] Such figures document a truly astounding increase in the number of registered lobbyists who influence, or attempt to influence, politics inside the Beltway. At the same time, one must be aware that federal law requires only those who plan to *directly* lobby Congress to formally register as lobbyists. Lobbying a congressman's staff, attempting to organize constituent pressure, lobbying executive branch agencies and lobbying the judicial branch through amicus briefs and other forms of pressure tactics are not regulated under federal law. According to some experts, only one-third of all lobbying in the nation's capital is actually regulated and formally monitored.[5]

Coterminous in proportion to the enormous increase in lobbyists is the huge increase in the number of special interest organizations operating in Washington. According to Hedrick Smith in his classic work *The Power Game*, "Business has led the new political rush to Washington."[6] In 1968, only 100 business corporations had offices in the nation's capital. By 1978, 500 corporations had opened offices, while by 1986 the number rose to 1300.[7] According to Edward V. Schneier and Bertram Gross, "By the 1980s virtually every large corporation in the United States was represented on the Hill."[8]

Trade associations, like business activity, have also mushroomed. In 1986, 3500 trade association headquarters were located in the Washington area. This was triple the figure recorded for 1960.[9] Needless to say, any American president who proposes legislation in any area affecting the interests of business or trade associations will be locked in a serious political struggle with a wide variety of organizations and associations represented by highly skilled and handsomely-paid lobbyists.

There has also been an explosion in the number of environmental protection organizations, consumer protection groups, senior citizen associations, religious organizations, single issue interests, educational groups, feminist groups, civil rights organizations, legal interest groups, and a multitude of other special interests. Simply put, the modern American president must contend with every conceivable economic, social, moral and ideological interest in American society. Frequently such interests work to block rather than support the president's policy agenda.[10]

In addition to fighting the thousands of lobbyists who represent the interests of domestically based organizations, American presidents are also forced to compete with the hundreds of lobbyists who work on behalf of foreign governments and foreign interests. In 1994, records show 749 individuals registered in the nation's capital as "foreign agents" or foreign lobbyists.[11] Foreign lobbying, although more restricted and regulated than lobbying on behalf of domestic concerns, is also a well-developed art in American politics. As Norman Ornstein and Shirley Elder put it, "Today, virtually every foreign nation of significant size has a lobbying agent or agents operating in Washington."[12] Foreign lobbyists, contrary to what one might expect, are typically American citizens. Often they are former congressmen or former State Department officials (many of whom have established thriving law practices in Washington) on the payrolls of foreign governments and foreign economic interests.[13] Such individuals, not surprisingly, know the subtleties and nuances of Washington politics far better than any new president. In fact, they are advantageously situated to challenge any presidential proposal that affects the interests of their foreign clients.

PAC Money

The ability of special interest groups and their lobbyists to thwart presidential initiatives is further enhanced by the vast amounts of money special interests invest in Congress. The American president is frequently made to feel the stifling effect of political action committee contributions. PAC dollars have so thoroughly saturated national politics that any American president, regardless of charisma, popular appeal and legislative skill, will inevitably discover that political allegiance in Washington is heavily conditioned by campaign contributions. A congressman's primary loyalty, regardless of party affiliation, is often to those special interests that have funneled money into his or her campaign war chest.

When President Clinton was inaugurated in January of 1993, there was a false notion that political "gridlock" had come to an end. This idea was predicated on the belief that a Democratic president and a Democratic Congress would engage in harmonious and creative policy-making similar, perhaps, to that which prevailed during the time of Franklin D. Roosevelt. Clinton suggested that he would depend on the party loyalty of fellow Democrats in Congress to govern the country. In his view, with comfortable legislative majorities in the House and Senate, Republican opposition could essentially be circumvented or even ignored. Throughout the 1992 presidential campaign, Clinton promised to break the political gridlock inside the Washington Beltway. Indeed, the end of gridlock was one of the principal themes associated with Clinton's presidential campaign.

President Clinton, however, naively underestimated the controlling power of campaign dollars and loyalty to special interests secured through PAC dollars. Consider, for example, what he was forced to deal with as a newly inaugurated American president. Figures compiled by the Center for Responsive Politics, a watchdog organization located in Washington, D.C., reveal that during the 1992 elections, Business PACs contributed $127 million to congressional candidates, Labor PACs $43.1 million, and Ideological and Single Issue PACs $18.6 million. Combining the three categories results in a total of $187 million flowing into the campaign coffers of congressional candidates—most of whom, it is important to note, were incumbents who were reelected.[14] In the 1992 election, 42 percent of all campaign contributions to House winners came from PACs. Compare this figure to that of 1976, an election year in which only 26 percent of contributions to House winners were in the form of PAC dollars.[15] "In 1974 a total of 608 PACs were registered with the Federal Election Commission; by the end of 1992 the total stood at 4,195. The dollars those PACs provide have continued to rise with each new election. In 1992 they grew to nearly $189 million, a $30 million leap over 1990."[16] The five most important special interest contributors in the 1992 race were the American Medical Association ($3,237,157), the National Association of Realtors ($2,950,138), the Teamsters Union ($2,514,056), the Association of Trial Lawyers of America ($2,366,135), and the National Education Association ($2,342,897).[17] How ambitious and creative American presidents can engineer meaningful change in the face of so many powerful special interests is a pertinent question as we approach the twenty-first century. The bar graph in Figure 1 documents the rise in PAC money in proportion to campaign contributions from private individuals.

Figure 1
Source of Campaign Revenues for House Winners
1976–1992

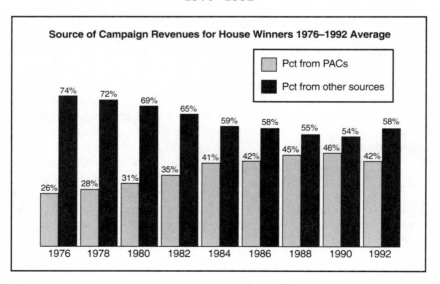

Source: Larry Makinson, The Price of Admission: Campaign Spending In the 1992 Elections, (Washington, D.C.: Center for Responsive Politics, 1993) p. 14. Reprinted with permission.

Iron Triangles and Issue Networks

Inside the Washington Beltway, operating deep within the bowels of the federal government, there exist mysterious political arrangements that in many ways control a significant part of the policy-making process. Political scientists refer to these arrangements as "iron triangles" because they involve three mutually dependent actors and because the triangular arrangements are incredibly inflexible. "Triple alliances" or "subgovernments" are terms also used to describe these tripartite policy-making associations.[18] One point of the triangle is composed of special interest lobbyists; the second of congressmen located in congressional subcommittees. The third point of the triangle is occupied by federal bureaucrats working within the maze of administrative agencies in the executive branch of government. The triangular relationship as it applies to defense policy is presented in Figure 2.

Iron triangles are found in several areas of the policy making

Figure 2
The Iron Triangle in Defense

Congress

(House and Senate Armed Service Committees and Defense Appropriations Subcommittees; Joint Committee on Defense Production; Joint Economic Committee; Government Operations Committees; House and Senate members from districts with interests in defense industry)

Executive Agencies

(Department of Defense; National Aeronautics and Space Administration; Department of Energy)

Defense Contractors

(Boeing, Lockheed, Grumman, McDonnel-Douglas, Hercules)

Source: Theodore J. Lowi and Benjamin Ginsberg, *American Government: Freedom and Power* (New York: W. W. Norton and Co., 1990), p. 552. Reprinted with permission.

process, including defense policy, agriculture, education, labor, and veterans affairs. As Hedrick Smith states: "All form their own iron triangles—iron, because the partners want an unbreakable lock on the policies most vital to them and they want to shut out outsiders. The object of the Iron Triangle is a closed power game . . ."[19] For example, within the realm of defense policy (as Table Two suggests), lobbyists who represent the interests of defense contractors, such as Boeing and Lockheed, work closely with key congressional committees responsible for the formulation of defense policy. These would include the House and Senate Armed Services Committees and the Defense Appropriations Subcommittees. At the same time, defense lobbyists would also work in conjunction with several defense related executive agencies in the formulation and implementation of defense policy. In the area of labor policy a detailed study would inevitably disclose labor lobbyists from the AFL-CIO working in close partnership with subcommittees of the House Education and Labor Committee, as well as with bureau chiefs of executive agencies of the Labor Department. A study of veterans' affairs legislation would reveal a triangular relationship between lobbyists for a variety of veterans' organizations working in close concert with the House and Senate Veterans' Affairs Committees, and also with the Department of Veterans' Affairs in the executive branch of government.

Lobbyists work closely with a small number of congressmen and key bureaucrats to meet the needs of their special interest group. At the same time, congressmen work with key lobbyists and bureaucrats to meet the needs of their constitutents and to secure a safe congressional seat. Executive branch employees interact closely with a handful of key legislators and skilled lobbyists in order to ensure the constant flow of federal funding so necessary to policy implementation and agency survival.

With each component of the triangle dependent upon the others to service its needs and interests, proposals that threaten the status quo will meet great resistance from the actors connected through the triangle. A president who attempts to reduce spending on behalf of veterans or agriculture will naturally face strong resistance from the iron triangles related to these policy concerns. Attempts to alter the defense budget will be met with extraordinary opposition from lobbyists representing defense contractors, congressmen, and senators on the Armed Services Committees whose constituents depend upon military spending for employment, and bureaucrats employed by the Defense Department.[20] The iron triangles operating in Washington have the potential and capacity to subvert, impede and sabotage the goals of any ambitious and reform-minded president.

Resistance to presidential initiatives from iron triangles is neither unpredictable nor random. It is an institutionalized condition that all modern presidents must contend with. As Hugh Heclo states: "People in the White House are aware of these subgovernments but have no obvious control over them. They seem to persist regardless of government reorganizations or, perhaps more to the point, they are able to prevent the reorganizations that displease them."[21] Harold Seidman captures the president's dilemma in a more dramatic fashion: "Sometimes the executive branch takes on the appearance of an arena in which the chiefs of major and petty bureaucratic fiefdoms, supported by their auxiliaries in the Congress and their mercenaries in the outside community, are arrayed against the president in deadly combat."[22] To complicate matters further, one often finds former congressmen or former executive branch officials working as lobbyists within the iron triangles, further strengthening the bond between the three components. This is the infamous "revolving door syndrome," a subject frequently discussed throughout the 1992 presidential campaign. The personal familiarity and camaraderie between the three sets of actors is truly extraordinary. For example, a congressman after spending most of his legislative career on the House Agriculture Committee and one or two specialized agricultural subcommittees, might retire from Congress and begin a new career as a lobbyist for an agricultural interest group. The former congressman is of course intimately familiar with the interest group's goals and objectives, the voting behavior and constitutent concerns of his former congressional colleagues, as well as the key players in the Agricultural Department of the executive branch. He has simply moved to another point of the triangle resulting in little change or disruption in agricultural policy-making.

It is important to note, however, that while iron triangles still characterize several dimensions of national policy-making, recent research regarding the interface between special interests, the bureaucracy and Congress has discovered that the tremendous infusion of special interests into the policy-making arena has disrupted many of the longstanding and predictable triangular relationships. The number of special interest groups now operating inside the Washington Beltway is so profound that it has become virtually impossible for one group, or even a small number of groups, to dominate one sphere of the policy process.[23] The vast array of senior citizen organizations, public interest groups, foreign governments, business enterprises, environmental groups, and other special interests, often converge and compete with one another over control of a specific policy area to the point where many of the tripartite policy relationships have either weakened or dissolved. In addition to the proliferation of group competition, one discovers multiple congressional committees and federal agencies competing with one another as well. Policy-making through "issue networks," rather than "iron triangles" is how several political scientists now describe the subgovernmental policy process. The process has become more competitive, crosscutting and less predictable. The unpredictable and fluid movement of policy-making participants in and out of the issue networks, according to Hugh Heclo, has made it "all but impossible to identify clearly who the dominant actors are."[24] As John R. Wright notes: "Unlike triangles, issue networks are not dominated by one powerful set of interests, and hence bargaining, negotiations, and compromise are much more important to the resolution of conflict."[25] The rise of issue networks in place of iron triangles should not be applauded, as this inevitable development has done little to strengthen presidential influence in the policy-making process. Rather than elevate presidential leverage, issue networks have further diminished the president's ability to mobilize the Congress and the executive branch on behalf of a coherent, national agenda.

The Bureaucratic Behemoth

According to Article II of the U.S. Constitution, the president of the United States is the nation's chief executive. In performing this critical constitutional role, the president is expected to ensure that the laws of the United States are "faithfully executed." To effectively execute or implement federal law, the American president must preside over, and guide the activity of, the executive branch of the federal government.

While the task of executing federal law might appear at first glance to be relatively simplistic, the reality of the matter is that modern American presidents are heavily constrained and frequently impeded by a bloated, overly secure, and even intransigent bureaucracy. The federal bureaucracy, due to its enormous size, bureaucratic complexity and growing authority, has the clear potential to either intentionally or unintentionally blockade implementation of creative and innovative presidential policies. All presidents, regardless of political party, are faced with this dilemma. Richard Rose states: "One of the first things a president learns after entering the White House is that he is a leader who has few certain followers within government."[26] According to Rose, the American president is in reality a "chief without an executive."[27]

In addition to iron triangles and issue networks which thwart and undermine presidential authority, consider the sheer size of the federal executive branch. As of January 1994, the federal civilian work force numbered precisely 2,925,819 employees.[28] Of this number, approximately 2,400 are political appointments or, put differently, part of the president's team. These are the high-ranking presidential advisors, cabinet secretaries, under-secretaries, assistant secretaries, agency heads, ambassadors, and underlings, who, along with a coterie of special appointees scattered throughout the executive branch, receive important posts within the executive branch due to personal and political loyalty to the president or the president's political party. They are part of the president's administration. Such individuals arrive with the president and will usually leave with the president. In some respects, therefore, one still discovers an element of patronage within the context of the federal executive appointment process. Political appointments, however, comprise a miniscule percentage of the federal civilian workforce within the entire framework of the federal bureaucracy. Working beneath the president's personal team of political appointees is the federal civil service, which comprises the vast majority of the federal executive work force. The work of the federal civil service is generally low-profile and attracts little media attention. It is conducted in bureaus located deep within executive departments and agencies. When presidential candidates campaign against the "federal bureaucracy," they are normally referring to the faceless and anonymous mass of career civil servants employed by the federal bureaus and agencies.

Contrary to what one might expect, the vast majority of federal bureaucrats, rather than working inside the Washington Beltway, are employed in offices located throughout the fifty states, territories and foreign countries. Civil servants receive employment not through political connections and political rewards but rather through a merit examination administered through the Office of Personnel Management, or by special examinations administered by the individual executive departments. The federal civil service, established with passage of the Pendleton Act of 1883 following the assassination of President James Garfield in 1881, was designed to ensure political neutrality and fairness with respect to the policy implementation process. Accordingly, federal civil servants are guaranteed extraordinary job security and protection.

A federal civil servant is essentially immune from pressures imposed by the president or the president's political appointees. A president who wishes to remove a civil servant due to personal dislike, or for political reasons, cannot do so. Therefore, the federal bureaucracy, in theory, functions as a competent, secure and objective administrative institution, but one which is largely beyond the reach of the American president.

While a federal civilian work force of approximately three million can potentially be harnessed to promote the policy agenda of the American president (and implement sweeping social and economic change), the reality is that the bureaucracy has in many ways stifled the ambitions of American presidents. This is not a dilemma exclusive to either Republican or Democratic presidents. Instead, the bureaucracy is truly bipartisan and politically neutral with respect to stalling and impeding the objectives of the nation's chief executive.

According to Harold Seidman, American presidents frequently find themselves frustrated by bureaucratic inertia and intransigence. "The bureaucracy is damned as 'uncreative' because it is unable to satisfy the White House appetite for immediate solutions to complex social and economic problems and dramatic imaginative proposals for the legislative program. 'Slow moving,' 'unresponsive,' 'disloyal' are among the milder epithets used to describe the bureaucracy."[29] In Clinton Rossiter's view, most American presidents if polled would probably agree that "the president's hardest job is, not to persuade Congress to support a policy dear to his political heart, but to persuade the pertinent bureau or agency or mission, even when headed by men of his own choosing, to follow his direction faithfully and transform the shadow of the policy into the substance of a program."[30]

In addition to the president, the president's political appointees heading the various departments and agencies also find themselves bewildered and shunned by the federal civil service. Discussing the seriousness of this matter, Hugh Heclo states: "Far from being a peripheral concern or a mere residue of nonpresidential details, the relationship of political executives and bureaucrats is a persisting and growing problem that goes to the heart of a modern democratic government."[31] According to Richard Rose, many of the president's political appointees, due to great frustration with bureaucratic obstacles and the iron triangles, as well as a perception that the White House offers few resources to achieve presidential objectives, resign after only two years of government service.[32]

Several American presidents, regardless of political ideology and partisan stripe, have commented on the integral relationship between presidential power and the president's relationship with the federal bureaucracy. President Harry S. Truman, a Democrat, viewed the federal bureaucracy in these terms: "There was too much duplication of functions, too much 'passing the buck,' and too much confusion and waste."[33] President Truman, like his predecessor Roosevelt, introduced legislation aimed at executive branch reorganization. As Truman stated: "I wanted to establish governmental lines so clearly that I would be able to put my finger on the people directly responsible in every situation. It was my intention to delegate responsiblity to the properly designated heads of departments and agencies, but I wished to be in a position to see to it that they carried on along the lines of my policy."[34]

President Lyndon B. Johnson, a Democrat who assumed the presidency following the assassination of President Kennedy, noted in his personal memoirs that in addition to winning the confidence of the Cabinet, Congress and the American people in the wake of President Kennedy's death, it was equally important that he gain the respect and confidence of the federal bureaucracy. As Johnson put it: "I had to prove myself."[35]

A more critical perspective of bureaucratic power was offered by Republican President Richard M. Nixon: "Sometimes it's said that all federal employees 'work for the president.' In fact, hardly any do, and some even work against him. In the huge bureaucracy, a few people are motivated by devotion to the president or to the cause he represents. Most are lifers who are motivated primarily by self-interest."[36]

President Ronald Reagan, also a Republican, campaigned throughout his political career as an opponent of "big government." He described the adverse impact of bureaucratic power on presidential leadership in the area of foreign affairs in this manner: "Whenever I wanted to send a message to a foreign leader, for example, copies of my message were usually first circulated to a half-dozen or more agencies at the State Department, the Pentagon, the Commerce Department, and elsewhere for comment and suggestions. And often the bureaucrats down the line (I'm sure in good faith) would try to add or change something—whether it was needed or not. The result: often a blurring of my original intentions."[37]

The growth and power of the federal bureaucracy must clearly be considered when analyzing and discussing the governing problems currently plaguing the American presidency. Bureaucratic power has become a major constraint on the creative capacities of the president. To complicate matters further, any president who attempts to exert personal control over the bureaucracy, as did Presidents Nixon and Reagan, will immediately be accused of "corrupting" and "politicizing" the federal civil service.[38] The American president, as Harold M. Barger put it, "finds it impossible to get a handle on government because there is no handle there."[39]

Figure 3
The Federal Executive Branch

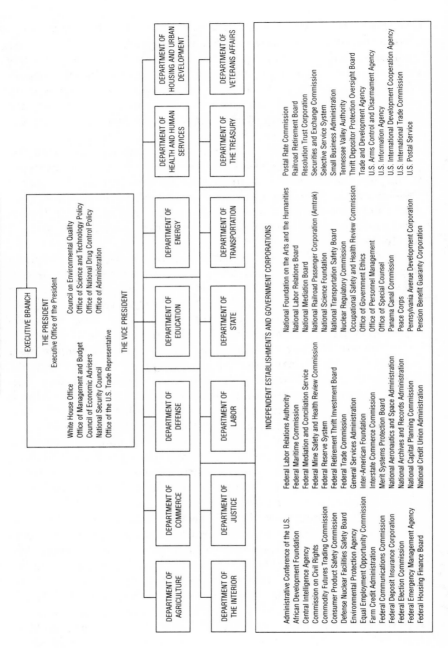

EXECUTIVE BRANCH

THE PRESIDENT
Executive Office of the President

White House Office
Office of Management and Budget
Council of Economic Advisers
National Security Council
Office of the U.S. Trade Representative

Council on Environmental Quality
Office of Science and Technology Policy
Office of National Drug Control Policy
Office of Administration

THE VICE PRESIDENT

DEPARTMENT OF AGRICULTURE

DEPARTMENT OF COMMERCE

DEPARTMENT OF DEFENSE

DEPARTMENT OF EDUCATION

DEPARTMENT OF ENERGY

DEPARTMENT OF HEALTH AND HUMAN SERVICES

DEPARTMENT OF HOUSING AND URBAN DEVELOPMENT

DEPARTMENT OF THE INTERIOR

DEPARTMENT OF JUSTICE

DEPARTMENT OF LABOR

DEPARTMENT OF STATE

DEPARTMENT OF TRANSPORTATION

DEPARTMENT OF THE TREASURY

DEPARTMENT OF VETERANS AFFAIRS

INDEPENDENT ESTABLISHMENTS AND GOVERNMENT CORPORATIONS

Administrative Conference of the U.S.
African Development Foundation
Central Intelligence Agency
Commission on Civil Rights
Commodity Futures Trading Commission
Consumer Product Safety Commission
Defense Nuclear Facilities Safety Board
Environmental Protection Agency
Equal Employment Opportunity Commission
Farm Credit Administration
Federal Communications Commission
Federal Deposit Insurance Corporation
Federal Election Commission
Federal Emergency Management Agency
Federal Housing Finance Board

Federal Labor Relations Authority
Federal Maritime Commission
Federal Mediation and Conciliation Service
Federal Mine Safety and Health Review Commission
Federal Reserve System
Federal Retirement Thrift Investment Board
Federal Trade Commission
General Services Administration
Inter-American Foundation
Interstate Commerce Commission
Merit Systems Protection Board
National Aeronautics and Space Administration
National Archives and Records Administration
National Capital Planning Commission
National Credit Union Administration

National Foundation on the Arts and the Humanities
National Labor Relations Board
National Mediation Board
National Railroad Passenger Corporation (Amtrak)
National Science Foundation
National Transportation Safety Board
Nuclear Regulatory Commission
Occupational Safety and Health Review Commission
Office of Government Ethics
Office of Personnel Management
Office of Special Counsel
Panama Canal Commission
Peace Corps
Pennsylvania Avenue Development Corporation
Pension Benefit Guaranty Corporation

Postal Rate Commission
Railroad Retirement Board
Resolution Trust Corporation
Securities and Exchange Commission
Selective Service System
Small Business Administration
Tennessee Valley Authority
Thrift Depositor Protection Oversight Board
Trade and Development Agency
U.S. Arms Control and Disarmament Agency
U.S. Information Agency
U.S. International Development Cooperation Agency
U.S. International Trade Commission
U.S. Postal Service

Source: Office of the Federal Register National Archives and Records Administration. The United States Government Manual, 3/1994 (Lanham, Maryland: Bernan Press, 1994), p. 21.

Most structural models of the federal bureaucracy place the American president at the apex of this vast institution. Beneath the president is the Executive Office of the President, which includes the White House staff, the Office of Management and Budget, the National Security Council, the Council of Economic Advisors, and other high level staffs and councils. These are the president's most immediate subordinates and advisors. Beneath the Executive Office are fourteen cabinet departments, such as the Departments of State, Treasury, Defense, Agriculture, Veterans Affairs and others. Beneath the cabinet departments lie a broad array of independent executive agencies, government corporations and independent regulatory commissions such as the CIA, U.S. Postal Service, and Nuclear Regulatory Commission. A standard textbook executive branch diagram is shown in Figure 3.

While the hierarchical model of the executive branch is useful for theoretical purposes, a more practical conception of executive branch relationships—particularly as applied to the exercise of presidential power—is presented in the work of Benjamin I. Page and Mark P. Petracca.[40] Rather than a pyramidal organization of neatly arranged agencies and departments with the president at the apex, Page and Petracca portray the executive branch as an administrative institution consisting of "concentric circles." The presidency, according to this view, is situated within the smallest innermost circle, tightly surrounded by personal advisors located on the White House staff. Beyond the White House Staff circle are several additional bureaucratic circles, including that of the Executive Office of the President, the Cabinet circle, the circle of Independent Regulatory Agencies, and the circle of Government Corporations. Each circle appears larger and farther from the president's influence and reach. It is evident that as the federal bureaucracy expands, the president's control over it declines.[41] According to this model, the president appears to exert little power and control in executive affairs beyond those of the White House staff (see Figure 4).

In the concentric circle model, the modern American presidency, rather than sitting atop an administrative pyramid, is instead surrounded by circles of powerful bureaucracy. To complicate matters even more, the vast majority of those who occupy agencies within the various circles cannot be removed by the president. According to Barger, "The rate of dismissal because of improper job performance or inefficiency is less than one-seventh of one percent. Rarely are federal civil servants given anything but positive job evaluations,

Figure 4
Presidential-Bureaucratic Relations
The Concentric Circle Model

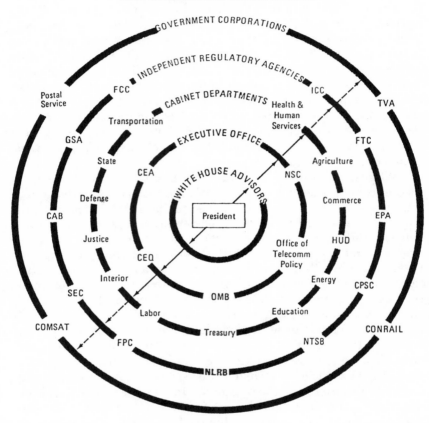

Source: Benjamin I. Page and Mark P. Petracca, *The American Presidency,* New York: McGraw-Hill, 1983, p. 205. Reprinted with permission.

and merit pay increases are virtually automatic."[42] Federal bureaucrats develop their own policy agendas and operate deep within the framework of iron triangles—often at direct odds with the goals of the president—and there is little the president can do to change the status quo. It is this ironclad condition that severely debilitates American presidents and is yet another reason why the modern presidency currently functions in a state of siege.

A Viperous Mass Media

The presidency is also marked by unprecedented tension between occupants of the Oval Office and mass media. In fact, the media, which include newspapers, magazines, radio, and television, often seem quite determined to undermine the character and reputation of American presidents, as well as individuals who seek the presidency. So focused is the modern mass media on the weaknesses of presidents and presidential candidates that journalists, according to Larry J. Sabato, seem at times "like sharks in a feeding frenzy."[43] This devouring, quasi-tabloid, and viperous style of journalism has claimed several presidencies over the course of the last twenty-five years. The Nixon, Ford, Carter, Reagan, Bush, and Clinton presidencies were, in one form or another, weakened and wounded as a result of overzealous journalism focused on exploiting and magnifying faults in presidential decision-making and, even more distressing, faults in human character. At this point in time, enough evidence exists to question whether Clinton Rossiter's 1956 perspective, portraying the president as "the chief gainer from the miracles of electronics" is still appropriate.

Clearly, a formerly effective tool has now become a major nemesis for all American presidents. Herbert Schmertz, discussing the end result of an overly aggressive mass media on public perceptions of the presidency, captures the situation this way: "As the public continually observes the media in hot and heated pursuit of the president, the public's perception of the office changes. We see a man pursued by a herd of irritable and irritating inquiries; barking at him like dogs after a bear, demanding answers to their questions, and soon—on a subliminal plane—we begin to see him as perhaps our opponent, our legitimate quarry, and perhaps even our foe."[44] To complicate matters further, of the three branches of government, the media scrutinize the actions of the presidency most intensely. One study of evening network news coverage discovers an average of 172 stories per month regarding the presidency compared to only 24 about Congress and 16 about the Supreme Court.[45]

Exactly when this style of aggressive media reporting first appeared with respect to American politics is somewhat difficult to identify. It seems to have developed gradually, rather than in an immediate and dramatic fashion. Tension between the president and the mass media certainly escalated throughout the Johnson presidency due to the president's handling of the Vietnam War. Johnson's relationship with the press became increasingly strained as presidential pronouncements regarding America's military progress and the supposed "light at the end of the tunnel" were exposed as fraudulent and unrealistic. The unexpected and massive Tet Offensive of 1968 launched by the Communists throughout the countryside and cities of South Vietnam, including the capital Saigon, dramatically revealed how hollow and misleading Johnson's reports actually were regarding American progress with the war. This was regardless of the fact that the Viet Cong and North Vietnamese army during the Tet Offensive experienced a crushing military defeat by American troops.[46]

However, most observers would probably agree that *institutionalized* tension between presidents and the media began not with the Vietnam conflict, but rather with the Watergate scandal in the early 1970s. As a result of Watergate, which resulted in the first resignation of an American president, the media developed a fundamental and profound suspicion of presidents and presidential candidates. According to Michael Baruch Grossman and Martha Joynt Kumar: "Revelations of criminal activities and other wrongdoing by the Nixon administration led many to the view that the White House often is occupied by mentally unbalanced power seekers and the sycophantic members of their clique who use the office of the president for their own ends."[47] Following Watergate, there appeared an institutionalized proclivity on the part of the press to disclose, dissect, and accentuate the weaknesses of presidents, rather than analyze presidential performance in a balanced fashion. As presidential scholar Richard Pious ominously warned in his seminal text *The American Presidency*, in 1979:

> The legacy of Watergate is wolfpack journalism, which will confirm the worst fears of the public. The White House will remain in a state of siege, as the normal transactions of the political system are unearthed, magnified, and then distorted by the media. Presidential attempts to control the national agenda seem destined to fail on most issues.[48]

Austin Ranney, in his revealing work *Channels of Power*, also notes that career promotions and awards are more likely to go to journalists who expose "moral lapses, lies and policy failures" rather than correspondents who present more positive and favorable political stories. Unfortunately, the American president, according to Ranney, "is the biggest game of all in the perennial hunt."[49]

As proof that an adversarial press had now become the norm,

consider the presidency of Jimmy Carter. Elected in 1976 in the aftermath of Watergate, Carter promised a more friendly, frank, and open relationship with the press and to restore trust and confidence in the American presidency. In light of Carter's emphasis on faith, character, and ethics, there was reason to believe that presidential-press relations would dramatically improve.

However, by the summer of 1977 the Carter presidency, in the view of reporters assigned to the White House, exhibited a "siege mentality."[50] To complicate matters, a scandal errupted involving Bert Lance, Carter's Director of the Office of Management and Budget, forcing Lance to resign. Not surprisingly, the media seized the opportunity to question the legitimacy of Carter's presidency: "Throughout this period, the media were filled with news stories, editorials, and columns that seemed to bring nothing but bad news for the White House."[51] Reflecting on the state of presidential-press relations in a television interview, Jody Powell, Carter's Press Secretary, commented: "The basic relationship between the president and press or the president and Congress has changed over the past decade . . . It will never be what it was."[52] After a single term in office, President Jimmy Carter was defeated by Ronald Reagan in his bid for reelection. The election was a landslide, with Reagan receiving 489 electoral votes to Carter's 49.

In order to survive intense press scrutiny, Reagan arrived in the White House with a strategic plan specifically crafted to keep the media at arm's length. The president's strategy, based on a memorandum issued by Professor Robert Entman of Duke University entitled "The Imperial Media," clearly reflected the mutual distrust that, by 1980, characterized the presidential-press relationship.[53] Press conferences were deliberately kept to a minimum, press access to the president was severely restricted, and the press, as a result of administration manipulation was practically forced to focus on the content of public policies, rather than the president's political motivations.[54]

Distrust of the media was also evident during the Bush presidency, particularly with respect to operations Desert Shield and Desert Storm. Controlled press conferences, press pools, and restrictions placed on the physical movement of reporters during America's war with Iraq clearly underscored the president's apprehension towards the ambitious and enterprising mass media. Reporters assigned to cover the Iraqi war frequently complained about press restrictions. Some reporters even suggested that the Bush administration violated their rights to press protection guaranteed under the First Amendment.

In addition to the Watergate crisis, the institutionalization of a hostile media, or "wolfpack journalism," has increased as a result of major changes in the electronic media industry. Television audiences today (unlike those of only ten or fifteen years ago) can choose between network television as well as a broad range of cable channels for newsworthy stories or personal entertainment. On a typical evening across the land, Americans can scan an increasing array of network and cable channels in the space of seconds.

According to one study, in 1980 only one-tenth of American households received cable television. By 1990, this figure had risen dramatically to 55 percent. With over half of American households receiving cable television (and most having access to twenty or more channels), viewing audiences of the three major networks declined precipitously. In less than a decade, the major networks had lost twenty-five percent of their viewing audience.[55]

So in order to secure a greater share of viewers (and increase ratings), the major networks have focused on the darker and more tantalizing dimensions of presidential conduct. Personal and character-oriented stories attract a large number of viewers. At times it is rather difficult to differentiate between ABC, NBC, and CBS evening news and such lurid shows as Current Affair, Hardcopy, and Inside Edition. Even reputable news magazines such as *Time, Newsweek,* and *U.S. News* periodically take on the luster of *People Magazine.*

At the time of this writing, President Clinton is besieged with accusations of financial impropriety and sexual harassment during his tenure as governor of Arkansas. Questions from the press routinely inundate Clinton regarding these personal matters. Such probing into pre-presidential conduct is without precedent in the history of American politics. No president, regardless of popularity or party affiliation, has ever had to respond with such regularity to questions from the press concerning personal behavior or public conduct prior to becoming president.

This unfortunate state of affairs is symbolized by the recent establishment of President Clinton's Legal Defense Fund, a special account established by the president and his advisors to assist with the cost of legal counsel. With respect to charges of financial impropriety, what is known as the "Whitewater Affair," the alleged misdeed occured a full ten years before Clinton was elected president. The sexual harassment suit filed by Ms. Paula Jones, a former state employee in Arkansas, is even more troubling in light of the distinct possibility that a sitting president could potentially be sued in civil court. Never in the history of the United States has a president been required to appear in court during his term of office.

A ruthless and sensationalist media has clearly become an omnipresent component of modern presidential politics. The pattern of journalistic abuse begins even before a president is sworn into office. Consider the press treatment of Bill Clinton during the 1992 Democratic nominating contest. Throughout the period prior to the New Hampshire primary, it seemed as though Bill Clinton's name was synonymous with that of Gennifer Flowers. Flowers, a former state employee in Arkansas during Clinton's tenure as governor, stated in a televised press conference organized by *Star Magazine* (a publication very similar to the *National Enquirer*) that she had a twelve-year love affair with then Governor Clinton. Following this revelation, the press throughout the days prior to the New Hampshire primary bombarded Clinton with questions pertaining to marital infidelity and his alleged relationship with Flowers. Leading analysts predicted Clinton's defeat in the presidential nominating contest and eventual withdrawal from the presidential race. Especially disturbing, however, was that the substance of Clinton's campaign platform was virtually lost in the frenzy over Gennifer Flowers.

Media coverage of the 1988 presidential contest had been equally torrid to that of the 1992 campaign. Once again, America watched an obsessed mass media relentlessly devour a leading presidential candidate. Not surprisingly, the lead story for the 1988 campaign involved sex and romance.

Former Colorado Senator Gary Hart, who captured the support and imagination of many voters during his unsuccessful bid for the Democratic nomination in 1984, was derailed in his second quest for the presidency following press exposure of a brief affair with actress and model Donna Rice. A photograph published in the *National Enquirer* showed Rice nestled into Hart's lap aboard the luxury yacht "Monkey Business." The two had spent time together at a posh vacation resort on the island of Bimini in the Bahamas. Senator Hart was a married man and a parent.

The tantalizing photo sparked a media furor that eventually led to Hart's political demise. Journalists, rather than focusing on Hart's innovative domestic and foreign policy platform, chose instead to concentrate on the senator's personal lifestyle. In one press conference after another, Hart was forced to answer pointed questions concerning Donna Rice and his relationship with his wife, as well as his overall philosophy of marriage. The American public heard very little from Senator Hart regarding his strategic and interesting proposals to balance the budget deficit, stimulate the economy, and reform American foreign policy. Those aspects of the Hart campaign were deemed unnewsworthy by the media. Unlike Bill Clinton, who managed to survive the media onslaught, Senator Hart withdrew from the nominating contest prior to the New Hampshire primary. Although Hart eventually reentered the race, the damage to his credibility proved irreparable. Gary Hart's promising political career was brought to an abrupt end.

Negative press treatment of presidential candidates has become a permanent feature of the modern presidential selection process. Indeed, as Thomas E. Patterson has demonstrated, negative press treatment of those who pursue the Oval Office has been steadily increasing with each decade. Compare, for example, press evaluations of presidential candidates in 1960 with those in 1992. During the 1960 presidential campaign, 75 percent of reporters' evaluative references to Kennedy and Nixon were favorable. In 1992, only 40 percent of press evaluations of Bush and Clinton could be classified in such terms.[56]

One has to seriously question what affect such intensive media scrutiny might have on the decisions of current governors, congressmen, and senators who aspire to the presidency. Talented politicians whose sights are set on the Oval Office are bound to have skeletons of some sort in their closets. Media revelations of questionnable business transactions, marijuana experimentation, marital infidelity, employment of illegal aliens or the like will undoubtedly destroy future bids for the American presidency.

If the mass media continues to focus its concerns on the private lives of those who seek the presidency and demands from them pristine and monk-like lifestyles, many talented and dynamic political leaders are bound to be dissuaded from seeking the presidential office. Would Franklin Roosevelt or John Kennedy have stepped forward as a presidential candidate if the mass media was as relentless and aggressive in their time as it is today? (Both individuals, it has been quietly acknowledged, were involved with women other than their wives.) Kennedy's bid for the White House would most certainly have ended long before the first presidential primary took place.

A Reactionary Congress

Healthy tension between the three branches of government was the intent of James Madison and other Founding Fathers in developing the constitutional arrangement of checks and balances. In allowing one branch of government to impose a check upon the others, political power is inherently constrained. At the same time, a system of checks guarantees a balanced distribution of power, with no one branch exercising dominance over the other two. As Madison wrote in Federalist #51:

> But the great security against a gradual concentration of the several powers in the same department consists in giving to those who administer each department the necessary constitutional means and personal motives to resist encroachments of the others. The provision for defense must in this, as in all other cases, be made commensurate to the danger of attack. Ambition must be made to counteract ambition.[57]

Theoretically, as a result of a three-branch system of government, tyranny is prevented and liberty preserved. Three branches of government, each having its own sphere of constitutional authority and capable of imposing checks, is clearly one of the most fundamental and distinguishing principles of the American Constitution. It is this unique doctrine that truly separates the American form of government from others around the globe.

With the collapse of the Nixon presidency, the popular cliche echoed by politicians, pundits, academicians, the press, and the public was that "the system worked," and that checks and balances were alive and well. A president who abused the privileges and powers of the presidency was, as a result of controversial judicial rulings,[58] exhaustive congressional hearings, intense press scrutiny and a tide of negative public opinion, forced to resign from office.

The national nightmare known as the "Watergate Affair" had a profound impact on press relations with the president and public perceptions of the presidency, as well as congressional orientations towards presidential power. In the view of many congressmen, particular those who entered Congress in the early seventies, presidential power in its current form posed a direct threat to representative democracy and good government. Such power was not to be trusted, and ought to be carefully monitored and constrained. In the interest of preserving the American republic, Congress (in the view of congressmen conditioned by the Watergate scandal) had a political responsibility to initiate reforms specifically designed to prevent further presidential abuses. Congress needed to take strident action as guardians of the political order.

The new attitude of Congress set in motion a tremendous reaction to presidential power. "Unprecedented reconsideration of presidential powers" is how constitutional expert C. Herman Pritchett described Congress' conduct in the immediate aftermath of Watergate.[59] A wave of reform legislation and resolutions limiting the powers of the presidency flooded the floors of the House and Senate. So vehement was the congressional reaction to the "imperial presidency" that close observers of the governing process raised questions regarding the wisdom of such measures. In his leading text *The State of The Presidency*, presidential scholar Thomas E. Cronin asked: "Could a vast new array of checks and balances cripple the presidency and undermine its potential for creative leadership?"[60] One by one, a plethora of bills specifically designed to constrain and reduce presidential authority was passed into law in the aftermath of Watergate. Two leading examples, which underscore the new congressional mood, are as follows.

In 1973 Congress passed the War Powers Resolution over President Nixon's veto. It provides Congress with veto power over the president's decision to deploy combat troops abroad. The president is also required to notify congressional leaders in writing of his intentions within forty-eight hours after a combat mission has been launched. Unless he receives specific authorization from Congress, troops must be withdrawn by the president within sixty days. President Nixon viewed the Resolution as inconsistent with the intent of the Founding Fathers. Crisis leadership, Nixon predicted, would be severely restricted,[61] and in fact, most American presidents since Nixon have viewed the War Powers Resolution as an unconstitutional infringement of the president's authority to make war. Reflecting on the War Powers Resolution more than fifteen years after its passage, former President Gerald Ford noted: "I continue to believe that my colleagues in Congress who enacted the War Powers Resolution had the wrong "cure" for the tragedy of Vietnam. Their antidote has produced some very serious side effects of its own." According to Ford, the statute encroaches upon the commander-in-chief power of the president and is "at odds with the Constitution."[62]

The constitutionality of the War Powers Resolution is of course a debatable issue. Louis Fisher, a leading scholar of presidential war powers, views the Resolution as potentially contributing to the "collective judgment" of the executive and legislative branches of government. In Fisher's view, this is desirable and quite consistent with the intent of the framers who had intended the war power to be shared between the president and Congress.[63] Fisher argues, however, that the War Powers Resolution, although potentially capable of constraining presidents, has, in reality, done little to restict presidents within the realm of war making and military intervention. According to Fisher, predictions of a diminished commander-in-chief have never materialized. "Presidents continue to wield military power single-handedly, agreeing only to consult with legislators and notify them of completed actions. That is not the framers model."[64] Christopher J. Deering shares the same perspective: "In spite of the act, presidents have frequently utilized American troops abroad—in and near actual combat—but on each occasion Congress has been unable because of time, or unwilling due to political disagreements, to articulate its own position."[65] Whether or not the War Powers Resolution has directly constrained presidential power, whether the Resolution is consistent with the intent of the Founding Fathers, and whether the Resolution is in the interest of the American people will remain a source of controversy and debate for many years to come.

The new congressional involvement in foreign affairs is further evident from the enormous increase in legislative restrictions placed on the president's conduct in this critial policy area. Prior to 1900, there was only one restrictive statute placed on the executive branch in the field of foreign policy. By 1950, approximately 30 restrictive statutes had been passed by Congress. Between 1950 and 1980, 189 statutes were enacted. Between the years 1980 and 1986, a total of 191 legislative restrictions regarding foreign affairs were placed on the executive.[66] The extent to which Congress now monitors the activity of presidents in foreign affairs tends to support the position of those scholars who question the current validity of Aaron Wildavsky's "two-presidencies" thesis—a seminal study published in 1966 in which the presidency is described as an institution far less restrained in foreign policy-making compared to domestic affairs.[67] It appears that the modern presidency functions within a constrained environment regardless of policy sphere.

Presidential control over the federal budget and appropriations was another dimension of presidential power targeted by congressional reformers. In the final days of the Nixon presidency, Congress passed the Congressional Budget and Impoundment Control Act of 1974. Permanent budget committees were established in each chamber of Congress. To assist Congress in budgetary matters, a new support agency—the Congressional Budget Office—was also created. A politically wounded Nixon on the verge of resignation reluctantly signed the bill into law.

By establishing budget committees and a new congressional support agency, Congress assumed a much greater role in preparing and analyzing the federal government's annual operating budget. The president's budget proposal must now be forwarded to the House and Senate Budget Committees which, together with the staff of the Congressional Budget Office, consider all facets of it. The budget is then scrutinized in great detail by an array of congressional committees and congressmen. Extensive compromises, deals and negotiations between the White House and Congress are now a routine feature of the federal budget making process. With passage of the 1974 budget act, congressional power of the purse has been considerably strengthened and, as a result, the president has lost considerable leverage. The intent of the 1974 Act is concisely expressed in the report issued by the congressional conference committee which constructed the final version:

> ... to assure congressional budget control; provide for the congressional determination of the appropriate level of Federal revenues and expenditures; provide a system of impoundment control; establish national budget priorities; and provide for furnishing information to Congress by the executive branch.[68]

So involved are members of the House and Senate in the budget making process that (in essence) three federal budgets are eventually proposed: that of the president, the House and the Senate. Commenting on the politics of the new budgetary process shortly after passage of the law, Allen Schick, a leading authority on the federal budget making process, had this to say: "There are signs that budgetary warfare—in particular, conflict between the president and Congress—has escalated in recent years, and the prospect is for more tension in the future than was customary in the past."[69] In the view of James A. Thurber, budgetary reform has not only increased the complexity of federal budget making, but has also afforded Congress with more opportunity to control a president's spending priorities.[70]

According to Margaret Davis, legislative assistant for budgetary affairs and Heritage Foundation scholar, since passage of the Budget Act, Congress, not the president, routinely controls the outcome of the federal operating budget. (In Davis' view, the exception was President Reagan's first federal budget presented in 1981 for the fiscal year 1982.)[71] With respect to the impoundment provisions of the 1974 law, there are now specific limitations placed on the president's power to impound federal appropriations; no longer can the president unilaterally freeze money appropriated by Congress for federal programs. In accordance with the 1974 law, the president must seek authorization from Congress prior to impounding appropriated funds.

To wrest even more power from the president in the area of fiscal policy making, Congress also passed legislation requiring the Director of the Office of Management and Budget to undergo Senate confirmation. This requirement further reflects the new congressional attitude towards the power of the American presidency. Budget directors are one of the most important actors within the president's entire administration and budgetary decisions are at the heart of the president's agenda. Senate confirmation of such a pivotal presidential appointee potentially undermines the capacity of the president to direct major change in tax and spending policies.

In addition to its constraint of presidential war making and fiscal powers, Congress has increased its activity within the realm of congressional oversight. The Senate Watergate Hearings institutionalized congressional suspicion of the activities of the president, close presidential advisors, and executive branch activity in general. As a result, the tradition known as congressional oversight, which allows Congress to conduct hearings and investigations into suspect executive action, has become a recurring feature on Capitol Hill over the course of the last twenty years. A study by Joel D. Aberbach of the Brookings Institution concerning trends in congressional oversight from 1961 to 1983 clearly documents the rise of oversight-related activity in Table 4.

As the Aberbach study reveals, congressional committees now

Table 4
Hearings and Meetings of Congressional Committees, January 1–July 4, 1961–1983

Year	Total Days	Oversight Days	Oversight as Percent of Total
1961	1,789	146	8.2
1963	1,820	159	8.7
1965	2,055	141	6.9
1967	1,797	171	9.5
1969	1,804	217	12.0
1971	2,063	187	9.1
1973	2,513	290	11.5
1975	2,552	459	18.0
1977	3,053	537	17.6
1981	2,222	434	19.5
1983	2,331	587	25.2

Percent Change

1961–71	15.3	28.1	11.0
1961–77	70.7	267.8	114.6
1961–83	30.3	302.1	207.3

Source: Joel D. Aberbach, *Keeping A Watchful Eye*, Washington, D.C.: The Brookings Institution, 1990, p. 35. Reprinted with permission.

devote increasing amounts of time to oversight hearings. In 1961 only 8.2 percent of committee hearings and meetings concerned oversight of the executive branch. By 1983, this figure had risen to 25.2 percent, comprising a full quarter of congressional committee activity. Between 1961 and 1983, oversight activity rose by an astonishing 207.3 percent!

Seeking explanations for this remarkable rise in congressional oversight activity, Aberbach discovered 55 percent of top congressional staffers cited the growth and complexity of the federal government while 22 percent expressed concern over the "accrual and abuse" of presidential power.[72]

There is currently an increasing amount of detailed congressional oversight activity in all areas of public policy, both domestic and foreign. Consider, for example, congressional inquiry into the activities of the Department of Defense. According to one source, the number of congressional requests for testimony and information from the Defense Department between 1975 and 1984 was three times higher than between 1965 and 1974. During the Reagan era, for example, Richard Armitage, Assistant Secretary of Defense for International Security Affairs was asked to testify before Congress over 150 times. The Pentagon, it is estimated, currently receives approximately 100,000 such official requests from Congress each year.[73] This relatively new trend in congressional oversight has led some observers to accuse Congress of "micromanaging" foreign and domestic policy, thus posing a direct threat to presidential leadership, good government, and the entire separation of powers doctrine.[74]

The institutionalization of congressional oversight in recent years is further exemplified by congressional investigations into the so-called Clinton "Whitewater Affair." At the time of this writing, congressional hearings concerning the alleged scandal have commenced. Several members of the Clinton administration have been called before the Senate Banking, Housing, and Urban Affairs Committee. The questioning thus far has been detailed, intense, and quite grueling. A special prosecutor has also been dispatched to Little Rock, Arkansas to investigate the matter. Thus far, the Whitewater controversy has resulted in the resignations of White House counsel Bernard Nussbaum, Associate Attorney General Webster L. Hubbell, and Deputy Treasury Secretary Roger C. Altman. As it was previously noted, what is especially distressing about the entire Whitewater Affair is that accusations of impropriety on the part of both President Clinton and his wife originated not from Clinton's conduct as president, but rather from activity during his service as governor of Arkansas. The alleged misconduct occurred ten years prior to Clinton's assumption of the presidency—- over a full decade ago. Nevertheless, Congress—determined to curb presidential malfeasance—continues to press forward with congressional hearings in spite of the fact that the Constitution does not expressly articulate the power of congressional oversight. Although the Supreme Court in 1927 upheld the right of Congress to mount investigations, this power is *implied* in the Constitution rather than enumerated.[75]

In addition to aggressive oversight, congressional encroachment upon the affairs of the president and the executive branch can be observed in the increasing number of appropriations bills which contain specifically described spending limitations, in distinct increases in temporary rather than permanent spending authorizations, and in the increasing use of the controversial legislative veto.[76]

Many appropriations bills now contain limitations restricting executive use of federally-appropriated funds to advance a specific area of policy. Congress increases its leverage over the executive branch through use of such spending limitations, curtailing discretionary spending by the president, his advisors and executive branch officials. As James L. Sundquist states: "By simply adding to an appropriation bill a sentence beginning 'No part of any appropriation under this Act shall be available for . . . ,' the Congress can effectively prevent an administrative agency from developing or enforcing a particular rule, or taking a specific action."[77] Riders on appropriations bills are a common congressional tool for limiting the discretionary scope of executive officials. In 1963, a total of 17 limitation riders were proposed in Congress, of which 7 (41 percent) were adopted. In 1980, 67 limitation riders were proposed, of which 60 (75 percent) were adopted.[78]

Temporary authorizations are also utilized by Congress more frequently than in the past. Rather than provide permanent funding for federal programs, Congress has resorted to authorizing funds on an annual basis. By the end of the 1970s, approximately 40 percent of the federal budget had come under such temporary authorization. Through providing annual rather than long-term funding, Congress exerts substantial control over the activity of the president and administration officials.[79]

The legislative veto is yet another measure used by Congress in its attempt to constrain the power of the president and executive branch agencies. Laws may contain specific provisions that allow Congress to periodically review the implementation of policy, delaying or terminating it as Congress sees fit, thus exercising a "veto" over the executive branch. The War Powers Act and the Congressional Budget and Impoundment Control Act are examples of laws that contain legislative veto provisions.[80]

In a controversial decision, the Supreme Court in Immigration and Naturalization Service v. Chada (1983) ruled the legislative veto unconstitutional. In the Court's view, the exercise of such a veto violated the separation of powers doctrine.[81] Interestingly, the Chada ruling (contrary to predictions) has not in any significant way restricted congressional control over implementation of policies. Various measures continue to be used by the legislature to maintain leverage over the executive branch.

Power authorized by Congress to the executive branch which prior to the Chada ruling had been subject to legislative veto is now simply withheld by Congress. Riders on appropriations bills that place specific limitations on executive discretion regarding spending priorities are another congressional tactic through which control over the executive is exercised. At the same time Congress continues to pass laws that contain legislative veto provisions, regardless of the Supreme Court ruling against such measures. Rather than force a confrontation with Congress (which could potentially result in less support for agency activity), the executive branch appears willing to live with the illegal provisions.[82] The Chada ruling, therefore, has not had the effect of strengthening the presidency and the executive branch that was initially anticipated. As a result of a Congress fully determined to diminish and in many ways control the powers of the American presidency, recent presidents have experienced much difficulty with respect to the policy making process. The governing process has become increasingly difficult for each succeeding president. As Allen Schick states "Ronald Reagan launched his presidency more encumbered by legal constraints than was Jimmy Carter. Carter was more limited by law than was Gerald Ford. Ford was more limited than was Richard Nixon."[83] To this, one should add that Bill Clinton began his presidency more encumbered than George Bush, while Bush was more encumbered than Ronald Reagan. Research professor Steven A. Shull reiterates this perspective: "A President today is inherently weaker in his dealings with Congress than Thomas Jefferson, or even Franklin Roosevelt or Lyndon Johnson."[84]

Exactly why the American presidency has evolved into a state of siege is difficult for any presidential observer to precisely identify. Why do special interest groups, lobbyists and PACs pose such a threat to effective presidential leadership? What explains this development? What political conditions have allowed for the growth of the bureaucratic behemoth that all presidents must contend with? What occurred within the context of American politics that so radically altered the president's relationship with the media? Why is the United States Congress so unwilling to cooperate with the president?

The Vietnam War and the Watergate crisis are frequently identified as the major historical events relevant to understanding the decline of the American presidency and presidential power. Such events resulted in a significant reduction of presidential power. Any attempt to explain the American presidency under siege must consider Vietnam and Watergate.

But are such events the *fundamental* reasons why the presidency has become immobilized? Is it possible that a besieged presidency can be attributed to a development even deeper within the fabric of American politics? Why is the American presidency really under siege?

CHAPTER THREE

Party Decline and Presidential Leadership

Parties and the Presidency

Modern presidents are having difficulty leading the nation due primarily to the decline of political parties as instruments in the governing process. Although this may not be the sole explanation behind the problems facing the modern presidency, enough evidence exists to suggest a close association between party decline and the resulting crisis in presidential leadership. As Robert Harmel states: "Although the American parties of old may have never afforded the president the kind of party loyalty that is assured to prime ministers, neither did they require as much of him as their leader. The American parties did aid their presidents in ways that we may only now—in the age of a relatively nonpartisan presidency—begin to fully appreciate."[1] Presidents can benefit from political parties in a number of ways.

To begin with, a system of strong political parties provides American presidents with *stability* in the governing process. According to William Nisbet Chambers, American political parties contribute to stable and firm relationships between governmental decision-makers, and between the decision-makers and their client groups within the electorate. Political parties bind governmental decision-makers with one another and bind those in government with the American people. Uncertainty and chaos in the policy-making process is reduced and the framework for governing becomes more predictable and stable.[2] American presidents governing within a predictable and stable system of government are more likely to foresee obstacles to policy proposals and can more accurately calculate their chances of legislative success. Failure and national embarassment will thus be less likely.

Teamwork is another result of a political system characterized by strong political parties. Presidents who can depend upon their parties in the governing process are more likely to function within a network of political allies and trusted lieutenants. A strong political party system provides a president with a crucial power base from which to govern. Presidential objectives are more likely to be accomplished when members of Congress, Cabinet officers, state governors, state legislators and even municipal officials perceive themselves as members of the president's team. The partisan link is especially important in a governmental system characterized by a separation of powers between three branches of government and a division of power between national and state authority. In the absence of a strong political party, there is virtually no means through which the president is united with other policy-makers.[3] Political parties, according to Godfrey Hodgson, "bound together the president and Congress, separated in constitutional theory, just enough to allow the president to emerge as the effective leader of the government and to respond, in the persons of the two Roosevelts, Wilson and Truman, to the great new challenges of the first half of the twentieth century."[4]

Political parties central to the governing process result in a greater likelihood of presidential *accountability*. A party-oriented electoral process tends to emphasize the content of party platforms as cues for the voting public. Presidential candidates presenting themselves to the electorate not only as competent leaders but also as "Democrats" or "Republicans," will be evaluated in light of party principles and the connotations associated with a party label.[5] While in office, the president, due to public expectations, remains sensitive to the articulated principles of the platform. The extent to which the president implements the party platform serves as useful gauge for presidential performance. A president perceived as faithful to the platform and principles of the party is deemed a more trustworthy and accountable national leader. Presidents perceived by the American people as accountable and true to their word can govern with more respect and power. As Hodgson notes: "Thirty years ago, the platform was a serious statement of common principle, and elected officials were expected to stand by it."[6] It is important, therefore, that American presidents emerge through a party system in which parties express a clear set of ideals and positions on issues. It contributes to effective and accountable leadership.

Linkage between the president and the American people is enhanced when political parties are strong and active. Beginning with the campaign for nomination and throughout the general election campaign and during his term of office, as a result of vibrant and visible parties the American people will feel closer to, and more involved in, the political process. The importance of linkage cannot be overstated, as the presidency serves to maintain an important public connection so vital in a democratic system.[7] As the country's only national representative, it is imperative that the president have a grassroots connection with the American people. A president who emerges through the party system is more likely to enjoy a broad base of public support, while the president who circumvents the party system will not. As Harmel states: "The 'automatic' base of party support that presidents could once depend upon in the electorate has diminished with the decline of the parties."[8] James MacGregor Burns believes strong political parties are not only essential for good government, but also central to the functioning of a democracy:

> Political parties can serve as the mainspring of democracy, as the vital link between voters and rulers. They organize and focus public opinion. They aggregate 'special' interests. They provide meaningful cues to voters, present them with alternatives at election time, propose programs, develop among party followers and party leaders in office support for such programs. They unify legislators and executives among themselves and with one another. They help hold government officials accountable to voters. They mobilize popular support for candidates and officeholders and hence are indispensible to democratic leadership.[9]

Thus, there is much to be said for the relationship between a strong political party system and an effective presidency. Stability, teamwork, accountability, and linkage with the American people are essential ingredients in the exercise of presidential power. A strong political party system clearly helps ensure these conditions. As John H. Aldrich puts it: "Parties are—or should be—integral parts of all political life, from structuring the reasoning and choice of the electorate, through all facets of campaigns and seemingly all facets of the government, to the very possibility of effective governance in a democracy."[10]

Recent American presidents, unfortunately, have not enjoyed the luxury of a strong party system. A strong presidency requires a strong political party system—an element no longer present in American politics. President Jimmy Carter reflects on the place of parties during his term in the White House in this manner: "I learned the hard way that there was no party loyalty or discipline when a complicated or controversial issue was at stake—none."[11]

The gradual atrophy of the American party system has allowed new forces to dominate the political scene—much to the detriment of presidential leadership.[12] As parties have declined, there has been a marked rise in the power of special interest groups, lobbyists, and PACs. Party decline has strengthened the potential for iron triangles, issue networks and the bureaucracy to sabotage the president's agenda. The media's political influence has increased tremendously as parties have surrendered their communicative power. Without a strong partisan link to the legislature, Congress has become more antagonistic and hostile to the president. The decline of parties has created a power vacuum, into which have stepped an array of forces which often impede, undermine and block creative presidential leadership. The decline of political parties therefore is directly related to the current failure of presidential leadership.

Why Did Parties Decline?

The decline of the American party system is a complicated phenomenon. Many developments, some in conjunction with one another and others independently, have contributed to the weakened state of American political parties. Although the roots of party decline can be traced to the early years of the twentieth century, the decline of parties as instruments in the governing process has clearly accelerated over the course of the last twenty-five years. To do justice to the subject of party decline, a detailed discussion is required.

Social and Economic Developments

Any discussion of party decline must identify broad changes in the American socio-economic system as having an adverse impact on the power of political parties. In this respect, the rise in socio-economic status among former immigrant groups, the decline in immigration, and the resulting breakdown of tight ethnic communities in urban areas is relevant for understanding the waning strength of political parties. As A. James Reichley, author of *The Life of the Parties*, states:

> Rising levels of income and education produced new generations of voters who had less need of their precinct captain's services and did not readily accept instructions, or pleas, on how to vote. Deep reduction in the flow of immigration greatly diminished the supply of foreign-born who would look to their precinct captain for help in

finding jobs or dealing with government. As children and grandchildren of immigrants lost interest in ethnic attachments and moved away from old neighborhoods, the machines lost some of their function of speaking for ethnic and religious solidarity.[13]

There was a time in American history when powerful party organizations known as "political machines" dominated the politics of America's urban areas. New York City, Boston, Kansas City, Chicago, Philadelphia, Los Angeles, and other densely populated American cities were characterized by strong party organizations capable of mobilizing masses of voters at election time. The urban machines were run by party precinct captains, ward bosses and county chairmen. These individuals were the forces "behind the scenes" in American politics, and they devoted their lives to the welfare and power of their respective political party.[14] Candidates and office holders at all levels of government could not ignore the immense political influence of urban machines.

The machines had the capacity to determine the outcome of mayoral, gubernatorial, congressional, and even presidential elections. While in office, mayors, governors, and presidents consulted county chairmen on policy issues. Politicians at all levels relied heavily on party machines to maintain a base of popular support.

To sustain their control over the urban population, party machines depended substantially on the administration of patronage jobs. Immigrant groups arriving from Europe, such as the Irish, Italians, Germans, and Poles, looked to the party machines for economic security. The local precinct captain could offer government jobs to impoverished immigrants in return, of course, for party loyalty and voter support.

But gradual changes in the fabric of the socio-economic system eventually reduced the dependence of ethnic groups on precinct captains, ward bosses and county party chairmen. Increased educational opportunities led to a rise in affluence among major ethnic groups thereby weakening the machine's grip over large blocs of voters. Millions of urbanites became less reliant on political machines for employment and voting cues.[15] Improvement in the social and economic status of urban ethnic groups also resulted in the physical movement of such groups to suburban America, further severing ties between the party machine and its natural constituency.

To complicate matters for the party machine, President Franklin Roosevelt offered the American people a "New Deal." One major component of Roosevelt's vast agenda was the Social Security Act enacted by Congress in 1935. With passage of the Social Security Act, a national welfare system was created.

Social security legislation, which included an array of entitlement and relief programs, significantly reduced the dependence of the poor on party organizations for the bare essentials of life. The unemployed and destitute, rather than turning to local parties for help as many did prior to the Roosevelt years, now looked to the federal government for economic relief and assistance.[16] In essence, as a result of New Deal measures, the federal government supplanted the political party organization as the principal provider of social insurance.

A rise in educational levels, economic affluence and the creation of federal relief programs combined to reduce the importance of political parties—especially the large urban machines—within the context of American politics. The organizational power base of American presidents eroded considerably as a result. These developments, however, only partially explain the demise of the party system.

The Loss of Patronage

Sweeping reform in the field of government employment also contributed to the decline of party authority. Federal, state and local public employment used to fall under the domain of the political party organization. The party in power rewarded the party faithful with an array of government jobs commonly referred to as "patronage appointments." The possibility of receiving a government job in return for election-related activity was a major motivating factor behind intensive party activism.

Individuals seeking government employment had to be approved by the local party chairmen. The local chairs determined whether the applicant was in fact a loyal Democrat or Republican. Serving as the "gatekeeper" for government jobs gave the local party chairman unique and quite extraordinary authority.

Flagrant use of the patronage system as a means of inducing party loyalty can be traced to the presidency of Andrew Jackson (1829–1837). The "spoils system," as it came to be known, was institutionalized under this powerful and highly controversial president. Unlike the aristocratic presidencies of Washington, Adams, Jefferson, Madison, and Monroe, government jobs under Jackson were allocated to the less wealthy and more common people.[17] Appointing the common party loyalist from the grassroots was consistent with Jackson's image as the "people's tribune." In his view, partisan loyalty rather than administrative expertise should be the chief criterion for appointment to government positions. The use of patronage for the purpose of party building flourished throughout much of the nineteenth century. While patronage appointments did not always result in the most qualified individuals assuming administrative positions, they did provide presidents with an important link to the grassroots, considerable control over public servants in the executive branch of government, and a degree of leverage over the legislature. The "clearance" function of local party chairmen connected the presidency to the foundation of the party organization and the party's rank-and-file. Federal employees unprotected by civil service laws were forced to comply with presidential directives. Presidents could reward congressional support with choice government posts for constituents. If administered strategically, patronage appointments could secure popular and legislative support for presidential initiatives.

A major turning point in the history of the patronage system was the assassination of President James Garfield in 1881. Garfield's assassin, according to most accounts, was a "disgruntled office-seeker,"—a man who believed he was owed a government job as a result of his partisan activity. The Garfield assassination served as the principal catalyst for passage of the Pendleton Act of 1883.

The Pendleton Act created the Federal Civil Service Commission to control the hiring of government employees. Merit, rather than partisan connections, became the criterion for filling a wide range of federal jobs. Individual competence for particular administrative posts was determined through civil service examinations. Government employment was now based on competence and political neutrality.

From the passage of the Pendleton Act to the present, an increasing number of federal jobs have been classified as "civil service" and thus politically neutralized.[18] The number of federal posts under the control of the president has systematically declined. This has significantly reduced the president's role as party leader and weakened his authority as the nation's chief executive. Needless to say, the role of political parties as avenues to government employment was also severely diminished. One study reveals that in 1891, only 21.5 percent of all federal government jobs were classified under the merit system. By 1990, this figure had risen to 81.0 percent.[19] State civil service legislation further reduced the patronage available to political parties at the state and local levels of government. Although reform at the subnational level proceeded somewhat haphazardly and varied from state to state, parties eventually lost control over a substantial number of government jobs. In some states (such as Wisconsin), civil service reform was engineered in the early decades of the twentieth century and served as a model for government reformers. In other states, reform of the patronage system did not receive serious attention for decades. Consider, for example, the blatant use of patronage by Governor Ross Barnett of Mississippi as late as 1959:

> When he was sworn in, office seekers trooped into Jackson from all over the state, and the waiting line wound around the capitol rotunda and down the street. Governor Barnett found hundreds of jobs, but not enough for everyone. Campaigning for re-election in Brandon, Mississippi, the governor met someone who had voted for him, and had influenced all his relatives to vote for him, and still couldn't understand why he didn't get a job. The governor answered that that was precisely, yes precisely, why he was running a second time—to find jobs for everyone he couldn't take care of the first time.[20]

Consider as well the state of Indiana. Until the 1960s, the patronage system was used by party leaders, not only to reward party loyalists with government employment, but also to bolster the party's treasury. Ten to twenty thousand jobs were controlled by the party in power, and job holders were routinely expected to donate two percent of their salaries to the party's treasury.[21] While reform of the patronage system proceeded slowly at the state level, all states eventually restricted the use of patronage appointments.[22] Most government employment at the state and municipal level is now regulated by civil service legislation.

To complicate matters for political parties, civil service at both the federal and state level was further neutralized by passage of the Hatch Act in 1939. According to this law, federal employees, except high level political appointees, must refrain from campaign-related activity. Government posts cannot be used by individuals to advance the interests of a political party. Sidney M. Milkis describes the impact of the Hatch Act on the Roosevelt presidency in these terms: "Until the passage of this bill, the Roosevelt Administration was developing the expanding executive branch into an inchoate national political machine. The Hatch Act, however, which in many respects was passed in reaction to the purge campaigns, made the full development of a presidential political machine less likely."[23]

According to Milkis, approximately half of all delegates to the 1936 Democratic National Convention were employees of the federal government. By 1940, only cabinet officers, congressmen, and other high level political appointments in the Roosevelt administration arrived as delegates.[24] In 1940, the Hatch Act was ammended to include state and municipal employees. Shortly thereafter, a number of states and municipalities followed the lead of the federal government by enacting laws and ordinances known as "little Hatch Acts."[25]

During the Clinton administration, Congress once again amended the Hatch Act, only this time for the purpose of allowing somewhat more freedom for federal employees to participate in party politics. Although there are still legal restraints on federal employees, it should be interesting to observe whether or not this newly acquired opportunity to engage in partisan activity will serve the interests of presidential leadership. There appears to be some promise in this recent reform for political parties and the presidency.

Reform of the patronage system and the creation of federal and state civil service commissions dramatically reduced the power of political parties. The capacity of party chairmen to offer government jobs in return for party support was a major resource relied upon by party organizations. Even in Connecticut, ranked on the low end of the spectrum regarding use of patronage jobs,[26] seasoned party officials lament the loss of patronage as a tool for political party maintenance.[27] This is not to suggest that patronage was, or is, the only incentive behind party activity in American politics. Psychological rewards and ideological commitment to the issues associated with a party are for some people far more important than the possibility of a government job.[28] Nevertheless, any discussion of party decline and the resulting diminishment of presidential power must consider the decline of patronage as contributing to this condition.

Direct Primary Elections

In addition to socio-economic developments and a series of legal reforms directed at patronage, the emergence of direct primary elections as nominating mechanisms has also weakened the power of political parties. The introduction of direct primaries in American politics reflected a deep concern among reformers with the power of party leaders in the internal affairs of party politics. Party chairs, often depicted as "party bosses" or "party chieftains," were percieved as wielding far too much authority during election campaigns, especially with respect to the process of selecting candidates for public office—the nominating process.

In the view of reformers, the nominating process required a more open and fair system in which the party's rank-and-file rather than a handful of party leaders determined the outcome. Smoke-filled rooms at nominating conventions in which party bosses brokered the outcome was an image common to the presidential nominating system during the heyday of powerful party organizations.[29] Primary elections posed a new and very direct threat to the power of the party bosses. As Theodore H. White notes: "People, ordinary people—so ran the thought—should have the right to go into closed voting booths and there accept or repudiate the party bosses in naming the party's candidates to govern them."[30]

The initial drive to democratize the party nominating process was spearheaded by The Progessive Movement, a political reform movement which surfaced during the early decades of the twentieth century. The Progressives directly challenged the vast power exercised by party organization leadership. In addition to advocating the direct primary as a nominating device, the Progressive agenda called for civil service reform, non-partisan elections, popular referenda, initiatives, minimum wage for women, prohibition of child labor, social insurance, and the establishment of a Department of Labor.[31] Progressives were active in electoral contests at the local, state, and national levels. Three presidential candidacies were launched under the Progressive banner—those of former Republican President Theodore Roosevelt in 1912 (also known as the Bull Moose Party), Wisconsin Governor Robert Lafollette in 1924, and former Vice President Henry Wallace in 1948.[32]

The proliferation of direct primary elections in state and national politics resulted in a more porous and fluid nominating process, much to the detriment of party organization leadership. Presidential, congressional, and gubernatorial candidates no longer had to win the approval of party leadership in order to secure the party's nomination. Candidates could appeal directly to the party's rank-and-file and become the nominee by winning the most votes in a primary election. In this way, candidates could circumvent the party organization during the nominating contest.

Although primary elections have been present in American politics for a good part of the twentieth century, their role as nominating devices in presidential elections evolved at a much slower pace compared with that of other elected offices. As recently as 1968, only seventeen states had adopted presidential primary laws.[33] In that year, most delegates to national nominating conventions were selected, not according to the results of primary elections, but rather through party caucuses or other closed delegate selection procedures dominated by state and local party leaders.

Even in states where presidential primaries were held, the winner of the primary contest did not necessarily win the state's convention delegates. The rules permitted party organization leaders to construct delegate slates to the national nominating convention regardless of primary election outcomes.[34] This condition was radically altered by the tumultuous and explosive events associated with the 1968 Democratic National Convention. This highly controversial episode in the history of American politics set in motion a series of internal party reforms which directly reduced the nominating power of the political party organization.[35] In addition, these reforms further weakened the relationship between presidential candidates and their respective parties. Election year 1968 is a story in and of itself.

1968: The Turning Point

1968 was clearly a powder keg year for American politics. President Johnson, in a televised speech from the White House, announced his decision not to seek a second term of office. Racial tension and civil unrest gripped the cities of America and the Vietnam War continued with no end in sight. The anti-war movement had reached its peak, protest was rampant in the streets and on college campuses, and a distinct counterculture opposed to authority had emerged. The hopes and dreams of millions of Americans were shattered by the assassinations of Martin Luther King and Robert Kennedy.

The Democratic Party, known for its heterogeneous membership and factional politics, reflected the turmoil of 1968. Alabama governor George Wallace, nationally known as a racial segregationist and supporter of states' rights, departed from the "liberal" Democratic Party to wage an independent and conservative campaign for the presidency.[36] But the more important story for the Democratic Party of 1968 is found, not in the candidacy of George Wallace, but rather within the internal politics of its presidential nominating process.

Following President Johnson's announcement, an intense factional struggle erupted between three presidential candidates: Vice President Hubert Humphrey, who represented the Johnson administration, Minnesota Senator Eugene McCarthy representing the anti-war and left wing of the party (whose near upset of president Johnson in the New Hampshire primary had dissuaded the president from seeking another term), and Robert Kennedy, a liberal Democrat with a substantial following among racial minorities, anti-war activists, and the party's poor. It was this fractious nominating struggle which eventually led to broad party reforms that fundamentally altered the presidential nominating process—even to this day. These reforms severely reduced the power of party organizations in the presidential nominating process and further severed the working relationship between political parties and the American presidency.

One of the major problems in the 1968 Democratic nominating contest was that the nominating process was, for all intents and purposes, closed to the party's rank-and-file. The majority of delegates to the Democratic National Convention were selected by party leaders in closed party caucuses. To complicate matters, in states where primary elections were held, the results were often meaningless. The number of votes received by a presidential candidate in a primary election were not reflected in the number of convention delegates apportioned to that candidate. Although a candidate might win in the primaries, there was no guarantee that the majority of the state's delegation would support him at the nominating convention.

Hubert Humphrey was nominated at the Democratic National Convention in Chicago based on the support of delegates handpicked by party leaders in closed party caucuses. This was the predominant method for selecting convention delegates in 1968, and in years prior. Equally disturbing was the fact that Hubert Humphrey had never entered a presidential primary contest. The nominating process was a closed process, controlled by party leaders who exhibited little respect for the will of the Democratic electorate. It was in essence sealed from the party's rank-and-file and dominated by autocratic party leaders. Eugene McCarthy and Robert Kennedy *had* entered primary contests and both had received sizeable shares of the primary votes. McCarthy and Kennedy were, therefore, identified by their supporters as the only legitimate Democratic contenders; Humphrey was an "illegitimate" candidate.

Kennedy's assassination in the immediate aftermath of his primary victory in California left only McCarthy to challenge Humphrey and the Democratic party's establishment. Followers of McCarthy believed that he, not Humphrey, was the rightful heir to the party's nomination because of his extensive campaigning and respectable showing in state primary elections. Party leaders, however, had other plans.

When the Democratic National Convention met in Chicago during August, Hubert Humphrey was nominated as the party's presidential candidate. The decision to nominate Humphrey was viewed by McCarthy supporters and the liberal wing of the party as the result of a nominating process dictated by "party bosses." This intolerable situation, combined with the Democratic establishment's continued support of the war, resulted in demonstrations in the streets of Chicago. Violent confrontations ensued between police and anti-war protesters. Chicago mayor Richard Daley, a "party boss" in the true sense of the term and a Humphrey supporter, ordered Chicago police to crack down hard on the demonstrators. Daley's orders served only to escalate the violence. As William Crotty notes: "The heavy-handed approach of the police combined with the determination of the demonstrators to make their point at whatever cost ended in a daily series of confrontations, clubbings, gassings, attacks, and counterattacks that stormed across the nation's television screens."[37] Americans watched in disbelief as the nominating procedure of the Democratic Party—the party of Kennedy, Truman, and Roosevelt—erupted into a full-scale riot on the streets of Chicago.

Events associated with the 1968 Democratic Convention triggered a series of dramatic party reforms. In its effort to "democratize" and improve the presidential nominating process, the Democratic Party created reform commissions to study nominating rules and procedures, make recommendations for promoting representative outcomes, and, more generally, to establish a nominating system that would empower the party's rank-and-file.[38] Among the many reforms resulting from the work of the reform commissions was a dramatic increase in the number of state presidential primaries.

Beginning with the presidential nominating contest of 1972 and extending to the present, a presidential candidate could no longer avoid primary elections, as Humphrey had, and still emerge as the party's nominee. Voting by the party's rank-and-file in a primary contest would also decide the outcome of the presidential nominating contest. The party's rank-and-file was clearly empowered, as many states after 1968 adopted primary elections as a means of determining the party's presidential candidate. Because primaries are enacted through state law, the Republican presidential nominating process was also affected by the recommendations of the Democratic reform commissions.[39] Like Democratic presidential candidates, Republican candidates must compete in primary elections. If a state decides to use the party caucus rather than a primary as the means of selecting convention delegates, that process must also be open to the party's rank-and-file.

Primary contests are now at the heart of the presidential nominating contest. As previously noted, in 1968 there were only seventeen state presidential primaries, and outcomes mattered very little in the eventual choice of the party nominee. By 1992, the number of presidential primary contests had risen to thirty-nine. Moreover, the results of the primaries now directly determine the party's presidential nominee.

In theory, primary elections should strengthen political parties. Nominating outcomes determined through primary elections should legitimize the party's choice of a presidential candidate. A candidate selected by means of primary elections ought to represent the demographic and attitudinal characteristics of the party's rank-and-file. By allowing the party's rank-and-file to directly participate in nominating outcomes, presidential candidates—and subsequently, the president—should enjoy a wide base of popular and partisan support. Theoretically, vibrant citizen-based parties that hold candidates accountable for their actions should develop as a result of primary elections. This, in fact, was one of the principal objectives of reformers after the 1968 Democratic Convention.[40]

Unfortunately, the proliferation of primaries has served to weaken, not strengthen, the American party system. Candidate-centered campaigns and a candidate-centered presidency are the end results of primary elections, phenomena unforeseen by party reformers. Candidates who aspire to the American presidency now form their own personal campaign organizations consisting of professional pollsters, fund-raisers, advance men, speech writers, and media consultants.[41] The typical presidential campaign organization is only marginally associated with the formal party organization and the party's professionals.

A presidential candidate is no longer required to have the support of the official party organization. How the party's national chairman, state party chairmen or thousands of county party chairs feel about a candidate is almost irrelevant in the modern nominating system. The opinion of party leaders in the House of Representatives and the Senate matter very little, and the views of state governors and local mayors have become much less important over the course of the last few decades.[42]

Due to opportunities afforded by primaries, presidential candidates today feel little obligation to work with those in the party hierarchy to secure the party's nomination. The candidate-centered process continues throughout the general election, with the "party's" nominee depending almost exclusively on his own cadre of consultants to manage and direct the presidential campaign. This development has had serious consequences for presidential leadership. Presidents, upon arriving in the Oval Office, find themselves essentially disconnected from those they need most for cooperation, guidance, and help during the governing process. The American president, due to the "candidate-centered" as opposed to the "party-centered" selection process, is in many ways a stranger to seasoned politicians with years of experience and a wealth of political expertise. With the exception of the White House staff, which often includes personal friends who managed the presidential campaign, the president has little if any close association with those he appoints to executive posts, or with members of Congress. As Lester G. Seligman and Carry R. Covington put it: "Each piece of legislation inititates a new 'game' to play for the president, requiring a rebuilding of the president's team repeatedly over the life of the presidency."[43] While one might expect primary elections to be an empowering device for presidents, the evidence regarding voter participation in these unique American nominating mechanisms suggests otherwise. Voter participation is normally very low in primary contests. A typical state presidential primary will record approximately twenty to thirty percent of eligible voters voting.[44]

Other problems are also evident in primary elections. In presidential primaries having several candidates, the candidate who "wins" the primary might receive nothing more than a small plurality of votes.[45] At the same time, primary winners are often candidates supported by well-organized factions within the party's rank-and-file—hardly a base upon which to build a strong presidency. In some nominating contests it appears that presidential candidates in the post-1968 era are building their base of popular support upon intra-party factions and special interest groups rather than a broad cross-section of the party's rank-and-file.[46]

Primary elections therefore have contributed very directly to the decline of political party organizations in electoral politics. Greater distance has been created between presidential candidates, party professionals and the party structure. This new system of electoral politics is evident in a more isolated, weaker, and confused presidency.

The Rise of Technology in Election Campaigns

The increasing role of technology in modern election campaigns is yet another development contributing to the decline of American political parties. Presidential candidates' reliance on media consultants and a range of other experts with techno-political skills has contributed to more distance between presidential candidates and their respective party organizations. In the process, official party committees have become relegated to marginal roles during the campaign. As John H. Kessel states, the "common pattern is to allow the existing candidate organization to conduct the campaign and have the national committee staff take care of 'other party business.'"[47] According to Stephen E. Frantzich in *Political Parties in the Technological Age*, new technology, particularly the electronic media, has diminished the pivotal function of party organizations in the electoral arena. The use of media, especially television, has allowed candidates to reach the electorate in a far more rapid and efficient fashion compared to the labor-intensive methods of political party organizations. Door-to-door campaigning, campaign rallies, and the traditional face-to-face voter mobilization tactics of party organizations have become almost obsolete in electoral contests beyond the local level.[48]

Frantzich also notes that increased reliance on electronic media for the purpose of conveying campaign messages to voters has resulted in a less partisan electoral contest. Due to the broad appeal of television, candidates have intentionally "standardized" their messages in order to avoid alienating large blocs of voters. They have "soft-pedaled their partisan ties" in the hopes of mobilizing a broad-based coalition.[49]

The infusion of technology into election campaigns becomes apparent in an examination of key personnel associated with a modern presidential campaign organization. No longer do national, state, and county party chairmen serve as chief strategists of the presidential campaign. Instead, within the ranks of a modern campaign organization, there is likely to be an array of political consultants with very specific technological skills. These skills, which command substantial salaries, are utilized to mobilize millions of voters.

Media consultants recruited from the field of commercial advertising, professional fund-raisers, direct mail specialists, pollsters, speech writers, and public relations experts appear to be the principal players in modern campaign organizations. Such individuals are frequently recruited from private industry where their skills have been employed for commercial profit. Kessel provides insight into the background of some recent public relations strategists:

> David D'Alessandro had risen from advertising to become president of the corporate sector of the John Hancock Insurance Company before John Sasso asked him to manage the Dukakis media campaign. James Travis, a partner in Della Feminia, Travisano & Partners,

a medium-sized advertising firm in New York City, organized the "Tuesday Team" that handled the Reagan media in 1984. Gerald Rafshoon Advertising, Inc., is a general advertising firm (that is, the bulk of its income comes from nonpolitical accounts) in Atlanta. Rafshoon, whose ties with Jimmy Carter went back to the first Carter gubernatorial campaign in 1966, was in charge of public relations in both Carter presidential campaigns. Peter Dailey formed Dailey and Associates in Los Angeles in 1968 after gaining experience in some very large advertising firms. He was in charge of the Nixon media campaign in 1972, worked on space acquisition during the 1976 Ford campaign, and was again in charge of the Reagan advertising in 1980.[50]

While public relations specialists, according to Kessel, do not always dominate the presidential campaign, the use of electronic media as a voter mobilization tool inevitably increased the influence of such individuals in the presidential selection process. With millions of dollars currently allocated for campaign commercials (television spot-ads),[51] it should come as no surprise that media consultants, rather than party organization personnel, now assume major campaign responsibilities. Larry Sabato characterizes the impact of professional consulting on political parties this way: "Political consultants, answerable only to their client-candidates and independent of the political parties, have inflicted severe damage upon the party system and masterminded the modern triumph of personality cults over party politics in the United States."[52]

In fairness to the parties, it should be noted that the national party committees have responded to the forces of technology by developing an array of sophisticated voter mobilization and campaign finance services. According to Sabato, the Republican National Committee in recent years has conducted telephone canvassing and instituted direct mailings in its effort to elect Republican presidents. Additionally, the RNC has provided sophisticated polling services and television commercials for national and subnational candidates. The Democratic National Committee, in response to a series of electoral defeats, has followed the lead of the RNC. Democratic candidates can, if they so desire, procure from the DNC an array of technological services throughout the course of the campaign.[53]

State party committees have also modernized to keep pace with technology. In Connecticut, for example, the Democratic and Republican state central committees have created highly sophisticated voter files which are readily available to candidates. These files contain voter registration figures, demographic information, and voting trends. Chairmen of both parties are sensitive to the technological requirements of modern campaigns and have worked diligently to modernize the operations of the state central committees. However, despite important technological advances, services provided by the committees are at best supplemental to those of the candidate's own personal organization. Presidential, congressional, gubernatorial, and even state legislative campaigns in most states are candidate-centered affairs. As Connecticut's Democratic State Chairman, John Droney, Jr. put it:

> This is a different political era . . . the voting population is not dependent on the two parties for the essentials of life; the party used to be their spokesperson for what they wanted out of life; the party was the vehicle for confronting elected officials, getting things they wanted through the rewards system. The old days are gone in Connecticut. Today candidates have direct access to media . . . and they can raise their own funds.[54]

Attitudinal Developments

Negative attitudes among the American electorate towards politicians, political institutions, and politics in general have further contributed to the demise of political parties. This disturbing development appears to be rooted in the politics of the 1960s. Scandalous political events of the 1970s and 1980s only served to reinforce negative public perceptions toward political institutions.

One of the first major studies to document the low level of trust and confidence exhibited by Americans toward political parties was a groundbreaking longitudinal study conducted by Jack Dennis.[55] Dennis' seminal study entitled "Trends in Public Support for the Party System," revealed a very weak base of public support for political parties as *institutions* of American democracy. The study utilized data gathered throughout the 1960s and 1970s. Some specific findings of the Dennis study were: the electorate was disenchanted with party labels; voters expressed preference for candidate-centered as opposed to party-centered politics; the electorate expressed a preference for the merit rather than the patronage system of government employment; and political parties were rated less favorably compared to Congress, the president, and the Supreme Court.

Trends discussed in the Dennis study also suggested that the disturbing loss of support for political parties had actually begun before, not after, the controversies associated with Vietnam and Watergate. Dennis issued an ominous warning regarding the future of the American two-party system:

> The data suggest that the mass base of institutional support is especially weak at this time; and this condition is worsening with each passing year. A mighty effort will therefore be required to reestablish for the parties the modicum of confidence and commitment that they once enjoyed, even a decade ago. Without such effort, we may be called upon in the not so distant future to witness the demise of a once prominent institution of American government and politics.[56]

Results of polls conducted throughout the 1992 presidential campaign—more than twenty years since the publication of the Dennis study—continue to suggest a low level of public support for political parties. The findings underscore why presidential candidates are currently waging candidate-centered rather than party-centered campaigns. Consider the following results generated by professional polling organizations.

In June of 1992, voters were asked to agree or disagree with this statement: "Both political parties are very much out of touch with the American people." Eighty-two percent of the sample agreed, while 15 percent disagreed. Three percent did not know or had no opinion.[57]

In July of 1992, one month after the presidential primary season, voters were asked: "Right now, would you say that the two-party system is serving this country well, or not?" Thirty-nine percent of the sample responded that the two-party system *is* serving the country well, while 59 percent responded that it *is not*. One percent of the sample was not sure.[58]

During that same month, voters were asked which model of electoral politics they preferred: a continuation of the two-party system, elections in which candidates run as individuals without party labels, or the growth of one or more new parties to challenge the Democrats and Republicans. Twenty-nine percent of the voters favored a continuation of the two-party system, 38 percent preferred candidates without party labels, and 30 percent favored the development of new parties to challenge the two major parties. Two percent were not sure.[59]

The low level of public support for political parties is further evident in recent trends regarding voter turnout, the strength of party affiliation among the electorate, and the pattern of partisan voting over the course of the last two decades. These trends, when taken together, suggest a growing disassociation between the American people and political party institutions.

Voter turnout has been in a state of decline since the 1960 presidential contest. In 1960, voter turnout among the eligible electorate was a respectable 63 percent. From 1960 to 1988, turnout declined in a steady and systematic fashion: 62 percent in 1964, 61 percent in 1968, 55 percent in 1972, 54 percent in 1976, 53 percent in 1980, 53 percent in 1984 and 50 percent in 1988. From 1960 to 1988, there was a 13 point drop in voter turnout. In 1992, voter turnout rose to 55 percent, a marked increase but by no means impressive.[60] Indeed, 45 percent of the eligible electorate chose not to vote despite the fact that three major candidates contested the presidential election. Although low voter turnout cannot be attributed solely to electorate antipathy toward parties, there does seem to be a correlation between low turnout and public displeasure with party politics.

Voting behavior of the American electorate further confirms a significant breakdown in partisan loyalty. In this respect, the steady and discernible rise in split-ticket voting during presidential election years seems especially relevant. Rather than vote a straight party line, a split-ticket voter will divide his or her support between the two major parties. For example, a voter might vote Republican for president and Democrat for Congress.

As the long-term influence of party affiliation has become less significant in determining voting behavior, short-term influences such as the image of the candidates and campaign issues become increasingly important with regard to structuring the vote.[61] Ticket-splitting is one result. In election year 1900, only 3.4 percent of congressional districts recorded split results for presidential and congressional candidates. Partisanship among the electorate was very strong during this period and served as the major determinant of the vote. By 1948, 21.3 percent of congressional districts recorded split results, a marked rise from the 1900 election. In 1988, split results were recorded in 34 percent of congressional districts.[62] It is clear that over the last several decades, the effect of the partisan label as a voting cue has diminished quite considerably for millions of Americans.

Split-ticket voting has unfortunate implications for presidential leadership. When partisanship was stronger among the electorate, there was a much greater chance that presidential candidates could carry congressional candidates of their own party into public office. Historically this is known as the "coattail effect." Presidential and congressional candidates on the ballot appeared to be members of the same Republican or Democratic team. With an attractive presidential candidate at the top of the ticket and an electorate favorably disposed towards party labels, many congressional candidates would be swept into office on the coattails of the president. This in turn contributed to a greater sense of congressional obligation towards the president during the policy-making process. The political bond between Congress and the president—so essential for cooperative policy-making—was rooted in the partisan dynamics of the election campaign. While presidential coattails have by no means disappeared in American elections, they have become much shorter. Nelson Polsby and Aaron Wildavsky describe the unfortunate consequences this way:

> This decline matters for governance because a coattail effect, in a system of separated powers, would operate to connect presidents and members of Congress of their own party more closely. In addition to replacing congressmen from the other party with members of the president's party, the belief on the part of congressmen that the president has support in the members' own districts creates incentives for them to support the chief executive's policies.[63]

In addition to declining voter turnout, split-ticket voting, and declining presidential coattails, there is a clear rise in the percentage of eligible voters who identify themselves as Independent. Rather than declare a party affiliation, large numbers of voters have currently chosen to identify themselves as Independent. Data from the Gallup poll, collected over six decades, reveal a distinct increase in the number of Independents among the American electorate (see Table 5).

In 1938, a mere 5 percent of voters identified themselves as Independent. By 1992, close to one-third of all voters polled preferred this self-description. During this period, the Democratic Party's rank-and-file declined from 49 percent of the electorate to 34 percent. Republican Party membership also declined from 46 percent in 1938 to 29 percent in 1992. Although there are small peaks and valleys for both political parties during this period, the larger pattern is one of an electorate increasingly detached from the two-party system.

This trend, when examined in conjunction with other recent developments indicative of a less partisan American electorate, raises important questions concerning presidential leadership. As political parties have become less meaningful for voters, the president's popular base of support has become correspondingly fragile. Presidents

Table 5
Party Affiliation Among the American Electorate
1938–1992

Year	% Democrat	% Republican	% Independent
1938	49	46	5
1940	44	37	20
1942	47	35	18
1944	42	39	19
1946	41	37	22
1948	41	35	24
1950	44	34	22
1952	42	33	25
1954	47	32	21
1956	44	34	22
1958	47	31	22
1960	48	30	22
1962	50	27	23
1964	52	26	22
1966	48	27	25
1968	44	28	28
1970	44	29	28
1972	43	26	31
1974	45	23	32
1976	47	22	31
1978	48	22	29
1980	46	24	30
1982	45	26	29
1984	40	31	29
1986	34	33	33
1988	39	32	28
1990	36	34	30
1992	34	29	32

Source: The Gallup Poll. The question was phrased as follows: "In politics, as of today, do you consider yourself a Republican, a Democrat, or an Independent?" Data obtained from the Roper Center at the University of Connecticut, Storrs.

find it increasingly difficult to sustain popular support for controversial policy proposals. The strong partisan ties that historically bound presidents to the public and provided a foundation for the exercise of presidential power have declined over time. This development has had serious consequences for presidential leadership. Unlike Presidents Jefferson, Lincoln and Wilson, recent American presidents are required to govern in an age of weak partisan attachment. The result is a less powerful presidency.

1974 Amendments to the Campaign Finance Act of 1971

The diminished role of political parties in presidential politics was further accelerated in 1974 with passage of important amendments to the Campaign Finance Act of 1971. Like so much legislation passed in the early 1970s, the amendments were the result of the Watergate crisis and, more generally, the abuse of power associated with the Nixon presidency.

In a broad sense, one of the principal objectives of the 1974 campaign finance amendments was to reduce the influence of wealthy individuals ("political fatcats") in presidential campaigns. Among the several disturbing aspects of Nixon's 1972 reelection campaign was the extraordinary influence wielded by a small handful of financial contributors. For example, W. Clement Stone, the largest single contributor during the 1972 election, donated $2 million to Nixon's reelection efforts. Richard Mellon Scaife, the second largest contributor, donated $1 million to the Nixon campaign.[64]

Another important aim of the new legislation was to reduce the power of corporate money in presidential campaigns. Although regulatory legislation was already in place by 1972, the influence of corporate dollars in conjunction with Nixon's reelection efforts, according to Herbert Alexander, had reached an entirely new level. "In funneling their money into the campaign . . . some companies 'laundered' cash abroad, disguised it in Swiss bank transactions or purchased nonexistent equipment in order to move cash from where it was available to where it was needed for political purposes."[65]

In the interest of cleansing presidential politics of the corrupting influence of "fatcat" contributions and corporate money, Congress created a system of public financing for presidential elections in 1974. Public funding for presidential candidates first went into effect during the 1976 presidential election. From 1976 to the present, presidential candidates have used federal funds to help finance their election campaign. In primary elections, presidential candidates can qualify for federal matching funds. The nominating conventions of the two major parties are also publicly funded. Nominees of the two major parties can receive full federal funding.

Since the passage of the 1974 amendments, every Democratic and Republican candidate with the exception of John Connally in

1980 has chosen to accept public funds. Candidates who accept public funding are subject to a broad range of legal restrictions. In the general election, for example, candidates who have accepted public funds cannot accept direct contributions from private individuals, special interest groups, or political parties.[66]

The provision for federal funding of presidential campaigns has further reduced the role of political party organizations in American electoral politics. Presidential candidates, rather than depending on their respective political parties for financial assistance, now turn to the federal government for campaign funds. Television commercials, radio advertisements, and other critical campaign activities are now funded primarily by American taxpayers rather than national, state and local party committees. The trend towards candidate-centered presidential campaigns with limited ties to the party machinery is encouraged through the system of public finance. Political parties, as Jeanne Kirkpatrick notes, were once again "the victims of reform legislation, which in its concern with correcting abuses, ignored the damage it might do to the parties."[67]

The preceding discussion indicates that party decline in American politics can be attributed to many diverse factors. When viewed collectively, the larger picture is one of relentless onslaught of anti-party forces throughout the twentieth century. Some developments have unintentionally weakened political parties, while others have reflected a specific desire on the part of reformers to reduce the power of parties in the political arena. Intentional or not, the end result of party decline is an individualized presidential selection process, and subsequently, an individualized American presidency. Presidential candidates now wage candidate-centered campaigns and presidents govern without reliable networks of partisan allies. It is this condition that explains the failure of recent American presidents. The decline of a strong political party structure uniting the presidency with Congress, the executive branch, state governments, and the American people has resulted in a more vulnerable and less effective American presidency. Even Thomas Jefferson, Abraham Lincoln, Woodrow Wilson, and Franklin Roosevelt would be unable to govern effectively within the current framework of national politics. Wilson's "New Freedom," or Roosevelt's "New Deal" would be accorded the same respect as that given to President Clinton's "New Covenant" (a noble vision which never materialized due to the instability of the political process).

Special interest groups have extraordinary leverage over the presidency. Lobbyists freely subvert presidential agendas. Political

Action Committees rather than political parties control political loyalty. Iron triangles and issue networks structure the policy-making process regardless of the president's agenda. Presidents without a firm partisan power base have become easy prey for the mass media. The bureaucracy is entrenched and immune from presidential pressure. Congressmen, rather than working as creative and constructive partners with the president, seem determined to block, impede, and compromise creative presidential leadership.

These are the conditions that emerge out of a weak political party system. In the absence of a strong partisan power base, American presidents have a more difficult time governing the nation. The president's ability to move the nation in new directions, to engineer profound social and economic change, and to effectively exercise the broad constitutional powers vested in the office of chief executive has been reduced. The American president's capacity to direct meaningful change seems less certain today than during any other period in American history. One very clear example of this is the death of President Clinton's health care reform bill in the 103rd Congress—an incredible development in light of the fact that Democratic majorities controlled the House and Senate. Health care reform was at the heart of the Clinton presidency. Yet the reform effort has failed.

However, support for President Clinton's health care reform plan is not the issue here. The issue is one of a presidency with less power. It is a recurring problem for Democratic and Republican presidents. Every president from Nixon to Clinton has experienced the negative consequences of a political process marked by party decline. The presidency of Jimmy Carter is a prime example of a failure in presidential leadership during the age of party decline.

CHAPTER FOUR

The Lesson of the Carter Presidency

Why was the average public approval rating of President Jimmy Carter, recorded at only 46 percent?[1] Why is the Carter presidency rated as one of the least effective presidencies in the history of the United States?[2] This is particularly perplexing in light of the fact that during Carter's term of office, the Democratic Party enjoyed a two-to-one majority in the House of Representatives and a three-to-two majority in the Senate. At the same time, within the electorate, Democrats outnumbered Republicans by a margin of two-to-one. When Jimmy Carter was inaugurated president in January of 1977, there was reason to believe that a dynamic and creative period of presidential governance was about to begin—similar in many respects to the inauguration of President Clinton in 1993. Like Clinton, however, Carter failed to lead. The end result was a one-term and largely discredited presidency.

Carter, like a number of post-Watergate presidents, was forced to contend with a post-Watergate Congress quite suspicious and perhaps even hostile to presidential leadership. Moreover, Carter, like all recent presidents, faced a press corps predisposed towards investigative journalism, lobbyists, and special interests opposed to progressive reform, iron triangles, and policy networks beyond the reach of the White House, and a large, self-interested and slow moving federal bureaucracy. To complicate matters, inflation had skyrocketed during Carter's term of office, unemployment rose, the nation grappled with an energy crisis, and Americans stationed at the United States Embassy in Tehran were held hostage by Islamic fundamentalists for over one year. A failed rescue mission ordered by Carter did little to improve the beleagured president's image. Thus, President Carter was constrained by a political process adverse to presidential leadership. At the same time, the president was hindered by

71

national and international dilemmas which seemed almost beyond his control.

However, to attribute the failure of the Carter presidency to systemic variables or policy dilemmas is to overlook what was at the root of Carter's governing problems. To be more specific, the genesis of Carter's failure as president can be traced to the deterioration of the American party system. The weakened state of political parties heavily conditioned the style and dynamics of Carter's presidential campaign. The style of Carter's campaign, albeit sucessful, did little to position the former governor from Georgia for a successful season of governing. To put the matter differently: weak political parties contributed to an individualized presidential campaign, which in turn resulted in an isolated presidency. The end result was a failure in presidential leadership. In some respects, Carter was a victim of political circumstance.

Jimmy Carter was a relatively obscure one-term governor from Plains, Georgia. He was not by any means a politician or personality associated with national politics—certainly not "the Washington establishment." As 1976 approached, Carter was not regarded as one of the Democratic Party's "leading" or "heavyweight" presidential contenders. When Carter announced his intentions to run for the presidency, he was considered one of the long-shots,[3] destined to be remembered as one of the "also-ran" presidential candidates. Indeed, Carter during the early stages of his campaign was referred to by the media as "Jimmy Who?"

Carter began his campaign for the Democratic Party's presidential nomination by forming his own personal, candidate-centered organization. By 1976, candidate-centered campaign organizations had become the norm in presidential politics. The Carter organization, like most presidential campaign organizations of the post-1968 era, featured a personal pollster, professional fundraiser, media consultant, field supervisors, issue specialists, and other campaign personnel who offered professional services related to voter mobilization. Most of the key individuals in the Carter campaign were close friends and associates who had established ties with Governor Carter during his years in Georgia politics. His tight circle of campaign advisors were sometimes referred to by pundits as the "Georgia Mafia." Several of these individuals would eventually assume staff positions in the Carter White House.

Throughout the campaign for the Democratic Party's presidential nomination, Carter presented himself as a "political outsider." His plan was to campaign as an outsider who had yet to be tarnished or corrupted by politics inside the Washington Beltway. By pursuing an outsider strategy, Carter was able to effectively distance himself from the field of Democratic contenders, several of whom had served in Congress for many years. Carter's competition included United States Senators with national constituencies. Idaho Senator Frank Church, Washington Senator Henry "Scoop" Jackson, Arizona Senator Morris Udall, Indiana Senator Birch Bayh, and Texas Senator Lloyd Bentsen were all Washington insiders with presidential credentials. California Governor Jerry Brown and Alabama Governor George Wallace were also high profile and nationally recognized contenders for the Democratic nomination. Among the various Democratic contenders, Carter's reputation was the least known.

Throughout the nomination campaign, Carter emphasized his agrarian roots and promised to restore trust and confidence in American government. Carter's populist themes resonated with the voters, who, in the aftermath of Watergate, were attracted to the image of an honest outsider from Plains, Georgia. As Burton I. Kaufman states: "Disgruntled Americans sought new ideas, fresh faces, and a style of leadership predicated on openness, truthfulness, and public responsiveness. Indeed, morality was the emerging keynote of the campaign—a desire to restore a sense of purpose, trust, fairness, and civic responsibility to American life."[4]

This was not the first time Jimmy Carter waged an election campaign based on trust and, more generally, an outsider strategy. In fact, Carter was quite good at it. In his bid for the Georgia governorship, Carter conducted a populist, outsider campaign in which he routinely railed against Georgia's political establishment.[5] During his many visits to small towns across Georgia, Carter consciously distanced himself from sheriffs, bankers, journalists, and those identified as the local political establishment. Carter's gubernatorial bid, according to Victor Lasky, "provided a preview of his later campaign for the presidency."[6]

In addition to a voting public highly receptive to the notion of a trustworthy outsider in the White House, Carter's campaign for the Democratic nomination also benefited from the nomination and election reforms that had taken place in the aftermath of the 1968 election. As previously noted, there was a proliferation of state presidential primaries following the events of 1968. The control and power of party organization leaders in deciding presidential candidates had been seriously diminished. The presidential nomination contest was no longer decided by party chieftans in smoke-filled rooms at nominating conventions, but rather by voters in primary elections. In

1976, a presidential candidate, such as Jimmy Carter, could appeal directly to the Democratic Party's rank-and-file to secure the presidential nomination. Carter, therefore, did not need to court and gain the support of the Democratic Party's leadership in order to win the nominating contest. Through intense personal campaigning, Carter was able to win the Iowa caucus, the first test of a candidate's strength in the presidential nominating campaign. Carter's win in Iowa was followed by a crucial victory in the New Hampshire primary. Although Carter received only 28 percent of the Democratic vote in New Hampshire, his primary victory catapulted the outsider from Plains to the status of frontrunner within the Democratic Party. As Gerald Pomper notes: "Cover photos on national magazines, television interviews, and increasing popular attention followed."[7]

Carter's presidential bid also benefited from the sweeping changes that had taken place with regard to federal campaign finance laws. During the presidential nominating contest, Carter, due to his political viability, qualified for federal matching funds. This was the first presidential campaign in American history in which federal funds were made available to candidates. Thus, Carter could depend not only on his own private fundraising efforts to meet campaign costs, which were substantial, but also on millions of dollars in matching funds from the federal government.

An appealing campaign theme, primary elections, and partial public funding contributed greatly to Carter's success in the 1976 Democratic presidential nominating contest. Carter's nomination symbolized the dawn of a new era in American politics. Indeed, under the old presidential nominating system, it would have been virtually impossible for a candidate of Jimmy Carter's stature to have emerged as the nominee of the Democratic Party. The post-1968 reforms, according to Carter's Chief of Staff Hamilton Jordan, "made it possible for an unknown like Jimmy Carter to win the big prize."[8]

Carter's general election campaign was quite similar to the Democratic nominating contest. Carter continued to emphasize themes of honesty and trust in government. More than ever, Carter cultivated the populist outsider image. He was not part of the Washington establishment, nor could he be corrupted. A typical campaign speech would normally begin with the words: "I am not from Washington."[9]

Media consultant, Gerald Rafshoon, was especially instrumental in securing Carter's presidential election victory. Rafshoon had worked for Twentieth Century Fox as a publicity and advertisng director prior to relocating in Atlanta. Impressed by Carter's sincerity and basic sense of decency, Rafshoon had joined the Carter campaign for governor.[10] In 1970, with the help of Rafshoon, Carter won the Georgia governorship. Shortly after George McGovern's crushing defeat in the presidential election of 1972, Carter and Rafshoon began to strategize for the 1976 presidential contest.

Throughout the 1976 presidential campaign, Carter delegated vast authority to Rafshoon regarding media production and campaign strategy. Rafshoon, like all media consultants in the post-1968 era, emerged as a central campaign advisor. Carter's spot-ads and extended commercials struck a responsive chord within the American electorate. Carter's image as an honest, populist outsider was at all times skillfully packaged. For example, in one five-minute campaign biography, Carter was seen walking through a peanut field in Georgia clad in blue jeans and workboots joking with Miss Lillian, his elderly mother.[11] The image was clearly that of an honest and simple farmer; a man of the soil with great integrity. Carter's spot-ads consistently focused on the related themes of trust and honesty: "Now listen to me carefully. I'll never tell a lie. I'll never make a misleading statement. I'll never avoid a controversial issue. Watch television, listen to the radio. If I ever do any of those things, don't support me."[12]

During the general election campaign, in accordance with the new campaign finance laws, Carter, like his Republican opponent Gerald Ford, was now entitled to full federal funding. In 1976, the Carter and Ford campaigns were each provided $22 million from the federal treasury. Of this amount, both campaigns allocated roughly half for campaign advertising. Within the advertising budget, approximately three-fifths of the money was directed towards television commercials.[13] The careful cultivation of candidate imagery, the millions of dollars directed towards television commercials, and the emergence of media consultants as principal strategists within the context of presidential campaign organizations was institutionalized during the 1976 presidential campaign. The Carter campaign marked an important turning point in the history of presidential politics. Television ads produced by media consultants would now be the principal means for mobilizing the voting population.

Thus, Carter's 1976 presidential campaign emerged as a model for post-Watergate presidential candidates: campaign as a political outsider, criticize the Washington establishment, appear as a populist, go directly to the voters in primary elections, use public funds to meet campaign costs, form an efficient candidate-centered campaign organization, employ consultants, and harness the power of television for the purpose of voter mobilization. The new road to the White House was radically different from that which existed prior to 1968.

What is ironic, however, is that the seeds of Carter's failure as president were planted in the very strategy that contributed to his presidential election victory. Carter's general election strategy was largely a candidate-centered campaign that operated on a separate level from that of the Democratic Party. To describe the Carter campaign as totally disconnected from the party structure would be inaccurate. Carter did head the Democratic ticket and throughout the fall campaign there was no way he could avoid campaign appearances with fellow Democrats running for Congress and state governorships. Nevertheless, although Carter performed the role of "party leader" during the 1976 campaign, he did so with little enthusiasm and with considerable reluctance. In an Oval Office interview with Jules Witcover, Carter discussed his dilemma in these terms:

> That caused me horrible trouble. That was the biggest problem we had. I finally made the difficult decision to be completely loyal to the Democratic nominees wherever I went; not to try to avoid them; to be on the platform with them; to share news coverage. It really hurt us in two or three states. In almost every instance, an incumbent governor, or incumbent U.S. Senator or state party chairman, even though they may be quite popular, my association with them in an overt way was damaging.[14]

The Carter campaign for president, despite standard homages to Truman and Roosevelt, and despite routine appearances with a variety of Democratic candidates, was not by any means a presidential campaign coordinated through the Democratic Party. As a result of primary elections, Carter did not require the blessings of the Democratic Party's hierarchy to win the party's nomination. Carter formed his own personal organization and went straight to the Democratic Party's rank-and-file. State, county, and local party committees were not responsible for bringing Carter to the forefront of the Democratic nominating contest. Voters in Democratic primaries were primarily responsible for this. In essence, Carter received the Democratic Party's nomination by establishing a very different power base compared to that which was required during the days of party-centered nominating contests.

The availability of public funding also allowed Carter to wage a nominating and election campaign apart from the formal party machinery. Carter did not require financial assistance from the Democratic Party in order to sustain a nationwide campaign. Public money, not party money, provided Carter with the necessary financial power to deliver his populist message to the American voter.

Heavy reliance on television commercials throughout the campaign also served to distance Carter from the formal apparatus of the Democratic Party. Voter mobilization efforts on Carter's behalf was accomplished primarily through the use of appealing spot-ads, rather than the efforts of party committees operating at the grassroots. Although Carter's media-based campaign reached millions of voters, such strategy did little to firmly connect Carter to party organization leaders and the many Democratic candidates running for Congress. The style of Carter's campaign distanced him considerably from the key players and power brokers within the Democratic Party.

The consequences of a presidential campaign conducted apart from the Democratic Party's power structure became readily apparent during the Carter presidency. Throughout his four years in office, Carter experienced great difficulty in establishing himself as a credible political leader. He never had the firm partisan base within the Washington establishment to sustain support for his presidential initiatives. He ran for president as an outsider and, consequently, was forced to govern as an outsider. His relationship with Congress was not at all harmonious and frequently revealed signs of tension and unusual strain. As Kaufman notes: "Because Carter had campaigned as much against the Washington establishment as against the Republican Party, few members of the new Congress felt politically obligated to him." [15] In the view of Walter Carp: "The real cause of Carter's failures with Congress stems entirely from one obvious and pregnant fact. He is the first modern president to scale the greasy pole unaided and unwanted by party leaders." [16] Reflecting on his strained relationship with Congress, President Carter put it this way:

> Some of the Democratic leaders promised me full support in implementing my general platform, but as we began to discuss the hard details, the support often evaporated. I had to seek votes wherever they could be found . . . Each legislator had to be wooed individually. It was every member for himself, and the devil take the hindmost. [17]

The experience of the Carter presidency reveals the inherent problems associated with a political process characterized by party decline. A weak party system inevitably leads to candidate-centered presidential campaigns and the emergence of political outsiders with limited ties to the Washington establishment. Although there is something quite refreshing about a populist outsider from Plains, Georgia pursuing and winning the American presidency, and in doing so reflecting the spirit of egalitarianism, such campaigns simply do not facilitate teamwork and presidential leadership. The nature of the modern presidential campaign, which thrives on outcomes in primary elections, public funding, media consultants, spot-ads, and outsider images, does little to promote presidential leadership. In an age of party decline and distrust of politicians, the political outsider can win the presidency—but, unfortunately, the outsider cannot govern.

Political scientists and close observers of presidential politics have commented at great length on the growing incompatibility between campaigning for president and serving as president. The two processes, once intertwined, have become separated. The emergence of a "gap" between campaigning and governing is one of the unintended and unfortunate consequences of party reform in the post-Watergate era. Political party decline appears to be the root of the problem. As political journalist Robert Shogan notes: "Unable or unwilling to depend on their parties, presidents have increasingly charted their own courses, relied on their own instincts and tried to fulfill their own ambitions. In the process they have inevitably made their office less accountable and less responsive to the electorate." [18] Lester G. Seligman and Cary R. Covington note that weak political parties in conjuction with a personalized presidential selection system "has sharpened the tensions and contradictions between winning the presidency and governing." [19]

Primary elections do not connect presidents with power brokers. Public funding does not connect presidents with party organizations. Personalized campaigns do not connect presidents with members of their party in Congress. Television commercials do not connect presidents with grassroots party volunteers—so critical for establishing a firm base of public support. The dynamics of the modern presidential campaign result in a presidency without the necessary political linkages required to govern.

President Carter and the NEP

President Carter's failed attempt at energy reform offers one concrete example of the governing difficulties inherent in a presidency with weak ties to the political party structure. The oil crisis of 1973, precipitated by the policies of the Oil Producing and Exporting Countries (OPEC), exposed America's dependence on foreign oil for the purpose of energy consumption. So severe was the energy crisis in the mid-seventies that President Carter upon taking office developed an ambitious and comprehensive legislative package designed to reform energy policy in the United States. Carter's ten point proposal, entitled the National Energy Plan (NEP), was designed to not only reduce energy consumption in the United States, but also to develop a long range strategy that would result in energy self-sufficiency. The NEP was introduced to Congress on April 20, 1977— only four months after Carter was inaugurated president.[20]

The legislative success of the energy plan would serve as the first test of Carter's ability to lead Congress. National press coverage of the NEP was extensive and the reputation of the Carter presidency was at stake.[21] The NEP was controversial and provoked much debate in both the public and the private sector. From an academic standpoint, the NEP would also provide evidence of the extent to which party discipline existed in the post-Watergate Congress. With a Democrat in the White House and with both chambers of Congress controlled by the Democratic Party, the NEP would provide rich insight into partisan teamwork and the current level of party loyalty.

The House of Representatives passed the NEP with very few modifications. House support was due primarily to the efforts of House Speaker Tip O'Neill, who insisted on Democratic unity and responsible party government. Seven of Carter's ten points remained intact following the House vote. House Democrats united behind O'Neill and supported a Democratic president.

The politics of the Senate, however, yielded a very different outcome, with only two of Carter's ten point plan generating support. Senate Majority leader Robert Byrd, a "fellow" Democrat, expressed only mild support for the NEP and did little in the way of mobilizing Senate Democrats on behalf of the president. Louisiana Senator Russell Long, Chairman of the Senate Finance Committee, and yet another Democrat, worked directly against the president's energy plan. Long's committee proved to be an insurmountable obstacle to the NEP resulting in a substantial dismantling of the Carter proposal. Party government in the Senate was for all intents and purposes nonexistent.[22]

A House and Senate conference committee eventually produced a compromised energy plan that bore little resemblance to President Carter's original proposal. The failure of the NEP, coming as it did in the early stages of the Carter presidency, severely undermined the reputation of Carter as a competent national leader. Press reports soon suggested that an "amateur" was in the White House.[23] As Martin B. Shaffer states: "The protracted nature of the negotiations in the Senate and, subsequently, during the House-Senate conference not only destroyed the NEP, but seriously hurt Carter's credibility and portrayed him as a weak leader."[24] In Shaffer's view, the debacle of the NEP is a principal reason why Carter to this day is perceived by scholars and journalists as a "failed" president.

The personal, rather than the partisan, dimension of the Carter presidential campaign had much to do with the failure of the National Energy Plan. In no way, was the NEP assocated with the platform of the Democratic Party, nor was the energy proposal regarded as part of a long-term component of the Democratic congressional agenda. The NEP originated in the Carter White House and was looked upon as the primary goal of the president's personal agenda. As Shaffer notes: "The fact that the energy package was 'Carter's NEP' rather than the 'Democratic Party's NEP' is illustrative of the personalized nature of the American polity."[25]

It should come as no surprise, therefore, that President Carter found himself with few political allies in the Senate during the NEP controversy. In the absence of a strong partisan connection between the president and Congress, the lawmaking process, particularly when it involves a contentious issue such as energy, is bound to result in factionalism and political fragmentation. Without a strong partisan bond between members of the same political party, lawmakers become vulnerable to the force of special interest money and the persuasion of lobbyists. Special interest pressure, rather than partisan considerations, ulimately structured the final outcome of the NEP. According to Shaffer: "A vast array of interest groups—including business and industry interests, state governments, and public interest groups, among others—were activated by the president's NEP. Although each particular lobby was only concerned with the aspect of the NEP which effected them, this intense effort had the combined effect of dismantling major portions of Carter's energy plan."[26]

Special interest pressure often prevailed over partisan loyalty throughout Carter's term of office. Indeed, it was to be a recurring problem for the populist from Plains. In addition to special interests opposed to energy reform, Carter encountered extraordinary and unexpected opposition from lobbyists representing weapons manufacturers and the health care industry. Carter's reforms regarding defense spending and health care often faced intense and intractable opposition in Congress due to the leverage exercised by special interest groups. In Carter's view, the flood of special interest money had so severely undercut party loyalty that a president's ability to lead the lawmaking process was in jeopardy. As Carter notes in his memoirs: "The lobbies are a growing menace to our democratic system of government."[27]

The experience of the Carter presidency underscores the problems inherent in a political process characterized by party decline. The teamwork dimension of governing, which only political parties can ensure, is severly compromised when parties fail to structure the course of politics. The consecutive failure of several post-Watergate presidents provides proof that a political process devoid of party authority promotes and sustains a personal style of politics which contributes very little to sound national leadership.

The experience of the Carter presidency demonstrates that presidents without a strong partisan base are largely on their own in the governing process. In an age of party decline, one also finds an unpredictable and individualistic Congress with little obligation or loyalty to the president. Party decay, it naturally follows, vastly escalates the power of special interest groups, as well as other forces operating within the Washington Beltway—often to the disadvantage of reform-minded presidents. The presidency of Bill Clinton, another ambitious Democratic president with visions of reform, offers another example of how presidential leadership is adversely affected by weak political parties.

CHAPTER FIVE

The Lesson of the Clinton Presidency

In 1992, presidential candidates who sought the Democratic Party's nomination were faced with the extraordinary challenge of competing in thirty-nine state presidential primary elections. Democratic voters in primary elections, not party elites in secretive nominating conventions, decided the outcome of the presidential nominating contest. Approximately eighty percent of the delegates who attended the Democratic Party's national convention in July of 1992 were chosen on the basis of primary election results.[1]

To be a viable contender for the 1992 Democratic nomination, a presidential candidate was required to construct a dynamic and efficient candidate-centered organization consisting of skilled campaign consultants and reliable volunteers. Organizational personnel had to be focused and thoroughly committed to the personality and goals of their presidential candidate.

The personal organization of Bill Clinton, assembled well before the start of the 1992 presidential nominating contest, consisted of very resourceful, savvy, and creative campaign strategists. Governor Clinton's inner circle of consultants included chief strategist James Carville, political communications director George Stephanopoulos, media advisor Mandy Grunwald, pollster Stanley Greenberg, and public relations specialist Paul Begala. Governor Clinton's wife, Hillary Rodham Clinton, served as a general coordinator and strategist throughout the campaign. Following the presidential election, several of the key actors within the Clinton campaign organization would be appointed to high level posts in the White House.

The Democratic presidential nominating contest began as a six man contest. In addition to Clinton, a five-term governor from Arkansas, the pool of Democratic candidates included the former senator from Massachusetts Paul Tsongas, former governor of California

Jerry Brown, Nebraska Senator Bob Kerrey, Iowa Senator Tom Harkin, and Virginia's Governor Douglas Wilder. Collectively, the six Democratic candidates were referred to by pundits as the "six pack."

The personalities of the individual Democratic candidates as well as their personal platforms provided Democratic voters with an array of styles and policies to choose from. At the same time, one detected a conscious attempt on the part of each Democratic candidate, including the two incumbent senators, to present themselves as a genuine political outsider, prepared and willing to fight the Washington political establishment. The outsider theme would reappear throughout the 1992 presidential campaign.

Clinton, well before the official start of the primary season in February of 1992, was identified in no uncertain terms by the media, political pundits, and party activists, as the Democratic Party's front-runner. The Arkansas governor had developed very meticulous plans for a presidential campaign long before his competitors had even considered running for the presidency.

Unlike Jimmy Carter, a one-term governor from Georgia, Clinton, through five consecutive terms as governor of Arkansas, had cultivated a national reputation as a dynamic and creative political leader with presidential credentials. For several years, Clinton was the Democratic Party's rising star, and not once did one hear the press ever refer to Clinton as "Bill Who?". It was Clinton who delivered the presidential nominating speech for Michael Dukakis at the 1988 Democratic National Convention. Moreover, it was Clinton who chaired the Democratic Leadership Council, an organization formed by centrist Democrats troubled over the leftward drift of the Democratic Party and the resulting inability of the party to elect a presidential candidate. Moderate, not liberal, policy positions were routinely advocated by the DLC.

As the New Hampshire primary approached—the first primary of the presidential nominating contest—Clinton appeared to be positioned for a very competitive and successful nominating campaign. The governor from Arkansas had raised a substantial sum of money; his youthfulness and speaking style was "Kennedyesque" and therefore appealing to young voters; his centrist policy positions attacted the support of moderate, middle-class Democrats; and his firm commitment to civil rights and social justice generated support from African-American voters. The governor from Arkansas had welded a coalition within the Democratic Party.

There was a certain freshness to Bill Clinton. He was a "New Democrat" who wanted to "reinvent government." At the same time, like Jimmy Carter, Clinton could claim outsider status unblemished by Beltway politics. There seemed to be few obstacles facing Bill Clinton as he launched his bid for the Democratic Party's presidential nomination—so it seemed.

The Character Question: An Unanticipated Explosion

In an age of political party decline, voter impressions towards presidential candidates have become increasingly conditioned by the mass media. Perceptions of presidential candidates are often based on the reports of media correspondents and commentators, rather than the campaign activity of grassroots party activists. As Thomas E. Patterson states: "The press's role in presidential elections is in large part the result of a void that was created when America's political parties surrendered their control over the nominating process."[2]

More specifically, it is television, more than any other comunicative medium, which is now educating the American electorate with respect to the character and policy positions of those individuals who aspire to the presidency. As David Broder, a seasoned and astute political journalist, notes in his classic work *The Party's Over*: "The 'tube' has changed the political process in several ways that make it more difficut for the parties to fulfill their functions. Indeed, in one respect, television has seemed to make one of the party's old functions irrelevant—that of serving as a bridge between the candidate or officeholder and the public."[3]

The power of television was more than evident in the 1992 Democratic nominating contest. The Clinton campaign, which had so effectively secured the necessary pre-primary momentum necessary for victory, almost came to an abrupt and unceremonious end in the days prior to the New Hampshire primary. The governor of Arkansas was savaged by the media to the point where experts were predicting an early withdrawal from the presidential race.

Several items, none of which had anything to do with policy positions, became the focus of intense media scrutiny as the New Hampshire primary approached: Clinton's use of marijuana as a college student, his draft evasion during the Vietnam War, and allegations concerning marital infidelity. Although Clinton attempted to rebut the charges, his answers often proved unsatisfactory to the press and the voting public.

Clinton admitted smoking marijuana when he was a young man,

but claimed that he did not inhale. Regarding the accusation of draft evasion, Clinton claimed that while he had in fact secured a student deferment which exempted him from the draft, he did eventually place himself in the pool of draft-eligible men only to draw a high lottery number. It was a complicated little story that was clouded by the chronology of events and a number of inconsistencies. To this day, how Clinton was able to avoid military service is unclear.

The marital infidelity charge, discussed in a previous chapter, involved a former state employee in Arkansas by the name of Gennifer Flowers. Ms. Flowers, in a widely publicized press conference claimed to have engaged in a long-term secret love affair with Governor Clinton. Clinton's response to this charge was somewhat evasive and murky.

The media's eagerness to pounce on the character questions surrounding Clinton was surprising in light of pre-campaign promises on the part of the press to focus on the substantive issues of the presidential campaign. In a fashion similar to the media's obsession with Senator Gary Hart's affair with model Donna Rice, the intensity of which eventually forced Hart to withdraw from the presidential race, the media in 1992 appeared once again to be absorbed in the private sex life of a presidential candidate. As Wilson Carey McWilliams put it: "The media's early resolutions to forego sensational inquiries into the private lives of candidates crumbled under the impact of the supermarket tabloids, and the whole of the press was soon engaged in what one British paper called 'sexual McCarthyism.'"[4] The media's obsession with Clinton's alleged marital infidelity, as well as other accusations, cast serious doubt over the integrity and character of the Democratic Party's frontrunner. Bill Clinton, the five-term governor from Arkansas, Rhodes Scholar, New Democrat, and future President of the United States, became known to the voting public as "Slick Willy."

To the surprise of many, the Clinton campaign was not derailed. Clinton placed second to Paul Tsongas in the New Hampshire primary. Indeed, the Arkansas governor's ability to overcome such adversity and to resurrect a collapsing presidential campaign resulted in yet another campaign nickname: "The Comeback Kid." Despite a formidable challenge by Tsongas in the early phase of the nominating campaign, as well as some unexpected opposition from Brown, Clinton was still able to secure the Democratic Party's presidential nomination. However, although Clinton was not prevented from winning the Democratic Party's presidential nomination, the question of character raised prior to the New Hampshire primary would continue to haunt his campaign. The media had once again inflicted severe political damage on a leading presidential candidate.

Consider the results of polls conducted during the 1992 presidential nominating contest in which the following question was asked: "Do you think Bill Clinton has the honesty and integrity to serve effectively as president?" During the primary season, the percentage of voters responding in the affirmative to this question was normally less than fifty percent. It was only after the field of presidential contenders had narrowed to two candidates did the percentage of Democratic voters responding in the affirmative rise above half.[5]

A New York Times/CBS News Poll conducted at the end of the primary season discovered that only sixteen percent of registered voters had developed a favorable impression of Governor Clinton. Forty percent of voters expressed an unfavorable view. As Ross K. Baker put it: "At the root of the problem was that at the conclusion of the primaries, few people knew much about Clinton and much of what they did know was negative."[6] Patterson notes that between January 1 and March 15, approximately one in every six stories involving the presidential campaign involved the character allegations against Clinton. According to Patterson, such stories were often unattributed or based upon the reports of other news organizations.[7]

A voting public with serious doubts about the Democratic Party's frontrunner could also be observed in the low level of voter turnout in primary elections. It was estimated that compared to 1988, primary turnout in 1992 declined by approximately three million voters.[8] The Committee for the Study of the Electorate, a committee based in Washington, D.C. that monitors voter turnout, reported that only 18.9 percent of eligible voters participated in the 1992 primary elections.[9]

Although multiple explanations have been offered concerning low voter turnout in primary elections, including the fact that modern nominating contests are for all intents and purposes decided by the end of March, and hence many potential voters find little reason to vote in primaries scheduled for the late spring, it is possible that the character issue surrounding Clinton had a suppressive impact on primary turnout. The style of media coverage not only reduced confidence in the Democratic Party's frontrunner, but also dissuaded voters from participating in the nominating contest.

Generally speaking, however, the extent to which the character issue undermined the credibility of Bill Clinton is perhaps more of a statement about the role of political parties in the modern age of presidential selection than it is about the character of Clinton. The extent to which the media was able to ruthlessly impugn the integrity of Clinton, and with such lasting consequences, was clearly a residual by-product of a presidential selection system that has become candidate, rather than party centered.

In an age of candidate-centered politics, the candidate has become the prime target of the media. Emphasis in media coverage has shifted from the platforms of political parties, and what it means to be a Democratic or Republican presidential candidate, to the candidate himself. The candidate's past life and personal character are now more important than the party's approach to policy-making. Presidential candidates who wage campaigns on the basis of a personal, candidate-centered organization have become susceptible to the type of media probing and "feeding frenzy" (to use Sabato's term) that was witnessed in 1992.

The candidate-centered campaign, unlike the presidential campaign coordinated by party organization leaders, practically invites journalistic sensationalism. If the candidate is found to have a character flaw, the media will exploit and magnify it. When a campaign places a premium on the candidate, rather than the party to which the candidate belongs, then it naturally follows that the electronic and print press will direct their time and energy to unearthing, and discussing the vices and weaknesses of those who pursue the presidency. Weak political parties invite this condition.

Although Clinton had secured endorsements from many Democratic party leaders and congressmen, he was for all intents and purposes on his own when it came to deflecting the barrage of character accusations. He did not enjoy the political shield that only a strong party organization could provide. Clinton was the Democratic Party's candidate for the presidency, yet the party did not come to his rescue.

It is doubtful that Clinton would have been so vulnerable to the media onslaught had his presidential campaign been initiated and organized by a strong Democratic organization. A strong party organization would most certainly have been able to counter the media scrutiny, and diminish the political damage inflicted on its presidential candidate. As Benjamin Ginsberg put it: "Traditional party oganizations had stable popular followings that could be counted on when their leaders came under fire." [10]

Despite the character controversy, Clinton's nominating convention, conducted in Madison Square Garden during the month of July, was well-organized and harmonious. According to convention watchers, the 1992 Democratic National Convention was a model of unity. The convention resulted in a significant boost in the polls for the Clinton/Gore ticket.[11] The Clinton/Gore bus tour launched immediately following the convention maintained the momentum for a vibrant fall campaign—perhaps the deciding factor behind Clinton's victory.

Throughout the general election campaign, the Clinton organization remained a candidate-centered affair. Although the Democratic Party mobilized resources and provided campaign services for its presidential candidate, the activity of the formal party apparatus still seemed supplemental to that of the candidate's own organization. Despite the fact that Clinton led Bush and Perot in public opinion polls throughout the fall,[12] his candidate-centered campaign accomplished little in the way of laying a firm foundation for future political teamwork. Clinton's connection with Democrats running for Congress seemed remote and distant—similar in some respects to the Carter campaign. Bill Clinton was the head of the Democratic Party's national ticket, yet there was little visible evidence of a partisan team campaigning together on the basis of a distinct party platform. Some commmentators speculated that as a result of the character issue raised during the nomination process, Democratic candidates for Congress consciously kept Clinton at arms length.

The candidate-centered aspect of the 1992 election was more than apparent in the general election results. In Senate elections, the Democratic Party failed to gain a single seat. In House elections, the Democrats lost ten seats. Studies following the election discovered that Clinton received more votes than House members in only 5 of the 435 congressional districts.[13] It was apparent that voters did not perceive the Democratic ticket as a united partisan team campaigning under a common party platform. The presidential and congressional campaigns were disconnected and election coattails were non-existent. The weak party connection between Clinton and Democratic candidates for Congress would have unfortunate consequences for the Clinton presidency. As John H. Aldrich and Thomas Weko note: "Democrats in Congress, most of whom had served only under Republican presidents, expressed their desire to cooperate with Clinton and claimed that their fortunes were tied to the success of his presidency. However, no members of Congress felt themselves beholden to or threatened by President-elect Clinton."[14]

Indeed, the consequences of a candidate-centered presidential campaign, with weak ties to fellow partisans campaigning for Congress, became very apparent during the first two years of the Clinton administration. This was especially evident during President Clinton's failed attempt to reform the nation's health care system.

President Clinton and Health Care Reform

Reform of America's health care system was the centerpiece of Bill Clinton's campaign for the presidency. The Arkansas governor, perhaps more than any other presidential candidate in history, stressed the need to overhaul a health care system which, in his view, had evolved into a "state of crisis." There was repeated reference to the forty million Americans who lacked any form of health insurance—the working poor. Voters throughout the campaign were constantly reminded of the plight of uninsured children.

Clinton vowed to the American public that health coverage for all Americans would be the top priority of his administration. The American system of health care, according to Clinton, was not only an immoral disgrace, but the costs associated with health coverage had profound ramifications for the economy. Reform of the health care system not only would ensure adequate health coverage for people in need of medical care, but such reform would promote economic growth and shrink the deficit.

President Clinton's intense and unwaivering commitment to health care reform could be observed during the early days of his presidency. In his first State of the Union address, delivered on February 17, 1993, the president identified health care reform as an urgent priority:

> The rising costs and the lack of care are endangering both our economy and our lives. Reducing health care costs will liberate hundreds of billions of dollars for investment and growth and new jobs. Over the long run, reforming health care is essential to reducing our deficit and expanding investment . . . Later this spring, I will deliver to Congress a comprehensive plan for health care reform that will finally get costs under control. We will provide security to all our families, so that no one will be denied the coverage they need . . . The American people expect us to deal with health care. And we must deal with it now.[15]

President Clinton's intense commitment to health care reform reminded one in many ways of President Johnson's War on Poverty:

the issue was at the center of his presidential agenda, and successful reform would secure his place in American history. President Clinton would forever be remembered as the president who directly confronted and ambitiously reformed a costly and inequitable system of health care.

In September of 1993, President Clinton, in a nationally televised address to the United States Congress, outlined his health care reform plan. Public opinion at the time was on the side of the president, and support for reform remained high throughout the fall.[16] There was momentum for health care reform.

The president's wife, Hillary Rodham Clinton, was appointed to spearhead the health care reform effort. Democratic congressional leaders were not deployed as legislative point persons, nor was the president's cabinet heavily relied upon for the purposes of policy formulation and legislative liaison. Under the direction of Mrs. Clinton, a large task force consisting of 500 persons was assembled and charged with the responsibility of developing a comprehensive health care reform plan. Individuals from the private and public sector with expertise in health care policy and health-related issues were recruited to serve on the White House Task Force On National Health Care Reform.[17]

To shield the task force from political pressure, Mrs. Clinton required that task force deliberations, as well as the task force's membership, be kept secret. The select and secretive nature of the task force was disturbing to many congressmen, for it was apparent from the start of the reform effort that the First Lady had little regard for the standard system of policy-making inside the Beltway. As Paul J. Quirk and Joseph Hinchliffe put it: "Evidently assuming that a workable plan could best be developed by experts insulated from political pressures, the task force avoided consulting with congressional leaders or representatives of many affected interests."[18] Ira Magaziner, a policy analyst with closer ties to academia than Capitol Hill was selected to serve as chief advisor to Mrs. Clinton. Although several congressional staff workers and executive branch officials were chosen to serve on the White House Task Force, it was evident that the legislative initiative for health care reform would emanate from a hand-picked and select group of individuals with marginal ties to the Washington establishment. In essence, political novices, rather than veteran politicians experienced in the art of compromise and bargaining, were assembled for the purpose of engineering one of the greatest reform efforts in the history of American government.

After many meetings and testimony before Congress, the White

House Task Force on Health Care Reform produced a very lengthy and complex legislative proposal entitled "The Health Care Security Act." The 1,350 page proposal was submitted to Congress in October 1993. The plan extended health benefits to all Americans, required small businesses to extend comprehensive health insurance benefits to employees, imposed controls on private insurance companies, and established a system in which quasi-public agencies known as "alliances" would manage competition between health care providers in the interest of ensuring quality care at competitive rates.[19]

In his second State of the Union message, delivered in January 1994, the president once again stressed the immediate need for health care reform. At the same time, he vowed to veto any health care reform bill that did not include a provision for universal coverage. The president stood firm in his commitment to reforming the nation's health care system. Two State of the Union Messages, a special address to Congress, a White House task force, and a comprehensive legislative reform proposal underscored in no uncertain terms the centrality of this policy objective to the Clinton presidency.

Health care reform, however, was never achieved. The legislative proposal essentially disintegrated within the context of the lawmaking process. Alternative health care reform plans were presented by members of Congress which not only factionalized both congressional parties, but diminished interest and support for the president's original proposal. Republican legislators, not unexpectedly, depicted Clinton's plan as yet another example of a Democratic reform effort that would result in more bureaucracy and big government. Although most of the verbal opposition emanated from Republican lawmakers, it was apparent that many congressional Democrats had serious reservations regarding the president's reform effort as well. The health care reform initiative was not by any means emerging through the Democratic Party.

To complicate matters for the president, the proposal, rather than assigned to one standing committee in each legislative chamber, was referred to a variety of legislative committees. House committees with legislative jurisdiction included Ways and Means, Energy and Commerce, and Education and Labor. In the Senate, the Finance Committee, as well as the Labor and Human Resources Committee were the two standing committees with principal juridiction over health care reform.[20] Multiple committee involvement did little to maintain the coherence of the President's reform proposal.

In a lawmaking process characterized by fragmentation and weak partisan teamwork between the White House and Congress, it should come as no surprise that lobbyists and special interest groups would also exert considerable influence over the president's reform plan. Indeed, the pivotal role of special interests during the failed reform effort is thoroughly documented in a study conducted by the Center for Public Integrity, a non-profit organization based in the nation's capital. According to the Center's investigative study, *Well Healed*, President Clinton's health care reform effort triggered one of the most intensive lobbying efforts in the history of American politics.[21]

The Center's report estimates that over $100 million was spent by special interest groups during the health care debate, with the vast majority of money directed against, rather than for, the president's proposal. Money from special interests associated with the health care industry was used to influence the position of congressmen in many ways, including direct campaign contributions to members of Congress, extensive television, radio and newspaper advertising, public opinion polling, the hiring of lobbying firms, and intensive grassroot lobbying in congressional districts.

Federal Election Commission records, cited in the Center's study, reveal that from 1993 through the first quarter of 1994, over $25 million was donated to congressmen from special interests affected by the president's plan. Contributions from Political Action Committees to congressmen serving on the five standing committees with jurisdiction over health care policy totalled $8,240,694. Members of the House Ways and Means Committee received a total of $2.7 million from health care organizations. According to the Center's report, organizations in the health care industry hired at least ninety-seven lobbying and public relations firms to influence congressional orientations.[22] Many organizations were visible during the fight to reform health care. Leading examples included the American Medical Association, the Health Insurance Association of America, the Pharmaceutical Manufacturers Association, and the National Federation of Independent Businesses.

Public relations advertising was intense during the health care debate. The Center identified the "Harry and Louise" ads as having an especially far reaching impact on public perceptions of the president's reform proposal. The ads, which were sponsored by the Health Insurance Association of America (HIAA), involved a middle class couple discussing the negative economic consequences of the president's health care reform plan. According to the Center's report, the dialogue between Harry and Louise was responsible for a twenty point drop in public support for the President's plan. Senator Jay

Rockefeller, a Democrat from West Virginia, described the ads as "the single most destructive campaign I've seen in 30 years."[23] The Center's report cites Kathleen Hall Jamieson's estimate that more than $50 million was spent on advertising during the health care reform effort.

In addition to the millions of dollars funnelled to congressmen, and the millions spent on lobbying and negative advertising, the Center also discovered that at least eighty former members of Congress and executive branch officials were working as lobbyists for the health care industry. Among the eighty former public officials, twenty-three had left government service in 1993–1994. Among the twenty-three, twelve were former members of Congress. The "revolving door" syndrome, an important campaign issue in 1992, was more than evident during the president's attempt to initiate health care reform.

Special interests also sponsored a number of trips across the United States and around the globe for members of Congress. Such trips were ostensibly for the purpose of health care fact finding. According to the Center's report, over eighty-five members of Congress from 1992–1993 participated in 181 trips sponsored by health care organizations. The American Medical Association alone sponsored 55 trips in two years. In addition to trips to California and Florida, congressmen traveled to Puerto Rico, France, Jamaica and Canada. Spouses were included in seventy-three of the trips.

Beyond sponsored trips to posh vacation resorts, the Center also discovered that 134 members of Congress, their spouses or children, had financial investments in the health industry. Investments were particularly evident in pharmaceutical companies. Within the congressional committees exercising jurisdiction over health policy, more than forty members of Congress, their spouses or children, had financial interests in health care companies.[24]

The Root of the Problem

On the surface, the disintegration of President Clinton's health care reform plan can be attributed to a number factors: a political amateur was placed in charge of the reform effort, the reform plan was sent to several standing committees, and special interest groups opposed to reform were simply too powerful for the president to compete with. While all of this is related to the president's failure to achieve reform, the important question which emerges is *why* did such conditions exist? Why was a political amateur and a secretive task force in charge of such a critical legislative proposal? Why did the reform proposal fragment upon its introduction to Congress? Why were special interests groups able to undermine the president's reform effort? Why did health care reform, which was at the center of President Clinton's domestic agenda, totally collapse?

The deeper answer appears to lie in the current weakness of the political party system. Weak political parties result in candidate-centered presidential campaigns. Candidate-centered campaigns accomplish little in preparing future presidents for the business of governing. Media scrutiny of candidates is more intense and frequently negative when the entire campaign revolves around a single individual, rather than the party to which the candidate belongs. Such scrutiny does little to enhance the image of a presidential candidate. Bill Clinton's reputation was permanently damaged in the very early stages of the presidential campaign. This did little to foster a positive connection between Clinton and fellow Democrats running for Congress.

In an age of party decline, presidential coattails have become much shorter. The candidate-centered presidential campaign, such as that conducted by Bill Clinton in 1992, does little to establish a firm party connection between presidential and congressional candidates. This has governing consequences, as short coattails do not help a new president engineer broad and controversial reform. Longer party coattails and a stronger partisan connection between the president and congressional Democrats would most certainly have helped President Clinton direct health care reform.

When presidential candidates form their own personal organizations and hire their own campaign consultants, it naturally follows that such individuals will be appointed to high level staff positions in the White House. Such individuals then become policy formulators and initiators of the president's agenda. While such individuals might be quite adept at managing presidential campaigns, it is doubtful if they have the experience necessary for guiding legislative measures through the many minefields of the congressional decision-making process. The arrogance of the White House Task Force on National Health Care Reform, demonstrated by secret meetings and undisclosed membership, the complicated and lengthy legislative proposal developed by the Task Force, the parceling of the proposal to five different standing committees, and the coordination of the reform effort by Mrs. Clinton and her chief advisor Ira Magaziner, reflected the work of individuals unfamiliar with the political terrain inside the Beltway. It is the candidate-centered campaign which lends itself to such political incompetency.

In the absence of a strong party connection between the presidency and Congress, special interest groups will inevitably dictate the terms of public policy debates. Without a strong partisan bond between the president and Congress, the political loyalty of a congressman is more likely to be influenced, or perhaps captured, by active and well-financed special interest groups. Weak partisan ties between the executive and legislative branches of government allow special interests to infiltrate the corridors of power and thwart creative presidential initiatives. Public opinion regarding presidential initiatives is also more susceptible to manipulation by special interest activity when political party allegiance among the electorate is less firm.

Thus, the Clinton presidency, like the Carter presidency, provides yet another lesson regarding the consequences that result from weak political parties. This is not to suggest that Democratic presidents in the post-Watergate years are the only presidents to have been affected in a negative way by a diminished party system. A stronger political party system would most certainly have bolstered the presidencies of Presidents Reagan and Bush in their efforts to implement conservative agenda. An unhealthy party system impedes presidential leadership regardless of party affiliation.

Weak political parties have unfortunate consequences for the governing process. Thus, it seems appropriate, to direct our thoughts toward reform proposals designed to restore the role of political parties in American politics. Prescriptive remedies are discussed in the following chapter.

CHAPTER SIX

Party Reform and Presidential Leadership

In this chapter, a number of reform proposals will be explored which either directly or indirectly strengthen the role of political parties within the context of the American political process. More important for the purpose of this work, these reforms have the potential to strengthen the bond between political parties and the American presidency. The proposals about to be reviewed are not abstract and unrealistic recommendations. In fact, some are based on political models currently in place at the state level of government, while others reflect bills pending in Congress. These reforms are viable and practical solutions to the current problems associated with weak parties and presidential leadership.

A common concern expressed by many political scientists and observers is that the current presidential selection system lends itself to shallow and factional power bases. The process of presidential selection, according to this argument, does little to establish a strong partisan base from which presidents can govern. As we examine the current crisis facing the American presidency, it seems logical, therefore, that reform efforts to reconnect the president with the party must begin with the presidential selection process. As Theodore J. Lowi notes in *The Personal President*: "Virtually every treatment of the modern presidency is respectful of the relationship between the selection process and the nature and conduct of the office." [1]

Presidential Nominating Reform

The element of the presidential selection process which appears to be the most responsible for factionalizing presidential support is clearly the presidential nominating process. This process needs to be reformed in such a way as to broaden the president's partisan base among the American public and strengthen the partisan bond between the president, party organization, and elected office holders at all levels of government. Nominating reforms must therefore have as their goal a stronger connection between presidents and their parties.

The plan which would effectively accomplish this objective is one of the most fascinating political reform proposals currently in existence. This is the controversial pre-primary national convention plan, which includes the possibility of a national primary election.[2] It is modeled after nominating processes currently found in several states, including Colorado, New York, and the author's home state of Connecticut.

This proposal is controversial because it "reverses" the current nominating process by placing the national nominating convention before, not after, the primary process. At the same time, the plan collapses state presidential primary contests (currently conducted over the span of five months) into one national primary election. Theoretically, the end result is a more party-centered and coherent nominating process which lends itself to presidential leadership.

According to this plan, nomination of a party's presidential candidate begins with precinct party caucuses. In these caucuses, delegates are elected to attend county conventions. The nominating process, therefore, begins at the grassroots of the party system. Moreover, only registered party members are allowed to vote for delegates.

At the county conventions, delegates are elected to attend a state convention. At the state convention, delegates are elected to attend the party's national nominating convention. The bulk of a state's convention delegates are therefore selected through a three-tier competitive process which is very party-centered.

Thus far, there is nothing really new about this system, even with respect to presidential politics. Currently, there are eleven "caucus/convention" states which select delegates to the national nominating conventions through a three- or four-tier process (Iowa and Maine are two).

In addition to those delegates chosen in caucuses and state conventions, this plan also calls for governors, mayors, congressmen, state legislators and party organization officials to serve as formal members of a state's convention delegation. A typical state delegation will therefore be a combination of grassroots party activists chosen by their peers and political professionals. The plan also calls for state delegations to be made up of pledged and unpledged delegates.

Some very promising features of this reform plan can now be highlighted. The delegate selection process begins at the grassroots level and is party-centered, not determined by the mass media. The party-centered and deliberative process prevents candidates from securing convention delegates through momentum generated by the media—a formula for quick victory under the current nominating process. State convention slates consist of ordinary citizens and professional political practitioners, and convention delegates may be either free agents or pledged to presidential candidates.

The delegate selection procedure of this reform plan is certainly more feasible than the current practice of selecting national convention delegates by means of state presidential primaries. Primary elections (as research has demonstrated) have the potential to be easily influenced by ideological factions. Moreover, state primary laws have become so flexible with respect to participation requirements that political professionals are relegated to minor roles at the nominating convention.[3] The current nominating process lacks party authority, which results in presidents without a broad partisan power base.

After the selection of convention delegates, a national convention would be convened. It would be filled with suspense and drama—unlike current ratification forums billed as "nominating" conventions. Two rounds of balloting would be required. The first would winnow the field to the top three presidential candidates while the second would determine the top two. These two candidates—provided each received at least 25 percent of the convention vote on the second ballot—would then face each other in a national primary election. The voters could therefore choose between a convention-endorsed candidate and a viable challenger. In the event that one candidate received more than 75 percent of the vote on the second ballot, no primary would be necessary—the party would have its presidential nominee.

The national primary would be held fairly soon after the national nominating convention. The two candidates would campaign vigorously across the country for the support of registered party members. What is especially significant here is that the primary's national scope does not in any way allocate a disproportionate amount of influence to one state or even one region within the country. This is fundamentally unlike the current system of primary elections, in which the outcome of the New Hampshire primary (the first primary of the nominating season) determines the fate of so many presidential contenders—many of whom are potentially excellent presidents. According to the reform plan, in order to win the party's nomination, a candidate must necessarily have a broad, national base of support and must be well-respected across the land—both essential requirements for national leadership.

At the time of this writing, the 1996 presidential nominating contest is about to begin. Quite clearly, there is evidence to suggest displeasure and frustration with the primary calendar. Witness, for example, the rescheduling of the California primary from June to March, and Arizona's attempt to compete with New Hampshire for the first primary of the season. An increasing number of states clearly wish to have equal power within the context of the presidential nominating process, rather go through the motions of conducting a primary long after the outcome of the nominating process has been decided. A national primary election would resolve this grossly unfair situation.

Restructuring the presidential nominating process appears to be a step in the right direction in order to broaden the partisan power base of American presidents. Presidential candidates would begin the long journey to the White House through cultivating the support of the party's rank-and-file, party organization officials, and fellow partisans in federal, state and local office. Delegate selection procedures would serve to cement a political relationship between the candidates and various components of the party structure. There would be little opportunity for candidates to circumvent the political party under this system.

The national party convention would regain its status as a decisive nominating mechanism. Convention decisions would be determined by a mix of pledged and unpledged delegates composed of citizens and political professionals. The winnowing process should lend itself to perceptions of legitimacy and fairness. Should the contest result in a national primary, voter turnout would be higher compared to the current system of state presidential primaries. At the same time, a broad cross-section of the citizenry, rather than small ideological factions, would directly nominate presidential candidates. No state would be irrelevant to the outcome of the nomination process, and the party's nominee would emerge with a mandate from a broad base of the party.

Advocates of this reform plan believe media coverage will tend to center on the issues of the campaign, rather than a candidate's political momentum during primary elections.[4] This suggestion seems logical, as the more structured, party-centered and shorter process could very well direct media energy and focus away from polling results and towards substantive issues of the presidential campaign. It is quite possible, therefore, that a more issue oriented nominating process will emerge—yet another feature of the plan which serves the interests of national leadership.

General Election Reform: The Electoral College

Efforts to strengthen the working relationship between political parties and the presidency cannot stop with presidential nominating reform. Like the nominating process, the party's presidential nominee needs to be drawn closer to the party structure during the fall campaign. Presidential candidates must come to depend more on their parties for electoral success, rather than waging candidate-centered campaigns which often lack reference to either party labels or platforms.

There are reform proposals which attempt to accomplish this very objective. Some reformers call for abolishing the electoral college and conducting instead a direct popular election.[5] According to the Direct Election Plan, a minimum of 40 percent of the popular vote would be required to win the presidency. If no candidate received the 40 percent minimum, a run-off election would be held between the top two candidates. On the second ballot, the winner would necessarily receive over 50 percent of the popular vote.

While there are possibilities for stronger political parties and national presidential mandates under this proposal, the risk of presidents consistently elected by a plurality of popular votes and the specter of third party candidates manipulating second ballot outcomes must raise serious doubts about abolishing the electoral college. Decisive victories in the electoral college promote the sense of a governing mandate (even though the popular vote may have been extremely close), thus enhancing presidential power. Abolishing the electoral college is not the answer for stronger parties or a stronger presidency.

Another reform proposal concerning the electoral college is to allocate electoral votes proportionally. Under this plan, a candidate would receive a percentage of electoral votes from each state in proportion to the popular vote he or she received. The Proportional Plan has the least appeal with respect to stronger political parties and presidential leadership. Proportional representation inevitably contributes to a multi-party system. Minor parties of a regional, ideological, or personal nature would blossom under this arrangement.

Presidential mandates in the electoral college would be less decisive and presidential elections would repeatedly be decided in the House of Representatives. The legitimacy of the presidency could very well be threatened under proportional representation.

Another proposed reform regarding the electoral college is already in place in the states of Maine and Nebraska. Rather than allocating electoral votes on the basis of winner-take-all, these are awarded according to statewide voting behavior and voting behavior within each congressional district. The candidate who wins the state's popular vote is awarded two electoral votes. Remaining electoral votes are then awarded according to election results in each congressional district. Theoretically, electoral votes are allocated to states according to the number of senators and congressmen who represent each state.

Of the various electoral college reform proposals, the District Plan offers the most opportunity for stronger political parties and presidential governance.[6] If adopted by the fifty states, presidential candidates would be required to campaign in each of the 435 congressional districts across the country. This would closely link party presidential and congressional nominees, a link which has been absent for quite some time in American politics. The concept of a partisan ticket campaigning together at the grassroots level could possibly be restored—a positive feature of the plan.

Presidential candidates, rather than focusing energy and resources in the large metropolitan areas of a dozen heavily populated and industrialized states, would be required to engage in a national grassroots campaign. Voters in the First Congressional District of Kansas would have the same political influence and contact with presidential candidates as voters in the First Congressional District of Florida. Moreover, no state could be considered lost or won based on results of statewide public opinion polls. Candidates would spend more time in states in order to secure electoral votes in the congressional districts. The District Plan has the potential to nationalize presidential campaigning, promote partisan tickets, and link the American people to the presidency. It is the one electoral college reform proposal which makes sense in light of the goals of stronger political parties and presidential leadership.

Campaign Finance Reform

If political parties are to serve a critical electioneering function during the presidential contest, then efforts must also be directed towards campaign finance reform. Indeed, nominating and electoral college reform will be effective only if political parties assume a more central financial role during presidential campaigns.

The current system of financing presidential campaigns not only diminishes the relationship between parties and presidential candidates, but actually encourages candidate-centered campaigns. To its credit, the system of public funding has leveled the playing field between candidates. The influence of special interests, and "fat-cat" financial influence, have been admirably contained. Unfortunately, however, public financing of presidential elections (so readily available to candidates, including those with only a modicum of viability) encourages candidates to bypass party organizations in their quest for campaign funds. Under the current campaign finance system, there is little if any incentive for presidential candidates to secure funding from party organizations. American taxpayers and the federal treasury now provide all that is necessary to wage a modern presidential campaign, replete with media consultants and high technology.

A variety of reform proposals have emerged which could potentially restore the financial role of parties in presidential campaigns. These range from outright repeal of the public funding provisions of the federal election law (which would force candidates to depend exclusively on private money, including party contributions) to the establishment of a new federal law that would provide public financing for political parties.

As with nominating and electoral college reform, one has only to look to the states for guidance. Currently, twenty-one states have some form of public finance policy for state elections. Among these, roughly a dozen allow for tax dollars (raised through a voluntary state income tax check-off), to be funneled directly into the coffers of political parties.[7] Exactly how these funds are utilized by the party organizations varies from state to state.

Among those states which channel voluntary tax contributions to parties, Iowa's state central committees appear to have the most flexibility concerning the disbursement of funds. Dollars directed to the Democratic and Republican central committees can be used for a variety of purposes, including administrative costs and media advertising.[8] Public funds in Iowa cannot, however, be used to make direct contributions to candidates, but can be used to pay staff workers to assist candidates in their fundraising efforts.[9] According to one Republican staff worker in Iowa, the public funding plan, enacted during the early eighties, has to some extent drawn candidates for a wide variety of state offices closer to the party due to the array of services available through the state central committees. Although many campaigns in Iowa are still candidate-centered, a closer party connection seems to have emerged in recent years.[10]

Is it feasible to replace the current system of direct public funding for presidential candidates with an entirely new system of public funding for political parties? Would the taxpayers be willing, on their federal income tax forms, to give a few dollars to political parties? This is unlikely in light of the fact that no more than thirty percent of taxpayers have ever contributed to the Federal Election Campaign Fund. The prevailing cynicism towards political parties expressed in public opinion surveys also lends doubt to the potential success of this plan.

Professor Larry Sabato's recommendation to *transfer* a portion of the Federal Election Campaign Fund into the treasuries of the Democratic and Republican National Committees is the most practical—and least dramatic—step towards a system of public funding for political parties. Currently, federal taxpayers who wish to participate in the public financing system can direct three dollars to the Federal Election Campaign Fund. Sabato proposes that surplus federal funds at the close of a presidential election year be given to the parties' national committees.[11] This is a practical and sensible proposal.

However, bolder measures are clearly necessary if parties are to gain a significant advantage over presidential candidates and policy platforms. Perhaps if one out of every three Federal Election Campaign Fund dollars was transferred to the DNC and RNC prior to the beginning of the presidential election—with the legal stipulation that such funds be used to assist the campaign efforts of presidential candidates—it is conceivable that the candidates and their national committees would interact to a much greater degree throughout the course of the campaign. National party committees would no longer be merely auxiliaries of the candidate organizations; instead, they would be integral to the presidential campaign.

At the time of this writing, it is estimated that $128 million will be available for the presidential nominees of the two major parties during the 1996 general election campaign.[12] If $43 million (approximately one-third) was directed towards the two major parties ($21.5 million each), the national committees would have added resources necessary to consolidate control over campaign content and strategy. If this reform proved successful, the policy might be further modified to designate two of every three Federal Election Campaign Fund dollars to be directed towards the party committees.

Obviously, there are many details of this reform proposal to be addressed. At this point in time, however, it is the broad concept of public financing for national party committees that is being advanced. The task at hand is to convince the American people and federal lawmakers that national party committees should assume a more important financial role in presidential campaigns, and that public funding of political parties (a practice found in several states) is a desirable course of action.

In addition to establishing a system of public finance for political parties, other aspects of the federal campaign finance code require modification as well. Here, the recommendations of the Committee for Party Renewal, an organization consisting of political scientists and political practitioners interested in the restoration of the American two-party system, will be presented.

In its "Position Paper on Campaign Finance Reform" of March 25th, 1990, the Committee presented a series of recommendations concerning federal campaign finance reform. At the time this paper was issued, the House of Representatives and the Senate were in the process of proposing reforms to the 1971 Federal Campaign Finance Act. Subsequent to the appearance of this position paper, the Executive Director of the Committee for Party Renewal testified before the House Task Force on Campaign Finance Reform in hopes of persuading federal lawmakers that campaign finance reform efforts should strengthen, not diminish, the financial role of parties in the election process.[13]

The bold recommendations set forth by the Committee for Party Renewal included stricter limitations on Political Action Committee contributions to *individual candidates*. This would reduce a congressional candidate's dependence on special interest money during the campaign. The vast influence of lobbyists on the legislative process would also be reduced.

The Committee also recommended raising the ceilings on PAC and individual contributions to national and state political parties. There are currently limits concerning the amount of money a PAC or private individual can contribute to a political party. The Committee urged easing these limits in the interest of strengthening the financial capacity of political parties during election campaigns. In the Committee's view, there is a substantial difference between a PAC contribution to a congressional candidate, and a contribution to a political party. Since political parties work towards the general interest, PAC contributions to parties should not be severely restricted.

The Committee also proposed that political parties be allowed to spend money without restriction in the interest of party building. (This is known as "soft money" and is used for activities such as voter registration drives and party advertising.) The Committee objected to components of the House and Senate bills which place restrictions on the use of soft money. If used in an ethical and legal fashion, soft money can serve as an important tool for party development. In recent years, unfortunately, soft money has been employed in ways that border on illegality.

Another recommendation of the Committee was the lifting of all ceilings on party contributions to individual candidates at all levels of government. Current federal law restricts the amount a political party can contribute to a federal candidate. A number of states restrict party contributions to state candidates as well. The Committee urged that such restrictions be lifted entirely.

To inject more party money into congressional elections, the Committee also advocated that Congress adopt a system of public funding for congressional elections. These funds would be channeled to candidates through party organizations.[14]

The campaign finance proposals discussed above are specifically designed to broaden the role of political parties in election campaigns. If the financial capacity of political parties is significantly increased, there will undoubtedly be a closer association between candidates for public office and their respective parties. The proposals have a tremendous potential for forging a firm and dynamic working relationship between the president of the United States on the one hand, and congressmen and perhaps even office-holders at the subnational level on the other. Presidential power and the capacity for stable, national leadership will most certainly benefit through restoring the financial power of political parties.

At the time of this writing, the 104th Congress is preparing to begin work. Campaign finance reform efforts during the 103rd Congress were unsuccessful, despite the fact that two versions of a campaign finance reform bill were passed by the House (HR 3750) and the Senate (S–3). Exactly what will become of campaign finance reform is difficult to predict. Although it is not a component of the Republican "Contract With America," House Speaker Newt Gingrich has alluded to future campaign finance reform efforts. While some version may be on the horizon, the important question is whether Congress in its reform efforts will be sensitive to the important place of parties within the context of federal election campaigns. Indeed, the national interest will be better served if reform efforts are launched with an eye towards a stronger and more vibrant party system. The Committee for Party Renewal's position paper is relevant here:

> As Congress reforms the existing campaign finance laws, the Committee for Party Renewal urges it to recall the unique and valuable role that political parties have in American society. A century of academic study supports the position that the health of a polity is directly correlated to the vitality of its political parties. The committee advises reformers to proceed boldly so that the political parties can better perform their essential democratic functions. We believe the proposals we favor enhance the essential role the parties play in the United States, and that they can be implemented in a framework acceptable to Democrats and Republicans. In an era when voter turnout is low, and Americans seem to hate politics, strengthening the political parties is not only in the public interest, it is in the national interest.[15]

Campaign Advertising Reform

One component of presidential campaigns which has become all but invisible during the last two decades, is the extent to which political parties advertise party platforms. It is quite evident that party platforms in the modern age of American politics have been subordinated to the candidate's personal platform in both federal and state campaigns. Although most voters can discern the positions and principles of individual candidates, identifying the central themes and policy positions of the political parties to which they belong is far more difficult.

During a presidential election year, voters receive multiple and confusing messages from presidential, senate and congressional candidates—not only from those belonging to the two major parties, but also from those within the same party and on the same ticket. Although the platform issued by the national party convention every four years theoretically unifies party candidates for federal office, the platform is often overlooked in favor of the personal platforms of the candidates. This leads to unfortunate consequences for presidential and congressional interaction, as disparate personal platforms and parochial agenda impede political teamwork.

It is essential therefore that Democratic and Republican party platforms be brought to the forefront of the presidential campaign. Showcasing the party's platform should draw presidential and congressional candidates closer during the election campaign and during the governing process. One proposal which is achievable and very practical for accomplishing this objective is to enact a federal law which allows blocs of free television advertising time for the two national party committees. The model worth emulating is found not among the American states, but in the political system of Great Britain—a polity, it should be noted, remarkable for its pattern of responsible party government.

In the British system, the two major parties are allocated blocs of free air time broadcast on the major networks. National party organizations must restrict their campaign message to their party platforms, without reference to individual candidates. Five, ten minute blocs of free air time are allocated equally to the two major parties, with smaller parties given fewer blocs based on their electoral strength.[16]

British law also prohibits political parties and individual candidates from buying special blocs of time for campaign advertising. This feature of British politics, in this author's view, is neither desirable or constitutional when applied to the American political scene. Clearly, parties need free blocs of air time, but not to the exclusion of purchased air time. A combined approach seems to be most desirable course of action for American politics.

One panel of political scientists and campaign consultants who testified before Congress recommended that every television and radio station, as a condition for renewing their broadcasting licenses, provide eight hours of free air time to political parties each year.[17] The two national party committees would each receive two hours of free air time, and two hours of free time would also be allocated to each of the party's state central committees. Cable stations would be required to provide four hours of free air time to the national party committees only. At least two-thirds of the time slots would be scheduled between September and November—the most intense period of the election campaign. Air time for the parties would consist of spot-ads ranging from ten to sixty seconds, as well as five minute commercials. The panel recommended that allocation of time be determined through negotiations between party organizations and the networks. Like the British system, air time for third parties would be based on the parties' electoral strength in the previous election.[18]

In addition to free air time devoted to party advertising, the Committee for Party Renewal has also recommended that Congress legislate free television time for party-sponsored presidential debates. This proposal, if enacted into law, would most certainly transform debates from candidate-centered affairs, emphasizing panache and one-liners to party-centered forums in which the principles of party platforms are substantively debated by presidential candidates. Partisan labels would have more meaning to individual voters under an arrangement in which the parties sponsored debates, and presidential candidates would be more closely identified with the principles of their party's platform. As the Committee's position paper states:

> The presidential debates, which have become an expected part of campaigns for our highest office, offer an opportunity both to make political parties more visible in the contest for the presidency and to enhance the process of voter education. Presidential debates are not a "news conference" and should not be organized as one. They are not a "nonpartisan forum," and it serves no purpose to pretend otherwise.[19]

Free air time for party-sponsored debates, combined with blocs of free air time for party advertisements, could potentially breathe new life into party labels. Platforms presented to voters by the Democratic and Republican parties would have greater relevance to the policy-making process. A stronger bond between voters, party platforms and federal decision-makers would most certainly develop. American presidents, therefore, would have a stronger and more stable partisan base from which to govern under this system.

Lobbying Reform

Attempts to strengthen the president's partisan power base must also address the extraordinary influence of lobbyists inside the Washington Beltway. Rampant lobbying in national politics is a principal reason why ambitious presidential agenda are routinely subverted and compromised. The activity of special interest lobbyists has a fragmenting effect on party unity in Congress and between the executive and legislative branches of government. Special and private agenda frequently interfere with the broad policy goals of the president and his party. Wedges are constantly being driven between federal decision-makers, much to the detriment of leadership and good government.

Like campaign finance reform, lobbying reform experienced a slow death in the 103rd Congress. Whether or not the Republican-controlled 104th Congress will change the federal lobbying law remains to be seen. Unfortunately, lobbying reform is not a component of the Republican Contract With America. The strong connection between special interests and congressmen raises serious doubts about the prospect of meaningful lobbying reform—regardless of which party is in power.

Nevertheless, lobbying reform should be a top priority of the 104th Congress. The original reform proposal presented to the 103rd Congress, entitled the "Lobbying Disclosure Act of 1994," which replaces the Federal Regulation of Lobbying Act of 1946, should be reactivated, passed by Congress, and signed into law. An examination of the proposed legislation reveals a number of excellent recommendations which would effectively restrain and more closely regulate the activity of special interest lobbyists.[20] If passed, the new law would emphatically restrict lobbying at the federal level.

Included among the many positive features of the proposed legislation is a ban on gifts that lobbyists are currently entitled to give members of Congress, such as meals and tickets to sporting events. Gifts to spouses of congressmen are also banned under this bill. The bill also imposes a ban on special interest contributions to congressional legal defense funds and bans expense-paid trips for congressmen to recreational events such as tennis tournaments and ski resorts.

Even more meaningful from the perspective of presidential leadership and party unity is the bill's requirement that lobbyists register and report biennially on their lobbying activity. Lobbyists would be required to register with the Office of Lobbying Registration and Public Disclosure, a watchdog office that would be created by the bill. The bill requires the registration of lobbyists who attempt to influence the policy process through contact with congressional staff workers or executive branch officials. Such activity is currently unregulated under the 1946 lobbying law—the result of a narrow judicial interpretation in 1954. Extending registration requirements to congressional staff and executive branch lobbying is critical in light of the General Accounting Office's estimate that two-thirds of lobbyists currently operating within the Beltway are unregistered.[21]

A serious point of controversy regarding lobbying reform during the 103rd Congress concerned an attempt on the part of congressional reformers to extend reporting requirements to "grassroots lobbying." Grassroots lobbying is an effort on the part of interest groups to generate public pressure by mobilizing public opinion. Phone banks, advertising, and direct mailings are tools employed by special interest groups for this purpose. This reform is long overdue given the substantial amount of special interest activity made possible by the availability of new technologies. Although the tactics and tools are different from standard methods of persuasion, such activity still meets the definition of lobbying. Regulation and reporting of grass-roots lobbying should therefore be included in any reform measure.

Lobbying reform efforts should extend to lobbying on behalf of foreign interests as well. Although foreign lobbying is fairly well regulated by the Foreign Agents Registration Act of 1938, congressional reformers should take the additional step and ban altogether lobbying on behalf of foreign interests. Domestic lobbying alone poses enough of a threat to party unity and presidential leadership. Allowing foreign lobbyists legal access to the corridors of power encourages fragmentation and failed leadership.

The First Amendment was never intended to protect the free speech of lobbyists employed by foreign governments or foreign economic interests, regardless of the fact that such lobbyists are often American citizens. To stretch the meaning of the free speech clause to include foreign lobbying is to grossly distort the meaning of this cherished amendment. In 1992, Japanese interests spent over $60 million in their attempts to influence congressional voting behavior. Canadian interests spent $22.7 million, while interests from Germany, France, Mexico and Hong Kong devoted more that $10 million each.[22] Such activity undermines national leadership, subverts the basic principle of a government for and by the people, and places the country's national security at risk. On matters pertaining to foreign policy, either economic or military, federal decision-makers should not be subjected to the special demands and persuasive tactics of foreign interest lobbyists. Repeal of the Foreign Agents Registration Act should therefore be a reform objective.

The final aspect of lobbying reform which ought to be aggressively pursued concerns the concept of the "revolving door." It is well known that many former congressmen and executive branch officials, upon retiring from public service, begin new careers as lobbyists. Such an arrangement serves to solidify special interest leverage over the policy-making process.

The Ethics in Government Act of 1978 limits, to some extent, how soon a retired legislator or executive official can commence work as a lobbyist. In most instances, a former public servant must be retired for at least one year. There are also lifetime bans on lobbying for very specific policies in which the former official was personally involved. Recently, top appointees under the Clinton administration took an oath not to lobby their former executive branch agencies for at least five years.[23] However, despite the Ethics in Government Act, and despite public outcry over the "revolving door," the transition from public servant to private lobbyist continues unabated. Lobbying reform efforts must therefore drastically revamp post-employment restrictions. The pledge taken by Clinton appointees should be the model for a new law which covers *all* former congressmen and former executive branch officials. Simply put, no person should be allowed to lobby any part of the federal government or any policy area for at least five years after retiring from public service. The lifetime ban on lobbying policy areas in which there was direct personal involvement should be retained as well.

Lobbying reform is a prerequisite for strengthening the place of political parties in federal decision-making. It is clearly one of the most direct ways to reduce the vast power of lobbyists and to break the vise-like control of the iron triangles. As special interest activity becomes more closely regulated, political parties will be able to structure and more thoroughly influence the course of the governing process. At the same time, the law-making process will become less fragmented, and presidential agenda will face less opposition.

Patronage Reform

Many people bristle at the thought of reintroducing the patronage system to American politics. Patronage is often associated with cronyism, party bosses, and political favoritism. Opposition to patronage is perfectly understandable—political hacks with limited educations controlling government agencies is not in the interest of good government. It is therefore unwise and unrealistic to suggest a restoration of the spoils system that existed prior to civil service reform. Who delivers your mail, for example, should not be based on which political party controls the White House.

However, if one subscribes to the perspective that strong parties contribute to a strong presidency, and that strong presidents serve the interest of American government, then it is logical to reform federal hiring practices in a manner which allows an applicant's partisanship and political connections to be taken into consideration. The extent to which the bureaucracy is politicized is a philosophical issue which has broad implications for governing. As James P. Pfiffner states: "The balance between presidential appointees and career executives in governing the United States is a fundamental question of who shall rule."[24] It is important therefore that reform efforts attempt to strike an appropriate balance between politics and merit (an especially relevant issue given the current power of public employee unions).

Any meaningful reform effort that attempts to reintroduce the use of patronage in dramatic fashion will undoubtedly meet with great opposition. Indeed, our highest court has been very protective of the current merit system. In *U.S. Civil Service Commission v. National Association of Letter Carriers* (1973), the Supreme Court upheld Congress' right to prevent federal employees covered under the Hatch Act from holding a party post and engaging in routine partisan activity. In *Eldrod v. Burns* (1976), the Court ruled that dismissal from public service based on partisan consideration was unconstitutional. The Court reaffirmed its position even more forcefully in *Branti v. Finkel* (1980), leading some scholars to suggest a "constitutionalizing" of the merit system.[25] The Supreme Court has thus far shown itself to be a principal ally of the merit system.

To complicate matters for advocates of reform, Congress has shown little inclination to reintroduce the spoils system. This is not surprising in light of public opinion regarding patronage. In one poll, 79 percent of respondents expressed opposition to government hiring on the basis of partisan consideration.[26] It is obvious that patronage reform will be met with sharp resistance.

Nevertheless, the time has come for a stronger partisan connection between the president and federal employees. If the president of the United States is to serve this nation as an effective chief executive, he must have more latitude in the hiring and firing of those who work beneath him.

In this author's opinion, the question is not *whether* patronage is desirable, but rather *how much* patronage is needed. This issue is more problematic. Sabato's recommendation to create more honorary positions, such as blue ribbon commissions and advisory boards is a good one. He also recommends that presidents utilize patronage to the extent that current court decisions and public opinion allows. These are useful recommendations.

However, for patronage to again become a powerful tool for presidents, sweeping reform is needed. Patronage should permeate federal agencies to the point where the president commands at least one hundred thousand federal employees. Accordingly, a number of high level civil service posts would have to be reclassified as political. This would strike a reasonable compromise between politics and merit. The federal government (consisting of three million civilian workers) would still primarily be comprised of career civil servants—a requirement for stability and the execution of technical jobs. At the same time, there would be a substantial number of employees who would owe their jobs to the president and to their party. Increased loyalty to the president and a greater motivation to implement the presidential agenda would inevitably result. Undoubtedly, a number of political appointees in the field would simultaneously hold state and local party organization positions. These appointees would work hard to ensure a favorable attitude on the part of the American people towards both president and party. Strong motivation would more than likely reduce bureaucratic intransigence.

It should also be noted that an infusion of patronage into the federal government will not necessarily result in uneducated and incompetent government administrators (a claim frequently advanced by defenders of the merit system). Unlike those of the nineteenth century, literacy and educational levels in the United States are currently quite high; it is doubtful that a typical patronage appointee would differ much from a career civil servant in terms of aptitude and educational attainment. In addition, the generalist orientation of the federal bureaucracy, which political scientists view as essential for popular control over the government, will be maintained.

The reintroduction of patronage must be included in any reform agenda designed to restore the place of parties in American politics. Patronage not only serves as an important incentive for partisan activity, but also has a direct relation to presidential power. Strong political parties contribute to a strong presidency, and a greater degree of patronage can help facilitate this condition.

Deregulation of Parties

For political parties to assume a meaningful role in American politics, laws that regulate the activity of parties must be relaxed. Party vitality demands parties free from oppressive state regulatory laws. Parties should be free to conduct their own internal affairs as well as adopt by-laws which are in their political interest. Political parties are quasi-private associations, and state laws imposing strict regulations on internal party activity should either be repealed, revamped, or challenged in a court of law.

Fortunately, a series of recent court challenges to regulatory legislation have been mounted by party reformers. Surprisingly, judicial decisions have favored political parties—one of the few trends in recent decades in the direction of party authority. In each case, internal party rules conflicted with state regulatory laws.[27]

Generally speaking, the Supreme Court has favored the rights of political parties to conduct their own internal activity. The Court's current position is that political parties are protected under the First and Fourteenth Amendments. These amendments guarantee a right of association to voluntary organizations, including political parties. Parties, in the Court's view, need flexibility in order to govern their internal activity—especially with respect to the establishment of nominating rules and procedures.

Four Supreme Court decisions highlight the current position of the judiciary regarding the rights of parties. In each case, party nominating rules conflicted with state law. In *Cousins v. Wigoda* (1975), the Court ruled in favor of the Democratic Party when a dispute arose between it and the state of Illinois regarding rules and procedures for selecting delegates to the Democratic National Convention. The Court ruled in favor of the nominating guidelines prescribed by the Democratic party's national committee, not the state of Illinois.

In *Democratic Party of the United States v. Wisconsin ex rel. La Follette* (1981), the Court extended the Cousins precedent and once again favored the right of a party to determine its own nominating rules. In this case, the party's rules requiring that national convention delegates be chosen in closed primary elections conflicted with Wisconsin's law mandating open primaries. The rules of the national committee prevailed over state law.

In *Tashjian v. Republican Party of Connecticut* (1986), the Court ruled that the Connecticut Republican Party could allow unaffiliated voters to vote in Republican primary elections. This rule, engineered by the liberal wing of the party, was in direct conflict with Connecticut state law requiring closed primary elections. The Court reasoned that the First Amendment, as protected by the Fourteenth Amendment, allowed political parties to determine their own associational boundaries in primary elections. Republicans in Connecticut have subsequently returned to closed primaries.

Most recently, in the case of *Eu, Secretary of State of California v. San Francisco County Democratic Central Committee* (1989), the Supreme Court ruled in favor of a party's right to issue endorsements in primary elections. In this case, California law prohibited political parties from issuing formal endorsements prior to primary contests. Once again, the First and Fourteenth Amendments, which, in the

Court's view, protect associational rights for political parties, served as the legal basis for the Court's decision.[28]

These decisions are certainly positive, especially in light of the anti-party political environment in which parties must operate. Nevertheless, reformers still have much work to do to free political parties from restrictive regulatory legislation. Sabato's analysis of data collected by the Advisory Commission on Intergovernmental Relations reveals only fourteen states as having light regulations with respect to political party activity—a most distressing finding. Seventeen states are classified as moderate regulators, while nineteen are heavy regulators. As Sabato says, "the United States has the dubious distinction of hosting the most governmentally fettered parties in the democratic world."[29]

Deregulation of political parties remains a principal challenge for party reformers. Legal challenges, of course, require extensive litigation which is at once time-consuming and costly. Lawyers fees, however, are a small price to pay for liberating institutions essential to democracy and national leadership. More litigation is clearly necessary.

The reforms discussed in this chapter—if implemented—should have the effect of revitalizing the role of political parties in American politics. Presidents, in turn, will be more likely to emerge through the party system and govern within a stronger partisan network. The reforms will lend themselves to the stronger partisan base for presidents essential for national leadership.

Although there are a number of additional reform proposals found in the political science literature and the popular press, those endorsed above are, from this author's perspective, the most desirable and perhaps the most achievable for the purpose of connecting the presidency to the party system. Reforms have been proposed with this mind. To be sure, there are proposals that have not appeared in this chapter which could potentially serve this purpose. Term limitations imposed on Congress, team tickets elected to four year terms, mid-term national party conventions, legislative cabinets, and a national party council empowered to promote responsible party government are among the many reforms proposed by political scientists to strengthen the hand of parties in the governing process.[30]

This author's review of reform proposals, however, resulted in the conclusion that several required a radical—and undesirable— change in the American constitutional structure. Moreover, some reforms would only modestly increase party power, or would be politically divisive. All, however, do have merit and should remain topics for rich scholarly debate.

Some Promising and Recent Developments

Before turning our attention to legal reform proposals that should have the effect of strengthening the authority of the presidency, it is important to note some interesting and recent developments regarding political parties that have attracted the attention of political scientists. Although there can be little doubt that parties as governing mechanisms have declined over the past several decades, there are some encouraging trends which suggest parties might be on the rebound. Such trends could potentially be to the benefit of presidential leadership.

In addition to the previously cited court rulings favoring party deregulation, two developments in particular merit discussion: 1) energetic fundraising and organizational development on the part of national party committees; 2) rising cohesion within both parties in the congressional lawmaking process. For those who view political parties as essential instruments in the governing process, such trends are quite promising. A brief discussion follows.

National Party Committees: Signs of Vitality

The national party committees, while still overshadowed and circumvented by the personal organizations of candidates, are admirably attempting to regain influence in the electoral process. This is most evident in the areas of fundraising, the development of professional staffs, modernization of committee headquarters, and the offering of campaign services to candidates for public office. The Republican National Committee (RNC) was the first of the two national committees to show signs of modernization and adaptation to the new age of American politics. The impressive efforts of the RNC persuaded the Democratic National Committee (DNC) to pursue a similar course of action. The Democratic Party, however, has lagged behind the efforts of the GOP.

From 1983–1984, the RNC raised $289 million, while the DNC raised $84.4 million. In 1987–1988, fundraising efforts for both parties resulted in $257.5 million for the RNC and $116.1 million for the

DNC. From 1991–1992, the RNC raised $272.9 million, while the DNC's fundraising efforts generated $163.9 million—still a sizeable gap between the two organizations, but not as severe as the early nineteen-eighties.[31] The millions of dollars raised by the two national committees have allowed both parties to maintain modern headquarters in Washington, D.C. replete with sophisticated state-of-the art technology. Full time staffs are now present at the national committee level, party building workshops are conducted, and Republican and Democratic candidates can go to their respective national committees for polling, direct mail, media and consulting services.[32]

In addition to the revitalization of the two national party committees, one also discovers very active legislative campaign finance committees in the Congress. Like the RNC, the National Republican Senatorial Campaign Finance Committee, the National Republican Congressional Committee, the Democratic Congressional Campaign Committee and the Democratic Senatorial Committee have all shown signs in recent years of impressive fundraising and organizational vitality. An increasing amount of money and campaign services are currently provided by the legislative committees to candidates for Congress—normally nonincumbents engaged in competitive elections.[33] The legislative campaign finance committees are primarily concerned with federal legislative races, while the RNC and DNC tend to fous their efforts on presidential elections as well as state and local party building.

It is difficult to predict if the dollars provided by the national committees will result in a closer association between the presidency, Congress, national party organizations, and the American people. Will a revitalized role for national party committees strengthen the president in his capacity as party chief and chief legislator? Sidney M. Milkis, a leading scholar, suggests that the recent trends towards party revitalization did contribute in a positive way to the leadership of President Reagan. According to Professor Milkis, Reagan, unlike several of our recent presidents, was able to cultivate and harness the Republican party organization in a manner that facilitated the implementation of a conservative political agenda. "Republican party strength provided Reagan with the support of a formidable institution, solidifying his personal popularity and facilitating the support of his program in Congress."[34]

However, according to Milkis, the bond between Reagan and the Republican Party was never exceptionally firm. The Iran-Contra scandal, and the significant number of unilateral presidential actions without any congressional consultation throughout Reagan's two-term presidency, suggest that the policy connection between the president and his party was far from institutionalized. In a 1987 interview, William Brock, the innovate former chairman of the RNC and Secretary of Labor under President Reagan, described to Milkis the state of party government during the Reagan years: "Too many of those around [the President] seem to have a sense of party that begins and ends in the Oval office. Too many really don't understand what it means to link the White House to a party in a way that creates an alliance between the presidency, the House, and the Senate, or between the national party and officials at the state and local level."[35] Thus, while party organization development is exciting and promising with regard to the potential for presidential leadership, it appears that it will take more than money and an impressive menu of campaign services from national party committees to create a long-term and stable policy relationship between presidents and their parties.

Party Cohesion in Congress

Another indicator of political party vitality concerns the voting behavior of congressmen on legislative roll calls. In this respect, it is the rise of party cohesion within both parties that requires discussion. Longitudinal data demonstrate a growing ideological solidarity among Republicans and Democrats on a number of controversial national policy issues.

The average percentage of roll calls in the House of Representatives in which a *majority* of Republicans have voted in opposition to a *majority* of Democrats, what is commonly known as a "party vote," has increased from 37 percent between the years 1971–1982 to 56 percent between the years 1983–1992.[36] Although party cohesion during legislative roll calls in the House of Representatives does not approach the extraordinary party unity found in the British House of Commons, it is quite evident that the congressional rank-and-file in both parties are banding together with more frequency in the lawmaking process. In the Senate, party cohesion has also increased, although not to the extent as that found in the House. From 1969–1980, an average of 41.6 percent of legislative roll calls resulted in party votes. From 1981–1992, party votes on roll calls rose to an average of 46.2 percent.[37]

Several explanations have been been offered to account for the rise in congressional party solidarity. The increasing role of political party money provided by the House and Senate campaign finance committees appears to be contributing to party unification on roll calls. There seems to be a relationship between the rise of party cohesion and the rise of national committee money in congresssional elections. The money provided to candidates for Congress appears to be fostering loyalty and support for the policy objectives of Republican and Democratic congressional leaders.

A second explanation regarding the rise of party unity involves the internal reforms that were adopted by congressional Democrats during the nineteen-seventies. Although the reform movement resulted in stronger congressional subcommittees, which was not to the benefit of party unity, reformers at the same time were determined to strengthen the place of the House Speaker within the policy-making process. This reform has contributed to party cohesion.

In essence, The Speaker of the House was provided with more authority over the scheduling and flow of the legislative agenda. The new reforms authorized the Speaker to determine membership on the very powerful and influential House Rules Committee. The Rules Committee structures the business of Congress, determines the length of debate on the House floor, and decides whether or not amendments can be added to bills. This reform was significant, as the ability to determine the composition of the Rules Committee essentially allowed Democratic House Speakers to manipulate the congressional agenda in a fashion that favored the goals of the party hierarchy.[38]

In the 1994 mid-term congressional election, the Republican Party captured a majority of seats in *both* chambers of Congress. "Political earthquake" was the term frequently employed by commentators to describe this historic election, as more than forty years had passed since the GOP controlled both the House and Senate. Newt Gingrich, a conservative Republican from Georgia and the former House Minority Leader, was named Speaker of the House.

Under Gingrich's leadership, the power of the House Speakership has been greatly expanded, even beyond that which existed when Democrats controlled the House. Chairpersons of strategic standing committees have been selected by Gingrich, and many committees have been packed with freshmen legislators who feel a personal sense of loyalty to the Speaker. A small and very tight group of Republican congressmen known as the Speaker's Advisory Group, "S.A.G." work closely with Speaker Gingrich in determining the legislative calendar.[39]

Some observers believe Gingrich is one of the most powerful

Speakers in the twentieth century, similar in some respects to that of the legendary Republican Speaker Joe Cannon who dominated the House of Representatives at the turn of the century. Although one person cannot exercise unilateral control over a chamber as diverse and as large as the United States House of Representatives, it is clear that many Republican legislators look to the Speaker for voting cues and guidance during the many stages of the lawmaking process.[40]

A third reason cited for the rise in congressional party unity concerns the gradual diminishment of intra-party factionalism within the two major parties. The partisan realignment of voting blocs, the issue positions of the two parties, and demographic changes over the course of the past twenty years are deeply related to this development. The decline of intra-party factionalism is a complex subject.

Northern and southern Democrats now share fairly similar views on an array of issues. More to the point, the issue of civil rights, which for decades pitted northern and southern Democrats against one another, no longer divides congressional Democrats into hostile regional factions. Passage of the 1965 Voting Rights Act, which dramatically expanded African-American voting rights in the south, the steady urbanization of southern states, as well as legislative reapportionment rulings during the nineteen-sixties profoundly transformed the character of southern politics. Such developments have had a moderating impact on election outcomes in many southern states and congressional districts. Democratic incumbents in the south, in response to the political and demographic transformation, have assumed a more moderate posture on many issues. At the same time, several congressional seats in the south have been won by Democrats who are ideologically compatible with liberal Democrats of the north.[41] The result is less sectionalism and more party cohesion among Democratic congressmen on legislative roll calls. For example, in 1957, only 14 percent of southern Democrats voted in favor of voting rights legislation. In 1981, 91 percent of southern Democrats supported such measures.[42] As Nicol C. Rae states: "Although still distinctive from the rest of the House Democratic caucus, southern Democrats have come much closer to the Democratic mainstream than they were a quarter century ago."[43]

White voters in the south who found it difficult to identify with a liberal Democratic Party, have realigned themselves with the Republican Party, as it is here where conservative social values and the doctrine of states' rights are firmly embraced.[44] Thus, the dynamics of southern politics is directly related to the rise in legislative cohesion among congressional Democrats.

Intra-party factionalism has declined within the Republican Party as well. The gradual diminishment of the eastern, moderate faction of the Republican party, and the national transformation of the party into a more homogeneous conservative movement, has resulted in more legislative unity among congressional Republicans. The voice of moderate Republicanism no longer commands the respect or power it once enjoyed on Capitol Hill and in presidential politics.[45] A conservative social agenda, which has its roots in Sunbelt Republicanism, now appears to drive the Republican Party.

The question that emerges, however, is whether or not the recent vitality demonstrated by the two national party committees as well as the discernible rise in congressional party cohesion will in fact be to the benefit of presidential leadership. In theory, such developments should strengthen a president's capacity to lead Congress and to implement a presidential agenda. This should result from party cohesion and organizational vitality.

Unfortunately, however, such developments have not in any appreciable fashion elevated the power of our recent presidents. Parties are certainly showing signs of unity in Congress, but presidents are not necessarily benefiting from such a trend. The first two years of the Clinton presidency, with both chambers of Congress under the control of the Democratic Party, offers evidence of this. Was health care reform enacted? Was government "reinvented?" Was the deficit cleaved in half, as Clinton promised during the presidential campaign? How much "change" actually took place?

In his book *Separate But Equal Branches*, Charles O. Jones observes that the many years of divided government, with Republicans in the White House and Democrats controlling the Congress, has "accentuated and strengthened the separation of the institutions."[46] According to Jones, the Congress, in response to a series of Republican presidencies, developed into a more active competitor with the White House. Over the years, Congress consciously acquired many new functions, such as agenda setting and program implementation. Such functions have historically belonged to presidents. Even within the realm of international affairs, the Congress has attempted to assert more influence and leverage over presidential decision-making. Moreover, the party affiliation of the president, according to Jones, does not necessarily alter this condition: "Thus, one legacy of the period of split-party government was a substantially more policy aggressive Congress, one that was unlikely to forego this new institutional positioning with the election of a Democratic president."[47]

Indeed, the policy assertiveness of Congress now appears to be a permanent feature of politics inside the Beltway. Since the Republican congressional victory in 1994, and a return to divided government, the Clinton agenda, particularly within the realm of domestic policy-making, has essentially ground to a halt. In 1995–1996, a protracted budget stalemate between Congress and the President resulted in two closings of the federal government.

Temporary stop-gap measures were relied upon to fund departmental operations. At one point in the budget conflict, approximately 800,000 federal workers were temporarily furloughed. The Republican Congress, led by House Speaker Newt Gingrich and Senate Majority Leader Bob Dole, was determined to challenge President Clinton's budget proposal. Cuts in federal entitlements were at the root of the disagreement, with Republicans demanding from the president deeper and more severe cuts in entitlements, especially Medicare expenditures. Resistance, tension and gridlock between the White House and Congress characterized relations between the two branches of government in the months following the 1994 congressional election. Cooperation was virtually nonexistent, and the two branches of government appeared more "separate but equal" than at any other time in recent memory.

There are those who suggest that a Republican President and a Republican controlled Congress could perhaps set the wheels of government in motion and break the budget gridlock. While there undoubtedly would be more cooperation between the branches of government under this political scenerio, there is no guarantee that a Republican president with a Republican majority in Congress, would enjoy a harmonious season of governing. As Jones noted, the institutional autonomy of Congress appears to pose a problem for all presidents regardless of party.

This is why the reform proposals presented in this chapter have such relevance. Such proposals, implemented by statute or internal party reform, would strengthen political parties in a fashion that would more firmly connect the president to Congress, as well as to the American people. In light of the many challenges that face the modern presidency, and in light of the fact that political parties can serve as powerful governing tools for presidents, such reforms seem worthy of serious consideration. While revitalization of the national party committees and rising congressional cohesion certainly should be applauded, it is evident that a more comprehensive approach to party reform is required if the presidency is to once again assume a decisive leadership role within the context of the policy-making process.

At the same time, it is equally important that reform efforts extend beyond the parties. Although the restoration of political parties is essential for dynamic presidential leadership, party reform alone is insufficent to elevate the power of the presidency. Statutory and constitutional reforms are also needed to enhance the leadership capacity of modern presidents.

CHAPTER SEVEN

Legal Reform and Presidential Leadership

While party reform should broaden the president's political base within Congress and the executive branch, legal reform directed toward the restoration of presidential power will strengthen the president's formal leverage within the context of the federal decision-making process. The combined thrusts of the two reform efforts should result in a presidency more capable of decisive national leadership.

What essentially is advocated in this chapter is a presidency rooted in the philosophy of one of America's most thoughtful founding fathers—Alexander Hamilton. It was Hamilton, more than any other delegate to the Constitutional Convention of 1787, who stressed that the American presidency be vested with broad legal authority. My discussion of reform proposals to broaden the president's legal authority emanates from Hamilton's conception of leadership. Thus, it seems fitting to begin a chapter concerned with strengthening the president's legal powers with the perspective of Hamilton as expressed in the seminal Federalist Papers. It is here one finds wisdom and guidance.

Energy in the Executive

One of the most profound series of essays written by Hamilton involved his staunch defense of the newly created presidency—an institution, it should be noted, which stirred much debate during the fight for constitutional ratification. In Federalist #69, Hamilton systematically refuted accusations that the presidency was tantamount to a monarchy, an argument associated with the Antifederalist point of view. Hamilton's essay is a brilliant and careful deliniation of presidential powers within the context of the checks and balances doctrine; fears of a potential monarchy are effectively laid to rest.

However, despite his staunch defense of checks and balances, Hamilton, in Federalist #70, advocated a presidency with broad governing powers. His contention that "energy in the executive" is absolutley essential for sound national leadership is among the many classic passages of the Federalist papers:

> Energy in the executive is a leading character in the definition of good government. It is essential to the protection of the community against foreign attacks; it is not less essential to the steady administration of the laws; to the protection of property against those irregular and high handed combinations which sometimes interrupt the ordinary course of justice; to the security of liberty against the enterprises and assaults of ambition, of faction and of anarchy.[1]

In this author's view, Hamilton's words, written during the fight for constitutional ratification, are more relevant today than they were in 1788. Political gridlock in Washington, as well as the repeated failure of post-Watergate presidents to implement creative agenda, raises serious questions regarding energy in the executive, or, more accurately, the lack thereof. As Hamilton perceptively noted in Federalist #70: "A feeble executive implies a feeble execution of the government."[2] Energy in the executive is therefore a relevant concern as we approach the twenty-first century.

Defining Energy

The concept of "energy," although somewhat ambiguous, is definable. Writing in Federalist #70, Hamilton identified four main prerequisites for executive energy: 1) unity, 2) duration in office, 3) adequate financial support, and 4) competent powers.

Unity, according to Hamilton, is achieved through the single executive model. A single chief executive, rather than a plural executive, lends itself to "decision, activity, secrecy and dispatch."[3] In recent years, political scientists have argued that the proliferation of staffs and councils throughout the Executive Office of the President, combined with the rising power of policy advisors, have resulted in a "plural presidency," the executive model opposed by Hamilton as well as other Founding Fathers.[4] Individuals who are theoretically subordinate to the president have carved out independent power bases within the Executive Office to the point where several chief executives now seem to occupy the White House. There is reason therefore to question the extent to which unity is characteristic of the American presidency.

With respect to duration in office, Hamilton advocated a presidency of considerable tenure. In his view, the four-year term, with no limitations on reelection, would contribute to a sense of security on the part of the president, reduce the potential for expediential decision-making, and ensure wisdom and experience in the presidential office. Moreover, the four-year term without term limitations would promote stability during domestic or foreign policy crises.

Some observers have argued that the Twenty-second Amendment, which prohibits presidents from seeking a third term, inherently constrains energy in the executive. During a second term, according to this argument, presidents are automatically perceived as lameduck—the result being a powerless second term. Although Ronald Reagan has been the only president since Dwight Eisenhower to complete a full second term, there is still merit in this point of view. As he approached the end of his second term, President Reagan was viewed primarily as a caretaker of the Oval Office. Reagan's agenda seemed less important towards the end of his second term, public approval ratings declined, and candidates from both parties launched campaigns for the presidency. The media shifted its focus from the president's goals and objectives to the forthcoming presidential election. President Reagan became old news and in many ways was retired long before the close of his second term. Perhaps it is time, therefore, to consider a repeal of the Twenty-second Amendment.

Hamilton's third component involved adequate financial support for the presidency. Expressed in Federalist #73, Hamilton's chief concern was that the salary of the president and the amount of funds directed towards the office of chief executive be sufficient to sustain the presidency as an independent branch of government. Adequate funding, in Hamilton's view, was a prerequisite for energy in the executive.

At present, the president receives an annual salary of $200,000. Moreover, enough funds appear to be directed to the White House and, more generally, the executive branch, to sustain a separate and autonomous branch of government. Current funding provisions therefore appear to be sufficient to maintain a vibrant executive office.

The fourth prerequisite of Hamilton's "energy in the executive" has become problematic for the modern presidency—the need for "competent powers." In Federalist #73–77, Hamilton devoted a substantial amount of attention to those presidential powers he considered essential for dynamic national leadership. Such powers, in Hamilton's view, included the ability to veto proposed legislation, the capacity to serve as the nation's commander-in-chief, the authority to negotiate treaties, and the power of appointment.

The foregoing powers are clearly required for firm presidential leadership, and few would dispute the delegation of such powers to the president. Less clear, however, is whether the president has enough "competent power" to effectively govern within the context of the modern American political process. This process has so radically changed over the course of the last two hundred years that it is currently necessary to reevaluate the scope of presidential constitutional power. Does the president, as the sole representative of the American people, have enough formal power to govern the republic?

The United States is currently a country of 255 million citizens. Federal bureaucracy is smothering the presidency, the media is bent on destructive and tabloid sensationalism, Congress seems determined to block presidential initiatives, and lobbyists together with PACs and iron triangles dominate politics inside the Beltway. This new era of American politics begs for an expansion of the president's formal constitutional authority. Reform proposals designed to restore presidential authority are therefore worthy of review.

As the twenty-first century approaches, three specific legal reforms appear to be in order: 1) expanded presidential authority over the structure and internal operations of the executive branch; 2) repeal of the Twenty-second Amendment; and 3) passage of the line item veto. These reforms, although by no means panaceas for curing the besieged state of the presidency, address three of Hamilton's prerequisites for energy in the executive: unity in the executive, duration in office, and competent powers.

Presidential Control over the Executive Branch

In the previous chapter, it was proposed that more layers of the federal bureaucracy be reclassified from civil service to political appointment. A healthy infusion of patronage should promote loyalty to the president and strengthen the president's hand in executive affairs. However, without serious structural reform in the executive branch, presidents will remain ineffective in performing the tasks of a chief executive. Structural reform must be implemented to provide the president with more direct control over executive branch activity. As Terry Eastland notes in *Energy in the Executive*: "The strong presidency is organized and staffed and managed in ways designed to ensure its energy in behalf of the president's policies, whether they are pursued legislatively, administratively, or in both ways at once."[5]

Watergate in particular revealed how powerful key staff personnel had become within the Executive Office of the President. John Dean, Bob Haldeman, and John Erlichman, among others, became associated with the growing power of the Executive Office, and more specifically, the White House staff. As the Watergate scandal unfolded, it became painfully obvious that the "American presidency" consisted of more than just President Nixon. Highly publicized hearings revealed how staff personnel had secured independent power bases within the Executive Office. The autonomy and power of certain staff members suggested not one, but several chief executives operating under the auspices of the oval office—essentially a plural, rather than a singular, executive. Powerful White House staff members operating independently of the president, were largely responsible for the collapse of the Nixon presidency.

The problem of unaccountable and autonomous staff surfaced once again during the presidency of Ronald Reagan. The Iran-Contra scandal, which involved a rogue foreign policy operation masterminded by Lieutenant Colonel Oliver North, a staff assistant to the National Security Council, was further proof of independent power bases deep within the Executive Office of the President. Although Iran-Contra did not result in President Reagan's resignation, the presidency was impugned by the highly publicized scandal.

The proliferation of powerful staffs and councils within the Executive Office of the President has been noted and criticized by several presidential scholars. Thomas E. Cronin describes this disturbing development as "the swelling of the presidency." The presidential establishment, according to Cronin, is now "a large complex bureaucracy itself, rapidly acquiring the many dubious characteristics of large bureaucracies in the process: layering, overspecialization, communication gaps, interoffice rivalries, inadequate coordination, and an impulse to become consumed with short-term urgent operational concerns at the expense of thinking systematically about the consequences of varying sets of policies and priorities and about important long-range problems."[6] Erwin C. Hargrove states: "It would be a mistake to think of the Presidency only in terms of personality. The office is a bureaucracy as well as a man."[7] Hugh Heclo describes the dilemma in more forceful terms:

> The office of the president has become so complex, so propelled by its own internal bureaucratic dynamics, that it now presents every new president with a major problem of internal management. Without a conscious effort to the contrary, he may not even perceive the prison that his helpers erect around him.[8]

The proliferation of subunits within the Executive Office does not result solely from presidential initiatives. Laws passed by Congress have created a good part of the White House bureaucracy. Recent presidents, rather than circumventing or ignoring the role of Executive Office personnel, have been expected to defer to those in staff positions. As Heclo states, "as President-elect Reagan prepared to take office, a key issue discussed was who would bring to him the work of staffs from the national security and domestic councils, not whether to have and to use these units in the first place."[9]

The problem of a proliferating bureaucracy is not confined to the Executive Office. Beneath this stratum of federal bureaucacy are fourteen cabinet departments—each created by acts of Congress—which have also evolved into autonomous operations independent from the President. The sheer number of cabinet departments, each with its own internal bureaucracy, impedes implementation of the president's agenda. As James MacGregor Burns states: "The chain of decision-making command between the president and final administrative action can be broken in many places. Heads of agencies may fail to overcome the parochial interests operating in their subordinate units, especially in long-existing bureaus that have developed close and mutually satisfactory relations with well-organized clientele groups."[10]

Cabinet departments, because of their dependence on Congress for funding (as well as their very existence), seem more inclined to work with congressional committees rather than the president in establishing policy priorities. The autonomy of cabinet departments and their lateral financial dependence is an arrangement which clearly serves the interests of Congress rather than those of the president. As Peter L. Szanton notes: Congress "prefers independent bureaux' to well-integrated cabinet departments, and autonomous departments to tightly run administrations; the resulting autonomy leaves the executive branch more accessible to congressional influence."[11] The autonomy of cabinet departments also allows lobbyists to influence executive agencies to such a degree that some cabinet departments are controlled by their client groups. The end result is the iron triangles described in a previous chapter. It is not surprising, therefore, to find a cabinet secretary's loyalty to the president severely compromised. Congressional leverage over cabinet departments, combined with special interest access, has resulted in cabinet officers with weak ties to the president.[12]

The federal bureaucracy, from the Executive Office of the president through the cabinet departments, is in desperate need of reorganization. American presidents are so constrained by the maze of autonomous staffs, councils, departments, bureaus, and agencies, that the time has come for Congress to transfer broad reorganizational power into the hands of the nation's chief executive. For the executive branch to truly serve as an arm of the president, rather than either that of Congress or a fiefdom for interest groups, presidents should have considerable discretion over the structure and internal design of the federal bureaucracy. The bureaucracy should be creatively employed by presidents to promote their agenda. As Dr. Henry Kissinger, former National Security Advisor to Presidents Nixon and Ford put it: "In the modern state bureaucracies become so large that too often more time is spent in running them than in defining their purposes."[13]

Congress, through statute, should loosen the reins on presidents with respect to control over the internal structure of the executive branch. Indeed, this proposal is among the many specific recommendations offered by the very distinguished Panel of the National Academy of Public Administration in its executive branch management report, "A Presidency For The 1980s." According to the NAPA: "To promote greater coherence and effectiveness in government, the president should be granted permanent reorganization authority by Congress, subject only to a two-house veto."[14]

In 1979, Congress approved President Carter's proposal to create a Senior Executive Service. This was a corps of high-level civil servants who could be transferred from one specialized task to another by the president. President Carter, who understood the constraints of bureaucracy, recognized the need for presidents to have flexible reorganization power. The SES was clearly a positive measure with respect to improving the president's leverage over executive branch operations.

However, the federal bureaucracy has become so large over the years, and its constraints on the presidency so severe, that reorganization efforts must extend well beyond the establishment of a Senior Executive Service. In this author's view, draconian reorganization measures are now justified. As Heclo states: "a modern president who cannot govern his own office is unlikely to be able to govern anything else."[15]

Fortunately there is no shortage of reform proposals seeking to restructure the executive branch. As Bradley D. Nash states, "a full half-dozen major studies have brought to the attention of the president, the Congress and the public, a multiplicity of proposals for innovation, organization, reorganization, simplification, coordination, expansion and even abandonment of many of the agencies surrounding and presumably supporting the chief executive in his manifold tasks."[16] Although it is beyond the purview of this work to propose an ideal administrative structure, primarily because staff and departmental structures should reflect the administrative philosophy and policy agenda of particular chief executives, there are guiding principles of executive decision-making which, if implemented, should serve the interests of any president—regardless of party and ideology.

First, collapsing staffs and councils within the Executive Office of the President is essential. This should improve the accountability of the president's immediate subordinates. Fewer units within the Executive Office is a logical step in order to facilitate greater presidential control.

The function of Executive Office personnel also requires redefinition. Szanton argues that EOP subordinates need to take a holistic approach to policy formulation, rather than duplicating specific expertise found in other components of the executive branch. The Executive Office "must therefore be so organized, staffed, and managed as to insure that it will regularly and reliably bring to bear on major issues, before they arrive on the president's desk, an understanding of their myriad dimensions—symbolic, substantive, administrative, fiscal, foreign, and domestic."[17] Thus, reorganization efforts should create a smaller Executive Office with tighter channels of communication to the president, and generate a more holistic and synthetic approach to policy formulation.

In 1952, Bradley Nash proposed reorganizing the activity of the Executive Office into a "Management Staff" consisting of three major offices. There would also be a "chief" reporting directly to the president who would, according to Nash, be the president's "sturdiest source of action and support in his conduct of his executive duties."[18]

The Management Staff would consist of the Office of Policy and Program Development, the Office of Coordination, and the Office of Budget and Review. After the creation of the Office of Management and Budget in 1970, Nash recommended that all major administrative activity in the Executive Office be subsumed under this office. "Mightily armed with the financial sword of monetary allocation, always deeply involved in reconciling potentially conflicting and duplicating programs, whose broad 'across the board,' all pervading presences have gravely handicapped clear cut policy and program formulation and direction, the 'new' Office would seem to offer the best vehicle at hand for successful coordination of government programs."[19] Nash's reorganization recommendations are controversial and offer a radically different structure from that currently existing. While reorganizing the Executive Office under the full control of the OMB is perhaps a little ambitious, Nash's original proposal of a Management Staff consisting of three units is appealing. The EOP would be streamlined, more connected to the chief executive, and in all probability more efficient. Following reorganization of the EOP, attention then must focus on cabinet reorganization. Cabinet reform should be guided with two goals in mind. First, a consolidation of cabinet departments is essential: are fourteen individual departments truly required? Second, cabinet departments need to be empowered and more effectively employed as direct arms of the president. Functions currently performed by staffs and councils within the EOP, which were at one time cabinet responsibilities, must be returned to the various departments. Fewer cabinet departments would clearly streamline the executive branch and reduce political fragmentation. Congressional committees and special interest groups would have fewer access points within the federal bureaucracy, which should improve the administrative control of the president. Concern has been expressed that consolidation efforts would result in fewer, but larger, departmental bureaucracies. This argument is predicated on the assumption that federal responsibility for domestic programs would remain the same. But by returning several federal responsibilities (preferably education, energy and social welfare) to state governments the risk of unwieldy and massive cabinet departments could be reduced.

One consolidation plan, now close to twenty-five years old, but which still has merit, is that put forth by the President's Advisory Council on Executive Reorganization under President Nixon—also known as the "Ash Council." Watergate paralyzed the Nixon presidency so severely that executive branch reform as an issue in Congress was totally overshadowed by the unfolding scandal.[20] As a result, reform efforts were never seriously considered.

According to the Ash Council's reform plan, cabinet departments would be consolidated into eight broad administrative units. The Departments of State, Treasury, Defense and Justice would stay. The remaining departments would be collapsed into Natural Resources, Human Resources, Economic Affairs and Community Development.[21] Despite the fact that several new Cabinet Departments have been added since the Nixon presidency, this proposal still makes excellent sense from an administrative perspective. A careful review of cabinet departments beyond State, Treasury, Defense and Justice will discover that each department could be credibly consolidated into one of the four recommended departmental structures. By consolidating cabinet departments and returning several major policy areas to state governments, while at the same time trimming the manpower of the federal government, the executive branch would be leaner, more efficient, and more manageable. Presidential authority, the ultimate target of this reform, would be strengthened.

Restoring the policy-making role of cabinet departments would depend primarily on the president's conception of their function. Since the cabinet does not have defined constitutional responsibilities, its power is contingent upon presidential discretion. Presidents should make a concerted effort to meet more frequently with cabinet secretaries to promote a sense of teamwork. Once powers are returned to cabinet departments, cabinet secretaries can then be brought directly into the policy-making process. Cronin's interview with a White House aide is particularly relevant here:

> One way to improve things is to have the president and the cabinet members, particularly in domestic areas, meet at least six or seven times a year and talk in great detail and in highly substantive terms about the major priorities of the administration. You have to have better communication. Basically you have to make the cabinet less insecure."[22]

Regularly scheduled meetings between the president and cabinet officers, either collectively or individually, to discuss the substance of policy initiatives is desirable. A closer working relationship with the president's "Management Staff" in the policy formulation process would result and cabinet secretaries, under this new arrangement, would once again be part of the president's administrative team. A more stable and vertical relation with the president would occur, while horizontal relations with congressional committees and special interest groups would weaken—a development clearly in the interest of presidential leadership.

Proposing executive branch reorganization is quite different, however, from achieving it. Congress, special interest groups, and public employee unions are served by the sprawling and fragmented nature of the federal bureaucratic stucture. Reorganization reform will face great resistance from Congress and the client groups served by executive departments. Presidents clearly need to win the confidence and support of Congress before any major reorganization efforts can commence. Creative administrative reform, therefore, is among the great challenges facing future presidents.

Repeal of the Twenty-Second Amendment

To further enhance the president's governing capacity, reformers should also consider repealing the Twenty-second Amendment. This Amendment was enacted in 1951 as a direct reaction to the four-term presidency of Franklin D. Roosevelt. Prior to Roosevelt, no president sought reelection beyond a second term. Although presidents were not legally prohibited from seeking a third term, the tradition was that no president, regardless of success and popularity, should hold office for more than two terms. George Washington's decision to retire from the presidency after two successful terms in office established this long-standing and honored precedent.

It is not this author's perspective that three or four-term presidencies are the way to achieve effective national leadership. Dynamic leadership should be possible during two terms or even one. The problem instead lies with the Twenty-second Amendment, which requires the president to retire after a second term. The president, shortly after the commencement of his second term, automatically becomes a lameduck leader. The knowledge that the president is legally prohibited from seeking a third term causes his legislative proposals to become vulnerable to political compromise and defeat. Given the extraordinary obstacles to presidential leadership now inherent in American politics, common sense suggests that the last problem a president should be saddled with is lameduck status. Lameduck presidents automatically lose their legislative leverage, as there is little incentive for lawmakers to rally behind the presidential agenda. Moreover, during a President's second term, media focus tends to shift from the policy efforts of the incumbent to the campaign pledges and plans of presidential candidates. Fund-raising efforts, poll results, rising stars, hypothetical matchups, highly publicized visits to Iowa and New Hampshire, and alternative policy platforms consume the attention of pundits, journalists and the American people long before the president completes his second term. Even more distressing, as James MacGregor Burns notes, is that "party and legislative leaders inevitably start moving into the orbits of other presidential candidates."[23] Although there is political divisiveness during a president's first term, the problem becomes particularly acute during the president's second term. The Twenty-Second Amendment, according to Burns, has a "pulverizing impact on presidential party unity."[24]

Consider, for example, the Reagan presidency. Approximately two years into President Reagan's second term (1986), national attention seemed to shift from the goals of the Reagan administration to the forthcoming 1988 presidential campaign. The candidacies and platforms of five Republican and seven Democratic presidential candidates consumed the attention of the media and the American public. Was George Bush a true conservative? Was Bob Dole too mean to win the election? Who was Michael Dukakis and what was the "Massachusetts Miracle?" The presidential race was on—long before the completion of the Reagan presidency.

The glaring difference in legislative success between Reagan's first and second terms clearly underscores this point. From 1981 to 1985, an average of 72.3 percent of the bills introduced by Reagan were passed by Congress. During his second term, however, an average of 51.7 percent of bills introduced by Reagan were successful—a drop of 20.5 percentage points. The final two years of the Reagan presidency were particularly distressing for the president, with average legislative success rates of 43.5 percent in 1987 and 47.4 percent in 1988.[25]

The Twenty-second Amendment is partially responsible for this unfortunate condition. Incumbent presidents and their governing agenda, not future presidents or presidential candidates, should be the center of attention for lawmakers, the press, and the American people throughout most of a second term. When the president is no longer viewed as the central figure in American government, his ability to construct coalitions and govern the nation significantly diminishes. Only at the end of a second term should political opponents know precisely what the president's reelection plans are. A constant but healthy state of uncertainty with respect to presidential interest in a third term will allow the president to conduct business on his own terms rather than those of his rivals. By keeping reelection plans secret, the president can maintain an important tactical advantage over his adversaries. As Harry Truman noted in his memoirs: "By the very nature of his office this is one secret a president must keep to himself to the last possible moment." [26] Marcus Cunliffe elaborates on the former president's perspective: "Most commentators have agreed with Truman that the Twenty-second Amendment was a mistake. Whether or not they are correct, it should be added to the list of factors that circumscribed presidential potency in the second third of the twentieth century." [27]

As previously noted, lameduck second-term presidents are not common features of contemporary American politics. John Kennedy was assassinated during his first presidential term. Lyndon Johnson chose not to seek a second term due to declining popularity and a less than impressive showing in the New Hampshire primary. Richard Nixon, as a result of the Watergate scandal, was forced to resign in the middle of his second term. Nixon's successor, Gerald Ford, completed the second term and was then narrowly defeated by Jimmy Carter. Carter served only one term and was defeated in his bid for reelection by Ronald Reagan. Reagan served a full two terms, the only president since Dwight Eisenhower to do so. George Bush, however, served only one term and was defeated for reelection by Bill Clinton.

Nevertheless, the issue of a lameduck second-term president should not be dismissed simply because two-term presidents are unusual. If a president is reelected, he should not be hamstrung by a constitutional amendment that constrains his ability to lead. A president is reelected because the American people are pleased with his leadership. Any constitutional amendment which adversely impacts the president's capacity to lead and which fundamentally interrupts the important business of government is neither in the president's nor the country's interest. The Twenty-second Amendment, therefore, should be repealed.

Provide the President with the Line Item Veto

In this author's view, the need to expand the veto power of the president is urgent. Fortunately for the presidency, the issue of veto reform is the subject of extensive debate and consideration in Congress.

At the time of this writing, the House of Representatives, as part of the Republican "Contract With America," has passed a bill providing the president with a modified version of the line item veto. The House bill (HR 2) is known as the "Line Item Veto Act." The vote on the floor of the House was 294–134 in favor of the bill; 71 Democrats joined with Republicans in support of the proposed legislation.[28]

HR 2 was passed on February 6, 1995, Ronald Reagan's birthday. Reagan was an outspoken advocate of the line item veto throughout his two-term presidency. Prior to Reagan, several presidents had expressed support for this reform measure, including Presidents Grant, Hayes, Arthur, Franklin D. Roosevelt, Truman and Eisenhower.[29] More recently, President Bush supported line item authority, and President Clinton, during his 1995 State of the Union Address, explicitly endorsed efforts to provide the President with this power.

HR 2 allows the president to sign an appropriations bill into law, and at the same time to rescind specific spending lines in the bill. Should the president decide to rescind components of the bill, he must submit to Congress within ten days (excluding Sunday) a separate message specifying those spending items he believes should be rescinded. Rationale must also be included in the President's rescission message. The proposed rescissions will automatically take effect unless Congress passes a disapproval bill within twenty calendar days. The president has ten calendar days to either sign or veto Congress' disapproval bill. Should the president choose to veto the disapproval bill, Congress can override the veto by a two-thirds majority in both Houses, the standard constitutional requirement for overriding a presidential veto.[30]

HR 2 is a pro-presidency proposal which shifts the advantage currently enjoyed by Congress with respect to appropriations legislation to the executive. Under the provisions of the Congressional Budget and Impoundment Control Act of 1974, which governs current practices, the president can request a spending rescission. Only if Congress formally approves the president's rescission request by passing an approval bill by a majority vote in both Houses of Congress within forty-five days will the rescission go into effect. If Congress takes no action, the appropriated funds must be made available for the designated programs.

In short, under existing law, if Congress takes no action the rescission request will die. The burden is on the president to win congressional approval for his recommended rescissions. Under HR 2, Congress must take specific action within a short time frame and pass a bill formally disapproving the President's rescission request;

otherwise, the rescission will take effect. The burden therefore is shifted to Congress to defeat the President's rescissions. This is a significant departure from the current rescission process and clearly serves the interests of the presidency. Critiquing the substance of the line item veto proposal, Louis Fisher, Senior Specialist with the Congressional Research Service, views the potential of such reform as resulting in "a fundamental shift in the constitutional relationship between Congress and the president."[31]

The fate of HR 2 in the Senate is difficult to predict. Analysts predict greater resistance among Democratic Senators compared to Democrats in the House. Republicans in the Senate appear to be divided into two factions. One faction is led by Republican Senator Pete V. Domenici from New Mexico who has proposed a milder version of the line item veto (Domenici is chair of the Senate Budget Committee). Another faction, led by Senator John McCain from Arizona, appears to be backing the House version of the bill.[32]

HR 2, in addition to broader efforts to provide the president with a more definitive line item veto either through statute or constitutional amendment, has sparked lively debate regarding the constitutional separation of powers. Advocates of the line item veto, the position supported by this author, view the measure as a necessary step towards restoring the leadership capacity of the presidency.

Judith Best views the line item veto as a reform that would most likely be supported by the Founding Fathers: "It is fair to say that the veto power created by the Founders has been displaced and debilitated, and that some form of item veto would be viewed by the Founders as necessary to reinstate the veto power they orignially envisioned . . . It is reasonable to assert that the Founders would not find the item veto to be a dangerous innovation but rather a rehabilitation of an original and essential check and balance."[33] In Best's view, presidential power has eroded to the point where the line item veto is now a necessary reform.

Best's argument is persuasive, for the line item veto *restores* the president's capacity to work with Congress. Indeed, the true value of the line item veto lies not in controlling federal spending, which is the more popular argument in favor of the proposal, but rather in providing the president with a legal tool that can be employed in promoting legislative loyalty. In an age when Congress is hostile to the presidency, the line item veto allows the president leverage in the legislative process. Empowered with the line item veto, the president can dissuade legislators from obstructing his administration's goals and objectives. It is this aspect of the line item veto, more than the potential for deficit reduction, which offers rich opportunities for presidential leadership. Fisher's statement against the line item veto is perhaps the very reason the proposal should be adopted: ". . . item veto authority would give presidents a coercive weapon to control not merely spending but also legislators. Presidents and their assistants would try to use the item veto to penalize members of Congress who are insufficiently supportive of White House desires. Through these threats, the executive branch could influence the votes of members of Congress on spending bills, authorization bills, tax measures, and even treaties and appointments."[34]

Conservative columnist George F. Will, a supporter of the line item veto, also finds value in the coercive aspect of this controversial proposal: "It would give the president an instrument of reward and punishment that he badly needs."[35] According to Will, the line item veto will allow the president to deny dams, post offices and other federal projects to congressmen if they seek to undermine his legislative agenda. In Will's view, the president, in order to effectively compete within the political process, must have the ability to instill fear.[36] Although such an argument might seem somewhat manipulative or even mean spirited, political dynamics inside the Beltway have evolved to a point where a legislative tool, albeit a coercive one, which allows the president to dissuade congressional conduct obstructive of national leadership is needed. The coercive potential of the line item veto is one reason the proposal should be adopted.

Another theme in the arguments raised by proponents of the line item veto concerns which branch of government most closely represents the national interest. The House of Representatives currently represents constituents in 435 congressional districts, while the Senate represents constituents in fifty states. Congressmen and senators are notorious for adding (pork) riders to appropriations bills to serve the unique needs of constituents in their own districts and states. Although parochial needs are certainly important, one cannot lose sight of the fact that the national interest must prevail.

The presidency, more than Congress and the Senate, seems most strategically situated to represent the nation as a whole. By virtue of the electoral process and American constitutional structure, the president is the only federal representative who can claim a national constituency. It seems logical, therefore, for the president to be vested with authority that will enhance his capacity to govern in the interest of the American people. The line item veto is a step in that direction. As conservative congressman Robert Dornan, an advocate of the line item veto, put it: "The President, being elected by all the people, has

a better vision of what is good for the whole nation . . . the president—
whether Democrat or Republican—is in the best position to make
that determination."[37]

Proponents of the line item veto also cite the fact that forty-three
state governors currently have this authority (approximately ninety
percent of chief executives at the state level). Although opponents
consistently raise the specter of executive tyranny, it is difficult to
locate, among the forty-three governors possessing this authority,
one with a reputation for tyrannical behavior. In fact, what one is
more likely to find is an array of creative governors from both political
parties who have won the respect of their legislatures, the media, and
their constituents. Once again, a practice in place at the state level
offers an excellent model for national reform.

The three reform proposals presented in this chapter, if implemented, should serve to strengthen the leadership capacity of modern presidents. Strengthening the president's hand with respect to
the structure and operation of the executive branch, eliminating the
lameduck status of second-term presidents by repealing the Twenty-
Second Amendment, and providing the president with line item veto
authority should serve the interests of presidential leadership. These
reforms provide a necessary base for realizing Hamilton's conception of "energy in the executive." Although proposals designed to
strengthen presidential power raise questions regarding constitutional distribution of powers, there is nothing in such proposals that
remotely threatens the system of separated powers or the system of
checks and balances. On the contrary, such reforms, particularly in
light of current political circumstances, serve to *restore* the model of
constitutional government envisioned by the Founding Fathers. In
this authors's view, if the Founding Fathers, were somehow able to
witness the current state of the American presidency, they would undoubtedly express support for efforts aimed at restoration of presidential power. Why a stronger and more capable presidency is desirable as we approach the twenty-first century is the subject of the next
and last chapter.

CHAPTER EIGHT

The Case for a Strong Presidency

The Articles of Confederation: A Failure in Self-Government

Most Americans are probably under the impression that the United States Constitution was adopted immediately following the War for Independence. Often forgotten, however, is the new nation's first experiment in self-government. This was the ill-fated and short-lived Articles of Confederation—1781–1788.

The Articles of Confederation were by most objective accounts a failure in good government. The thirteen states were loosely knit together in what was described as a "league of friendship." Power and governing responsibilities resided not in the national government, but rather in state legislatures. The national government consisted of only a unicameral Congress with limited authority. There was no president or federal judicial system under the Articles of Confederation. The nation's capital was in New York City.

The Articles of Confederation proved to be deficient in several respects. The new system of government was very inadequate with regard to promoting economic prosperity. Congress under the Articles did not have the power to regulate interstate commerce or trade with foreign nations. Commerce between the states failed to flourish as a result of highly protective tariffs and separate state currencies. There was no indication of a strong national economy. The thirteen states functioned like thirteen separate nations under this form of government. Indeed, England, according to Wilfred E. Binkley, "was refusing to negotiate with the feeble Confederation and threatened to open diplomatic relations with the thirteen states." [1]

The Articles were also deficient in providing for a system of national security. American ships were under constant threat of piracy, while settlers in the south and west lived in fear of Indian attacks.

British troops still occupied several garrisons in the Northwest Territory. A serious deficiency in federal revenue created difficulty for maintaining a viable standing army. The inability to meet a military payroll led units in Philadelphia and New York to threaten mutiny.[2]

The deficiencies of the Articles of Confederation became further apparent in the winter of 1786 in western Massacusetts. Rebellious farmers, angered over the foreclosure of their farms, revolted against the government of Massachusetts. The rebellion, was led by former revolutionary war captain Daniel Shays. A court house was seized and an attempt was made to gain control of the federal armory in Springfield. Although the uprising was not by any means a large-scale and bloody revolt, political historians to this day still regard "Shays' Rebellion," as the catalyst behind the Constitutional Convention of 1787. After six years of economic stagnation, inflation, piracy and Indian attacks, the uprising in Massachusetts served to convince the political elite that the Articles of Confederation required serious revision. There was fear of a rebellious chain reaction throughout the thirteen states and the emergence of anarchy.[3] The time had arrived to establish a more effective system of government.

In 1787, a convention was in held in Philadelphia. Fifty-five delegates from the various states, with the exception of Rhode Island, attended. The business of the convention was conducted from May to September. It was a sweltering summer with most of the convention's activity conducted in secrecy within the confines of Independence Hall. Shutters were often closed and the press was banned from convention deliberations.

Although the convention was originally called for the purpose of revising the Articles of Confederation, a consensus was soon reached among a majority of delegates that a new form of government was required to resolve many of the deficiencies associated with the Articles. The delegates chose to establish a federal system of government. The power of government would be separated into three branches of government with checks and balances. The government would be empowered, yet constrained, by a constitution. Thus, as the delegates went about their task of writing the new constitution, the Articles of Confederation began to fade into American history.

A New Presidency: The Intent of the Framers

One of the most contentious issues regarding the structure and power of the new national government involved the question of a presidency. Should there be a presidency? How long should a president serve? Should there be a single or plural presidency? How should the president be chosen? How extensive should the president's powers be? A number of delegates expressed great reservation regarding the presidential office. As Henry Steele Commager notes: "Contemporary experience reinforced the teachings of history, and the framers were determined that the United States should never have a Louis XIV to ruin his nation by his extravagance, a Frederick the Great to plunge his people into ceaseless wars, a George III to currupt elections."[4] In matters related to presidency, the delegates were deliberative and exceptionally cautious.

What exactly did the framers of the Constitution envision with regard to the presidency? It is clear that the delegates ultimately supported a single executive chosen not by direct popular vote but rather through an electoral college. It is also evident that a consensus was achieved in favor of a four year term. Less clear, however, is the the original intent of the framers regarding the scope of presidential power. Precisely what the framers of the Constitution envisoned with respect to presidential authority remains to this day a debatable subject.

According to Professor Donald Robinson, a noted expert on the American presidency, among the fifty-five delegates to the Constitutional Convention, twenty-one played an important role regarding the creation of the American presidency. Among such delegates, however, only a dozen or so arrived at the convention with clearly defined ideas regarding presidential authority.[5]

Robinson places the twenty-one delegates involved in the lengthy presidency debate into one of three categories. The first category consisted of "the Radicals." The Radicals were those delegates who "wanted something new in America," including a strong and independent presidency. "In a culture, the leading political conviction of which was that power was dangerous and ought to be atomized and distributed into countervailing hands capable of restraining one another, the Radicals proposed to gather all executive power into one place and commit it to a single individual."[6] The Radicals favored a popularly elected president, a lengthy term of office and very broad powers. James Wilson, Gouverneur Morris, James Madison, Alexander Hamilton, Elbridge Gerry, and Rufus King were the leading voices among the Radicals. George Washington, who quietly presided over the Convention and who rarely voted, allied himself with the Radical faction as well.

The leading opponents of a powerful presidency, who directly engaged the Radicals in extended debate were "The Old Republicans." The Old Republicans were older men deeply fearful of aristocracy and executive power. Constantly reminding the delegates of monarchial treachery and despotism, the Old Republicans "used a voice that resonated with the themes from the American Revolution and from dissident circles in eighteenth century England."[7] These were men, according to Robinson, who "were determined to hold the line." A plural executive, chosen by Congress, vested primarily with administrative responsibilities was the model of executive leadership preferred by the Old Republicans. George Mason, Roger Sherman, Benjamin Franklin, Hugh Williamson, and Edmund Randolph were the most ardent spokespersons within this category of delegates.

In between the two competing factions of delegates, one finds what Robinson labels "The Men in the Middle." Within this category of delegates one finds, among others, John Dickenson, Oliver Ellsworth, Charles Pinckney, and William Paterson. Such delegates arrived at the Convention without a clear vision of executive power. However, The Men in the Middle, in Robinson's view, proved to be a critical bloc, frequently determining the balance of power on vital issues regarding the presidency. In some respects, the Men in the Middle were the swing vote.

Although debate regarding the presidency was robust and heated, it is Robinson's position that The Radicals ultimately prevailed. Elements of The Radicals' position were compromised in some instances, but, generally speaking, this young and energetic faction of delegates were able to secure in Article II of the Constitution a presidential office potentially capable of exercising significant power within the framework of the governing process. To allow flexibility for future presidents, the constitutional powers of the presidency were purposely described in very vague and broad terms. As Sidney M. Milkis and Michael Nelson note: "During the course of the convention, the pro-executive group won victory after victory."[8]

In retrospect, it is quite fortunate for the United States that the pro-presidency faction prevailed at the Constitutional Convention. History demonstrates that the interests of the United States, and even the world, have been served by presidents who were able to rely upon the broadly defined powers of the presidency for the purpose of resolving domestic and international dilemmas. Although the locus of power has from time to time shifted between Congress and the presidency, the evidence is persuasive that the presidency, not Congress, has been the institution of government most capable of responding to the major crises that have confronted the United States over the course of two centuries.

As Arthur Schlesinger Jr. states: "As a tiny agricultural country, struggling along the Atlantic seaboard, turned into a mighty continental, industrial and finally world power, the problems assailing the national polity increased vastly in size, number and urgency. Most of these problems could not be tackled without vigorous executive leadership. Throughout American history, a robust presidency kept the system in motion."[9] In the view of Adlai E. Stevenson III: "American history is largely the history of the American presidency. It is a history of men rising to the demands of their time in an office which afforded them the power to govern."[10] George McGovern places the presidency in this historical context: "When the United States has stood tall in the world—it has usually been because of strong presidential leadership. To a great extent the President helps set the moral, as well as the political, tone of the country."[11] Long before the United Sates emerged as a mighty industrial and world power, the positive aspects of a strong presidential office became readily apparent.

America's First Presidency: Power Set In Motion

President George Washington (1789–1797)

George Washington, who quietly aligned himself with The Radicals at the Constitutional Convention, understood the need for a strong and energetic presidency. Although Washington's conduct as president calmed fears of tyranny and executive abuse, it is clear that presidential power under Washington was advanced and solidified. Two events of historic importance are relevant with respect to the institutionalization of presidential authority: Washington's Neutrality Proclamation in 1793 and his bold action during the Whiskey Rebellion of 1794.

In 1793, shortly into Washington's second term of office, a naval war developed between Britain and France. Precisely what position the United States should assume during the conflict became the subject of much controversy. Factions rallied around the two leading figures of the Washington administration, Treasury Secretary Alexander Hamilton and Secretary of State Thomas Jefferson. Time after time, Hamilton and Jefferson would disagree over questions of national and international policy. Such fundamental disagreements eventually resulted in the formation of the American two-party system.

Hamilton was an admirer of the British monarchy and a staunch supporter of a political aristocracy. He never looked favorably upon mass empowerment nor political movements which threatened the power of a political elite. Not surprisingly, Hamilton viewed the French Revolution as a reckless and dangerous development. Thus, when war developed between Britain and France, Hamilton supported a position that would ultimately serve the interests of Britain. Recognizing the naval superiority of Britain, Hamilton urged Washington to proclaim neutrality. A neutral and noninterventionist position on the part of the United States would ensure a British victory.

Jefferson, unlike Hamilton, was a firm believer in the ideals of the French Revolution. The United States, in Jefferson's view, should offer support to a nation whose revolution was waged in the name of freedom, liberty and mass democracy. Jefferson, who authored the Declaration of Independence, had little regard for monarchy and aristocracy. He urged Washington to support France.

President Washington responded to the debate by issuing a bold proclamation of neutrality for the United States—ultimately supporting the position of Hamilton.[12] This was a controversial decision on the part of the president, in light of the fact that Article II of the Constitution does not explicitly authorize the president to issue independent proclamations without the consent of Congress. Washington's proclamation, as Milkis and Nelson state, "provoked a bitter exchange of views about the executive's proper role in foreign affairs."[13] Washington's decision to go beyond the express letter of the law and exert power in a unilateral fashion was of historical significance, for his action established an important precedent for future presidents within the realm of foreign affairs. The president's authority as chief foreign policy maker was strengthened as a result of the proclamation. Washington's actions the following year were equally significant with respect to extending the powers of the newly formed presidency.

In 1794, militant farmers in western Pennsylvania, angered over a national excise tax on whiskey, threatened an armed rebellion against the federal government. The "Whiskey Rebellion," as it became known, represented the first open and defiant challenge to the authority of the federal government. The potential for armed insurrection against the federal government became a distinct possibility as tension escalated between the rebels and federal revenue agents. A revolution of some magnitude seemed to be on the horizon. According to James Thomas Flexner: "Techniques which had nurtured the Revolution against England were being imitated: an illegal assembly, elected from several counties, had convened at Pittsburgh, had threatened revenue officers, and had established 'committees of correspondence' to keep the rebels in touch and extend the rebellion." [14]

Rather than depend on the governor of Pennsylvania to quell the rising rebellion, or depend on Congress to resolve the pending crisis, President Washington assembled and personally led a multi-state militia into rebel territory. The impressive display of force, combined with the personal presence of Washington, resulted in a quick and decisive victory for the federal government. The actions of Washington were historically significant, as the rule of law and federal supremacy, two critical doctrines for the newly formed republic, were considerably advanced. [15]

George Washington is regarded by historians and political scientists as a great president because his actions during the Whiskey Rebellion and the war between Britain and France served the interests of the new republic. At the same time, and perhaps more importantly, Washington is rated as a great leader because the presidency, during his two terms, emerged as the source of national leadership. It was Washington who set the powers of the presidency in motion. Additional presidential precedents established under Washington include, among others, the use of executive privilege, the customary two-term limit, the presidency employed as a symbol of national unity, and "a bevy of protocols between the president and Congress, the states, and foreign nations, many of which serve quite well for our far less intimate contemporary institutions." [16] The Washington presidency therefore served to institutionalize presidential power. Such power would prove beneficial to future presidents for resolving an array of domestic and foreign policy crises.

There is, however, a major difference between the Washington presidency and many subsequent presidents classified by scholars as great national leaders. Washington, unlike his successors, did not govern through a political party. The two-party system was in an embryonic stage during Washington's tenure as president. Political parties were not fully developed and had yet to be harnessed as a governing tool. Although Washington's political views were compatible with the emerging Federalist party, he depended primarily on his own prestige and reputation, which was beyond reproach, to exercise the powers of the newly formed presidency.

With the development of the two-party system, political parties became indispensable to presidential leadership. Presidents who wished to lead Congress, initiate reform, and sustain a base of popular support could do so by depending upon the support of their party and by performing in vigorous fashion the role of "party chief." Party leadership and presidential leadership became inextricably linked. As James W. Davis notes: "Not all presidents have been strong party leaders, but it is beyond dispute that no president can be rated as a dynamic chief executive unless he is a strong party leader." [17] The history of the American presidency clearly supports the assertion that presidential leadership has been enhanced through a system of strong political parties.

President Thomas Jefferson (1801–1809)

The paradoxical presidency of Thomas Jefferson is proof of how presidential leadership, operating in conjunction with a strong political party, can advance the interests of the nation. Although Jefferson was a firm believer in the virtues of limited government, he interpreted the powers of the presidential office with the intent of advancing broad national objectives. Thus, Jefferson's philosophy of government did not fully coincide with his actions as president. While most people associate Jefferson with the eloquent articulation of values related to liberty and freedom, it is really Jefferson's use of presidential power, more than his ideological rhetoric, which distinguishes his presidency.

Jefferson's use of executive power served the interests of an expanding and restless country. It was President Jefferson who purchased from France for $15 million the vast tract of land known as the Louisiana Territory, thereby extending the continent of the United States from the Mississippi River to the Rocky Mountains. The United States nearly doubled in size as a result of this monumental decision—and France no longer posed a threat to American national security. It was also President Jefferson who commissioned the famed Lewis and Clark expedition. The expedition, led by Meriwether Lewis and William Clark, succeeded in gathering vital geographical information in the newly purchased territory which proved helpful for westward migration and commercial expansionism. [18] As Morton Borden notes: "Jefferson envisioned an American empire covering the whole northern, if not the southern continent, 'with a people speaking the same language, governed in similar forms, and by similar laws.' The purchase would be a giant step in the direction of democracy's inevitable growth." [19]

Acting as the nation's commander-in-chief, President Jefferson waged an undeclared naval war against the Barbary Pirates, who were routinely engaged in raids against American ships off the coasts of Algiers, Tunis, Morocco and Tripoli. Jefferson's decision to take direct military action against the pirates in the port of Tripoli served to free American ships from terrorism and extortion on the high seas. Jefferson's bold foreign policy action was vital to the security of American merchant ships and foreign trade.[20]

What were the conditions that contributed to the success of the Jefferson presidency? Certainly Jefferson's stature, moral attributes and stunning intellect contributed to his success. He was without doubt a man of great talent and character. However, to more thoroughly understand the Jefferson presidency, it is important to examine Jefferson's role as party leader.

Jefferson's presidential authority was in many way derived through his political party activity. He not only formed his own party, which provided him with a unique political advantage, but routinely utilized his party as the chief instrument for governing. (Jefferson's party, known initially as the Republican party, eventually became known as the Democratic-Republican party. This is the genesis of the Democratic party in American politics—the oldest political party in the world.)

Acting as "party leader" during his two presidential terms, Thomas Jefferson maintained exceptionally close ties between himself and Republicans at all levels of government. He personally drafted bills sent to Congress, recruited political allies to run for public office, directly participated in decisions regarding congressional leadership positions, and persuaded the Speaker of the House and congressional floor leaders to serve as point men for the president's agenda. Additionally, Jefferson controlled his congressional caucus, harnessed the power of congressional committees and employed cabinet officers as principal liaisons between himself and the legislature.[21]

George Fort Milton captures the relationship between Jefferson's party leadership and his presidential leadership in these terms: "In retrospect, Jefferson chiefly influenced the presidency through establishing the importance of Party leadership . . . He was perhaps the most skillful Chief of Party among all the presidents."[22] It is also important to note that Jefferson not only exercised extraordinary control over his political party, but also demonstrated acute sensitivity to majority rule. Rather than alienate opponents of Jeffersonian Democracy and preside over a deeply divided nation, Jefferson was able to enlist the support of many political opponents. He did so by forging a majoritarian coalition based on a firm commitment to moderate policy positions. As Burns states: "In letter after letter he made his plan crystal clear—to bring over moderate Federalists into the Republican camp and thus to create an invincible majority behind the new administration.[23] Party government, energy in the executive, and majority rule were central to Jefferson's success as president. The result was a very impressive presidency which shaped the country's future.

President Andrew Jackson (1829–1837)

One of the most controversial and certainly powerful American presidents was Andrew Jackson. Depicted as "King Andrew" by his political opponents, Jackson's use of presidential power far surpassed that of his predecessors, including Jefferson and Washington. According to Edward S. Corwin, the presidency under Jackson was "thrust forward as one of three equal departments of government, and to each and every of its powers was imparted new scope, new vitality."[24] The "Age of Jackson," distinctly characterized by an aggressive, abrasive, and powerful president, is truly a milestone in the history of American democracy.

Prior to the two-term presidency of Jackson, American government was largely the domain of a political and economic elite. The common man or "masses" exerted little power within the context of national and state decision-making. This condition changed drastically as a result of the Jackson presidency. Majority rule, egalitarianism, and power to the people were themes consistently reiterated by President Jackson in his official proclamations and messages to Congress. Pro-Jackson newspapers echoed the president's perspective, while the Democratic Party, officially formed by Jackson, served as the president's personal tool for converting democratic rhetoric to public policy.[25]

Jackson's role as party leader was central to his success as president. As William N. Chambers states: "At the core of Jackson's importance for the American tradition are four great themes or issues: egalitarianism, democracy, and—as instruments—strong presidential leadership and political party action.[26] According to Corwin, "Jackson was a more dominant party leader than Jefferson."[27]

Political reform swept the nation during the "Age of Jackson." Property qualifications for voting were lowered, presidential electors became popularly elected rather than chosen by state legislatures, many public offices normally filled by appointment were transformed into elected posts, and extensive use of partisan patronage contributed to greater rotation among those employed as government administrators. As Robert V. Remini states: "By 1837, the word democracy had largely supplanted the term republicanism in national discourse."[28] The egalitarian and democratic thrust of Jacksonian democracy, according to Remini, was in many ways a prelude to Populism, Progressivism, the New and Fair Deals, the New Frontier and the Great Society.[29]

In addition to Jackson's contribution to the rise of democracy in American politics, one must also consider his role in conjunction with the cause of nation building. When South Carolina in 1832 declared federal tariff legislation "null and void" and "not binding upon this State or its citizens" and threatened to secede from the Union, President Jackson took decisive action designed to dissuade South Carolina, as well as other southern states, from further nullification proclamations and secessionist action. In an impressive display of force, the president deployed a flotilla of ships to Charleston's harbor. "They anchored off the Battery, their guns commanding the fashionable water-front lined with homes and brick-walled gardens of the city's elect."[30] President Jackson's actions during the "nullification crisis" is regarded by scholars as instrumental for preserving a federal union. As Remini states: "His view, along with its underpinning of constitutional law, provided the basic argument that Lincoln would use in 1861 to deny southern states the right to secede."[31] Jackson's vigorous use of presidential power depended heavily upon his ability to lead and unify the Democratic Party.

President James Polk (1845–1849)

In between the Jackson and Lincoln presidencies is the relatively obscure, but very impressive, presidency of James Polk. Polk, according to Clinton Rossiter, "is the one bright spot in the dull void between Jackson and Lincoln."[32] Polk is an exception to presidents normally classified as "strong" in that he served only one presidential term. The actions of Polk, like those of Jackson, and Jefferson, lend further support to the argument for a strong presidency. Also like Jefferson and Jackson, Polk governed through a strong political party. According to Charles A. McCoy, Polk "understood the necessity of shaping the Democratic Party into the instrument of the new governing class in America: the workingman in the cities, the pioneer on the prairies, and the farmer in the hinterlands."[33] The Democratic Party during Polk's presidency served as a critical power base for launching bold and aggressive presidential policies.[34]

Polk understood the necessity of a strong presidency for the purpose of achieving broad national objectives. "As Norman A. Graebner states: "He accepted the dictum of Alexander Hamilton that the American system provides no substitute for energy in the executive."[35] Polk, rated among the best presidents, is remembered primarily for his policies related to territorial expansionism—one of the clear goals of his administration. Polk initiated and waged a formally declared war against Mexico. Victory in the Mexican-American War resulted in the acquisition of vast new lands throughout the southwest and California. Through diplomatic, rather than forceful means, Polk also acquired the Oregon territory from Great Britain. At the close of Polk's one presidential term, the borders of the United States stretched from the Atlantic to the Pacific oceans.

With respect to securing support for his legislative proposals, Polk, to this day, is regarded by scholars as one of the most successful chief legislators. Every leading measure of the Polk administration passed Congress. This included tarriff reform, creation of an independent federal treasury, acquisition of the Oregon territory, and matters pertaining to the Mexican-American War.[36] According to Paul H. Bergeron, President Polk at all times kept members of Congress clearly informed regarding his legislative intentions. In private meetings with congressional leaders and in his messages to Congress, Polk outlined in a clear fashion precisely what items were included in his forthcoming legislative agenda. He participated directly in the congressional decision making process.[37] In the view of Charles Sellers, President Polk displayed "a brand of presidential legislative leadership that the country would not see again until the time of Theodore Roosevelt and Woodrow Wilson."[38]

In addition to extraordinary legislative leadership, Polk is remembered as one of the very best administrators of the federal executive branch. As McCoy states: "He was not content to rely upon his Cabinet members in their capacity as department heads to carry out the executive will; instead, he established for the first time the right and duty of the president to control personally departmental activity of the executive branch."[39] Broadly exercising the president's constitutional powers, most notably that of commander-in-chief, chief legislator and chief executive, James Polk, the first "darkhorse" chosen as president, emerged as one of the country's preeminent national leaders. Like Jefferson and Jackson, Polk's power as president was also bolstered through his role as leader of the Democratic Party. As James W. Davis states, the Polk presidency is further evidence "that a president with firm control over his party can compile a remarkable record of achievement."[40]

President Abraham Lincoln (1861–1865)

The experience of the Lincoln presidency further confirms the important place of presidential power and strong political parties within the context of American government. Indeed, among all American presidents, Lincoln is regarded as the most powerful and clearly the greatest. Historians and political scientists routinely rate Lincoln as America's best president.[41] Even George Washington and Franklin D. Roosevelt, do not command the respect that is exhibited toward Lincoln. As Alexander J. Groth put it: "Lincoln stands on a historical pedestal in certain respects unmatched by all other incumbents. His memory is surrounded with a reverence only occasionally accorded to prophets and spiritual leaders."[42] The Gettysburg Address and the Emancipation Proclamation, two by-products of the Civil War, represent the essence of the Lincoln presidency and his vision for America.

Lincoln's rating as America's greatest president is well-deserved. No other president in the history of the United States has ever been faced with the complex task of preserving the Union and the supremacy of the United States Constitution. The American Civil War, fought over the related issues of slavery and states' rights claimed the lives of 630,000 Americans—the bloodiest war in American history. The Union cause prevailed due in large part to the manner in which Lincoln vigorously prosecuted the war. A strict construction of constitutional powers could very well have resulted in a negotiated peace between North and South or victory for the Confederacy. Although federal courts declared unconstitutional Lincoln's decision to suspend the writ of habeus corpus[43] as well as his use of military tribunals to try civilians,[44] the end result of the Civil War justified the extended use of presidential power. In the words of Professor Groth: "The ends which Lincoln sought were, and are likely to be always regarded, among the most worthy in the American national experience: union and freedom. They are at the very core of the identity of Americans as one nation."[45]

While Lincoln's exercise of constitutional authority, as well as the industrial power of the north, were central to the Union victory, it is equally important to credit Lincoln's success in preserving the Union to the system of party politics in which the Lincoln presidency functioned. In this respect, President Lincoln experienced a significant advantage compared to Confederate President Jefferson Davis.[46] Although factionalism existed within the ranks of the Republican Party, particularly among radical and moderate Republicans, President Lincoln nonetheless enjoyed a firm partisan base from which he could prosecute the war. Horizontally and vertically, Lincoln could depend upon fellow Republicans to support his war initiatives. Among cabinet officers, congressmen, state governors, and within the ranks of the general population, Lincoln could routinely depend upon broad and enthusiastic partisan support.

Throughout the Civil War, there was a strong Republican link between the president, the machinery of the federal and state government, and residents of northern states. According to James W. Davis, party patronage at all levels of government proved to be one of Lincoln's principal resources for maintaining cohesion within the ranks of the Republican Party. Appointments to the post office as well as an array of military appointments were skillfully controlled by Lincoln in his effort to establish a firm power base and to preserve the Union.[47] It was the partisan base that strengthened Lincoln's capacity to wage war and join the northern states in a common cause.

This was not the case for the president of the Confederacy. By the time South Carolina seceded from the Union in 1861, the southern wings of the Democratic and Whig parties were in a state of disarray and even disintegration.[48] During the war years, Jefferson Davis' cabinet (which was based upon state representation) was in a constant state of fragmentation and turmoil, evidenced by numerous resignations and dismissals. Indeed, the Davis cabinet during the war years consisted of six secretaries of war, five attorneys general and four secretaries of state.[49]

In addition, centrifugal political tendencies erupted throughout the Confederacy. Southern state governors, extremely protective of state sovereignty, resisted centralized efforts to conscript soldiers and control armament production. Tension even existed between state governments and the Confederate government regarding which had the authority to suspend the writ of habeus corpus.[50]

At the same time, the Confederate Congress did little to assist Davis in the war effort. Its lack of clearly defined party organization resulted in unpredictable tension, mixed political messages and confusion for President Davis. Throughout the war, Davis experienced surprising disloyalty regarding presidential goals and objectives. Support in the Confederate Congress seemed to ebb and flow, leaving Davis in a constant state of uncertainty concerning his political allies. Unlike the Lincoln presidency and the Republican-controlled Congress of the north, the Confederacy was characterized by weak partisan linkage between the executive and the the legislative components of government. Unlike President Lincoln, Jefferson Davis could not depend on an established system of partisan teamwork.[51] In short, the outcome of the Civil War was determined to a significant extent not only by Lincoln's extraordinary use of presidential power, but also by the character of northern v. southern party systems. A president with broad powers combined with a strong partisan base explains Lincoln's success as president.

In the post-Civil War years, the country witnessed a strong congressional backlash to presidential power. The excessive use of executive power during the Lincoln presidency may very well have triggered such a response. The impeachment of President Andrew Johnson occurred only two years after the close of the Civil War and Congress, not the presidency, assumed the mantle of national leadership for the remainder of the nineteenth century. Not surprisingly, it was during this period where one finds several unsuccessful and weak presidents. Presidents Ulysses S. Grant, Benjamin Harrison, and Chester Arthur are representative of the era.

The era of "congressional government," according to James MacGregor Burns, was characterized by a "poverty of policy." Tariff legislation was the only policy area which consistently evoked major political controversy. However, while party platforms were quite distinct regarding the tariff issue, the positions supported by congressional Democrats and Republicans were often unclear and somewhat unpredictable. Tariff policy in Congress resulted in nothing more than "a series of compromises, now skewed in certain directions, now in others, as senators, congressman and presidents came and went."[52] Even the currency controversy involving gold and silver, despite great rhetoric suggesting "a titanic struggle between rich and poor, easterner and westerner, farmer and financier," was simply too crosscutting to result in clear legislative battles with winners and losers. Like the tariff, currency policy reflected "weak compromises and even vacuity."[53] It was also during this period in American history in which business mergers resulted in vast wealth for a tiny fraction of the population. Despite passage of the Sherman Anti-trust Act in 1890, which prohibited the formation of monopolies, leadership in the nation's capital was simply too weak to prevent business tycoons from acquiring unprecedented wealth and economic power. As Burns puts it: "an enfeebled government enabled a few to amass colossal riches."[54] Policy drift, unrestrained accumulation of wealth, and a powerless and enfeebled government came to an abrupt end with the succession of Theodore Roosevelt to the American presidency in 1901.

President Theodore Roosevelt (1901–1909)

The case for an empowered presidency bolstered by a strong system of political parties is further advanced upon examination of the first Roosevelt presidency. The presidency of "TR," as he was fondly known, is truly a major turning point in the history of American politics. As Nathan Miller notes: "Unlike the complaisant McKinley and all his predecessors since Abraham Lincoln who had abdicated leadership to Congress, Roosevelt believed that the president should be the ultimate authority in government."[55] The presidency of Theodore Roosevelt marks the emergence of "the modern presidency."

Although Roosevelt is frequently depicted as a brash political maverick, which in many respects is true, a closer inspection of the Roosevelt Presidency will discover considerable sensitivity on his part to the value of political parties in the policy-making process. Indeed, Roosevelt believed that effective presidential leadership and party leadership were deeply intertwined.[56] Roosevelt's perception of parties was formulated during his illustrious experience in New York politics. According to Willard B. Gatewood, Jr., as governor of New York, Roosevelt "accepted the Republican Party as the vehicle for implementing his ideas and learned to thread his way among various contending interests without disrupting its basic unity."[57] As president, Roosevelt made it a top priority to cultivate and secure the support of congressional Republicans. This was not an easy task in light of the tension that existed between Roosevelt and the Republican leadership. This was due not only to Roosevelt's assertive and domineering style, but also to his positions on tariff reform and corporate regulation, which, for the most part, were at odds with the Republican Party's conservative platform.[58] However, the president, by moving cautiously and steadily, successfully "transformed the party of McKinley into his own party."[59] In the view of Nicholas Roosevelt, cousin of the president: "TR's experience in various political offices had taught him that even a strong and willful executive cannot have his way without the cooperation of the legislative branch of government. In the presidency TR consistently made it a point to work with the Republican leaders in both houses of Congress, without whose approval and help needed legislation would be unobtainable."[60] Generally speaking, the relationship between the president and Republican leaders in Congress, although somewhat strained, was productive. Lewis Gould notes that over four hundred presidential messages were sent to Congress by Roosevelt during his tenure in office.[61]

Roosevelt's succession to the presidency in 1901 and his subsequent election in 1904 occurred at a time when the United States was emerging as a major industrial power and influential force in global affairs. It was also a time in which the Progressive Movement, a reform effort committed to economic fairness and political equality, was gaining ground among middle class voters. Theodore Roosevelt, by broadly employing the powers of the American presidency, admirably responded to the new era—"like a blast of fresh and bracing air in the fetid atmosphere of Washington."[62]

On the domestic front, Roosevelt challenged the extraordinary power of big business, particularly the ironclad grip over the economy exercised by railroad companies. Roosevelt was the first president to actively challenge the existence of concentrated economic power and corporate monopolies. Roosevelt's position towards the power of trusts is captured in his autobiography: "The power of the mighty industrial overlords of the country had increased with giant strides, while the methods of controlling them, or checking abuses by them, on the part of the people, through government remained archaic and therefore practically impotent."[63] In Roosevelt's view, America at the turn of the century had fallen under a "tyranny of plutocracy."[64] In addition to his assault on monopolies, Roosevelt personally resolved a national coal strike, established new measures to protect the environment, prosecuted corruption in government, and initiated policies designed to reduce exploitation in the work force. Roosevelt's ambitious domestic agenda, known as "The Square Deal," reflected his commitment to economic and social justice.

In the area of foreign policy, the Roosevelt presidency was even more remarkable. By broadly interpreting and exercising the powers of the presidency, the United States emerged as a major force in global affairs. It was Roosevelt who linked the Atlantic and Pacific Oceans by constructing the Panama Canal. The Canal was central to Roosevelt's strategy of increasing American political and economic influence in Latin America and the Caribbean.

President Roosevelt also intervened and negotiated a peace settlement in the war between Japan and Russia, an act for which he was awarded the Nobel Peace Prize. Moreover, to display American might and to further the cause of world peace, Roosevelt dispatched sixteen white battleships, known as the "Great White Fleet" to ports around the world. While such policies have been critized by some scholars as "imperialistic," Roosevelt's actions set precedent for future presidents to directly engage the United States in international affairs.

Thus, the presidency of Theodore Roosevelt underscores the

value of an empowered presidency. A broad interpretation of presidential power, combined with Republican Party leadership, served the national interest. Rated among the best presidents, Roosevelt, according John Morton Blum, "established a foundation upon which both Wilson and Franklin Roosevelt built."[65]

President Woodrow Wilson (1913–1921)

The presidency of Woodrow Wilson lends further support to the argument that a strong presidency is vital to the nation's welfare. The Wilson presidency also serves as an excellent example of how a strong party system and party leadership contributes to energetic and dynamic national leadership. Wilson, like other presidents discussed in this chapter, is rated among the best in American history.

Wilson's perspective concerning executive leadership and the role of political parties in the governing process was philosophically rooted in his admiration for the British parliamentary system.[66] In the British model, the chief executive is an integral component of the legislature and exerts political leadership through a system of highly disciplined political parties.

In Wilson's view, an individual's effectiveness as president depended heavily on his capacity to harness his political party in Congress. This would require an almost symbiotic relationship between the president and Congress, similar to that of the prime minister and the Parliament. For Woodrow Wilson, the Democratic Party served as his link to the legislature. Indeed, it is the prime ministerial approach to government which distinguishes Wilson from other twentieth century presidents. The Democratic Party was President Wilson's mechanism for initiating, guiding and engineering broad domestic reform. Skillful use of his political party was Wilson's strategy for executive leadership. Wilson adhered to this philosophy, it should be noted, long before he became president. As one journalist perceptively noted just prior to his inauguration: "He is not without party sympathies and not insensible to party obligations."[67]

Wilson's ambitious domestic agenda was launched under the banner of the "New Freedom." The president's partisan approach was immediately evident. His speech on tariff reform, delivered on April 8, 1913, was the first presidential message personally delivered to Congress since that of John Adams in 1800.[68]

In addition to personal appearances before Congress, President Wilson conferred frequently at the Capitol and the White House with congressional Democrats and cabinet officers. He was fully involved in the fine details of legislation and served as a mediator between Democratic factions in Congress. Wilson used patronage appointments effectively, as well as the power of the House and Senate Democratic caucuses to ensure party discipline.

Even before taking office, Wilson began conferring with congressional committee chairmen and Democratic leaders in order to establish the groundwork for his future legislative agenda.[69] The partisan bond between the president and Congress was quite extraordinary. As Wilson biographer Arthur S. Link states: "He won control through sheer force of personality and by using all the inherent powers of the party leader."[70] According to Link, Wilson's influence over the Democratic Congress was so pervasive that only once between 1913 and 1917 was he forced to appeal directly to the American people in order to secure legislative support. Tariff reduction, establishment of the Federal Reserve Board, anti-trust legislation, creation of the Federal Trade Commission, child labor legislation, and workers compensation for federal employees were among some of President Wilson's major domestic accomplishments.[71] According to Burns: "His management of Congress during 1913 and 1914 still stand as the copy book model of how a strong president drives his program through Congress."[72]

In addition to broad domestic reforms, Wilson's impact on American foreign policy was profound. Wilson's use of emergency powers and the powers of commander-in-chief during the First World War mobilized the nation in a fashion never experienced before by the American people. Wilson's war time efforts thrust America directly into the heart of a European international crisis. In doing so, Wilson completed the transformation of America as an isolationist country to that of a major world power and global actor. Although many of Wilson's wartime programs and emergency provisions were suspended following the war, his actions established important precedents upon which future presidents could depend to confront international crises.[73] Wilson also deserves much credit for envisioning a permanent international organization committed to crisis resolution and world peace. Wilson's League of Nations, although an unsuccessful experiment in world order, provided the model for the eventual creation of the United Nations in 1945.

Wilson's actions further contributed to the institutionalization of the modern presidency. The American people now expected presidents to be the driving force behind domestic and foreign policymaking. The powers of the presidency had been elevated to new levels under two very progressive presidents. Domestic reform and international crisis resolution depended on presidential, not congressional, leadership. At the same time, political parties and, more importantly, the ability of the president to lead his party, remained a critical component of the governing process. Power was lodged in the presidency, and parties were highly instrumental in advancing presidential agenda.

President Franklin D. Roosevelt (1933–1945)

Following in the tradition of Woodrow Wilson, Theodore Roosevelt, and Abraham Lincoln, Franklin Roosevelt, broadly employed the powers of the presidency to lead the United States in bold and new directions. Indeed, presidential power reached new levels under the second Roosevelt presidency. Roosevelt's exercise of power reflected a firm commitment to resolving the grave domestic and foreign policy crises that had beset the nation in the nineteen-thirties and forties. With the exception of Lincoln, no president, before or after Roosevelt, has ever been faced with such extraordinary challenges. The Roosevelt presidency is yet another example of how presidential leadership has served the interests of the American people.

Roosevelt was inaugurated as president in 1933, three years after the United States had plunged into the Great Depression. Economic conditions were extremely bleak: banks were collapsing, farm prices had declined, factory production and retail trade were far below normal levels, the value of stocks and bonds had plummetted, unemployment had risen from two to fifteen million, and farms across the country were facing foreclosure.[74] William E. Leuchtenburg captures the nation's despair in these terms:

> At least a million, perhaps as many as two million were wandering the country in a fruitless quest for work or adventure or just a sense of movement. They roved the waterfronts of both oceans, rode in cattle cars and gondolas of the Rock Island and the Southern Pacific, slept on benches in Boston Common and Lafayette Square, in Chicago's Grant Park and El Paso's Plaza. From Klamath Falls to Sparks to Yuma, they shared the hobo's quarters in oak thickets strewn with blackened cans along the railroad tracks. Unlike the traditional hobo, they sought not to evade work but to find it.[75]

To complicate matters for the newly elected president, Adolf Hitler and the Nazi Party had come to power in Germany, while in Japan militarist expansionists gained control of Japanese foreign policy.

Roosevelt would be the second American president to engage the United States in world war.

For the purposes of this work, it is important to emphasize the key role of the presidency in responding to economic collapse and fascist aggression. Roosevelt essentially transformed the presidency into the driving force behind American government—a radical departure from the placid presidencies of Hoover, Coolidge and Harding. As Leuchtenburg states: "Under Roosevelt, the White House became the focus of all government—the fountainhead of ideas, the initiator of action, the representative of the national interest."[76]

On the domestic front, Roosevelt initated a comprehensive presidential program designed to stimulate the economy and alleviate the suffering of the American people. In the tradition of Theodore Roosevelt's Square Deal and Woodrow Wilson's New Freedom, Franklin Roosevelt introduced a national reform program entitled The New Deal. Although New Deal measures initially faced stiff opposition from a conservative Supreme Court wedded to the status quo, the president ultimately prevailed in implementing major components of his controversial agenda. Social Security, signed into law in 1935, is but one example of the president's ambitious agenda. Many policies of the New Deal remain to this day.

In his response to German and Japanese aggression, Roosevelt's actions as commander-in-chief were equally dynamic and forceful. Although victory required a massive allied effort, including the historic leadership of Churchill and Stalin, the actions of President Roosevelt were absolutely central to the final defeat of the Axis powers. Roosevelt, according to Burns, "husbanded military resources in both the Atlantic and the Pacific until the enormous power, industrial and technological, of the nation could be brought to bear on the military scene."[77] In the view of Clinton Rossiter, President Roosevelt was "a commander in chief no less awesome than Lincoln himself."[78]

Party leadership was also relevant to the Roosevelt presidency, although the record indicates a somewhat uneven and at times less than successful attempt to lead the Democratic Party. Grassroots party organization revolving around the New Deal was not a top priority for President Roosevelt and loyalty to the President among conservative congressional Democrats was often less than firm.[79] Moreover, Roosevelt served as president for thirteen years, during which time the Democratic Party swelled to an enormous electoral coalition consisting of many diverse "have-not" constituencies. Roosevelt's coalition included poor northerners, urbanites, southerners, unions,

Catholics, Jews, and African-Americans. Thus, it is not surprising that Roosevelt, during such a long tenure as president, would encounter tension from within an exceptionally hetergeneous party. Roosevelt's personal charisma and direct popular appeal, rather than his role as party chief, often served as the source of his presidential power. Nevertheless, although in his role as party leader Franklin Roosevelt does not compare to Wilson and Jefferson, his partisan leadership, albeit uneven, was still instrumental to his legislative success. As Rossiter notes, Roosevelt was able to weld the Democratic Party's coalition into a "catalyst of congressional action."[80]

President Harry S. Truman (1945–1953)

During the course of Franklin Roosevelt's leadership, the power of the American presidency was significantly elevated, the size and responsibilities of the federal government vastly increased, and the United States emerged as the leader of democratic nations around the world. An expanded government, revolving around the presidency, with vast domestic and international commitments, is the legacy of Franklin Roosevelt. Roosevelt died in office in 1945. His successor was Vice President Harry Truman—"the little man from Missouri."

Although the American people did not have high expectations for Truman, he ultimately emerged as one of the nation's most effective presidents. Truman's use of presidential power as well as his ability to effectively employ the Democratic Party for governing purposes were highly instrumental to his success as a national leader. According to Donald R. McCoy, Truman "entrenched the presidency as the centerpiece of the nation's government by institutionalizing the trends in this direction that had been initiated under earlier presidents."[81]

Truman's domestic agenda was entitled The Fair Deal, reflecting the president's commitment to economic and social justice. Truman not only advanced the principles and policies of the New Deal, but also introduced a range of new and controversial domestic measures. According to David McCullough, "No more progressive program had ever been put before Congress than the Truman program."[82] The Fair Deal included extended social security coverage, minimum wage legislation, federal aid to education, aid to agriculture, increased support for public housing, federal unemployment benefits, anti-merger legislation, a system of national health care and protection for civil rights. As McCoy notes: "Whether it concerned civil rights, education, health, housing, migratory labor, natural resources, or a dozen other questions, the Truman administration constantly pressed the nation to consider making changes."[83]

Truman's leadership in the area of foreign affairs also reflected a man of courage and great vision. Indeed, the foreign policies of the Truman presidency are primarily why Harry Truman is rated among the best presidents. President Truman ordered the Atomic Bomb to be dropped on Japan—a deadly decision, yet one that saved thousands of American lives and rapidly brought closure to World War II. During the post-war years, Truman's policies were highly instrumental in containing communist aggression and preserving democracy in Western Europe. The Marshall Plan, The North Atlantic Treaty Organization (NATO), The Truman Doctrine, and The Berlin Airlift are prime examples of Truman's great resolve during the Cold War. At the same time, communist aggression on Asian soil was repelled by President Truman during the Korean War. The president's swift decision to send combat troops to Korea demonstrated in clear terms America's willingness to challenge the expansionist ambitions of the Soviet Union. Rossiter assesses Truman's foreign policy contributions in these terms: "Not one of his grave steps in foreign and military affairs, not even the fateful and controversial decision to use the atom bomb on live targets, has yet been proved wrong, stupid or contrary to the best judgment and interests of the American people."[84]

Truman's historic accomplishments must also be considered within the context of his ability to utilize the Democratic Party for leadership purposes. The Democratic Party provided Truman with an important power base from which to launch The Fair Deal and pursue an ambitious foreign policy agenda. Like Roosevelt, Truman encountered resistance from within the Democratic coalition, particularly from among southern Democrats opposed to the president's support for civil rights legislation. Despite the resistance, however, Truman was still able to maintain enough partisan support within Congress and among the party's rank-and-file to effectively implement a creative agenda. President Truman's perception towards parties as governing instruments is captured by Godfrey Hodgson: "At his last press conference as president in 1953, Harry Truman admitted that he did not expect 100 percent support from all those elected to Congress on the same platform with him. But he did believe, he said, that once the platform had been adopted by the convention, those who ran on it 'should generally abide by its detailed construction by the national candidate,' meaning the president."[85] Although

Truman's public approval ratings are among the lowest in recorded history, this president's extraordinary record provides one of the best examples concerning the interface between presidential power and the national interest.

Presidents John F. Kennedy and Lyndon B. Johnson (1961–1969)

The case for a strong presidency bolstered by a political party can be further advanced by examining the presidencies of John F. Kennedy (1961–1963) and Lyndon B. Johnson (1963–1969). Although the Vietnam War casts a legitimate shadow over the Kennedy and Johnson presidencies, the positive accomplishments of both presidents, domestic and foreign, would have been virtually impossible had the presidency not been empowered to initiate and direct bold reform.

President Kennedy understood, appreciated, and effectively utilized the powers of the modern presidency. Kennedy's support for a strong chief executive was rooted in his appreciation of past presidents and their contribution to the welfare of the American people. As a United States Senator, Kennedy routinely supported congressional attempts to increase the foreign policy powers of the president as well as the president's emergency and legislative powers. At the same time, he simultaneously resisted legislative efforts to limit presidential authority. In his writings, Kennedy often praised the powerful and activist presidents, particularly those who stretched and broadly interpreted the powers of the presidential office. As a presidential candidate he often concluded campaign addresses with references to the importance of presidential responsibilities and national leadership.[86] The following excerpt from a 1960 presidential campaign speech captures Kennedy's perspective:

> If this nation is to reassert the initiative in foreign affairs, it must be presidential initiative. If we are to rebuild our prestige in the eyes of the world, it must be presidential prestige. And if we are to regain progressive leadership on our domestic problems, it must be presidential leadership. If the president does not move, if his party is opposed to progress then the nation does not move—and there is no progress.[87]

During the course of his presidency, Kennedy, like those presidents he admired, broadly interpreted presidential powers. What Kennedy could not accomplish through normal legislative channels, he resolved by employing the alternative tools of the chief executive.

This included use of "executive orders, proclamations, contingency funds, inherent powers, unused statutes, transfers of appropriations, reorganization plans, patronage procurement, pardons, presidential memos, public speeches and private measures."[88] As James N. Giglio states, Kennedy "sought to be a strong, active president in the Democratic tradition of Woodrow Wilson, Franklin Roosevelt, and Harry Truman."[89]

Kennedy's leadership stands as positive testimony to an empowered presidency. President Kennedy challenged the American people to embark upon a New Frontier. Kennedy's domestic agenda addressed the issues of racial inequality, medical care for the elderly, increased aid to education, public housing, poverty, and space exploration. In some respects, the New Frontier was a modern extension of the Fair Deal and New Deal, although Kennedy's commitment to social justice and civil rights went far beyond that of previous presidents. Although the president's legislative record is one of mixed success,[90] Kennedy's legislative proposals, either those that were passed or defeated, sparked the debate and established the foundation for the landmark policies of President Johnson's Great Society.

In the area of foreign affairs, Kennedy, like his predecessors, remained firmly committed to a strong military and the containment of Soviet aggression. The president's bold and steady actions during the Cuban Missile Crisis clearly protected the national security of the United States. The crisis was the defining moment of the Kennedy presidency. The formation of the Peace Corps, and the Nuclear Test Ban Treaty demonstrated how presidential power in the right hands can advance the interest of humanity and world peace.

Following Kennedy's assassination on November 22, 1963, Vice President Lyndon B. Johnson assumed the office of the presidency. Johnson, had served as Senate Majority Leader for a number of years prior to becoming vice president. He was an experienced politician who understood, perhaps more than any other president, the dynamics and intricate strategies associated with the lawmaking process.

Johnson proved to be a formidable national leader. His extraordinary legislative skills, combined with the power afforded to presidents during this time period, resulted in one of the most impressive domestic records since the days of Franklin Roosevelt. Building upon the New Frontier, as well as extending the principles of the Fair Deal and New Deal, President Johnson proposed a most ambitious domestic agenda. The Johnson agenda was entitled The Great Society.

Elimination of racial inequality, eradication of poverty, aid to education, and health care for the aged were among the central goals of the Johnson presidency. Johnson's intense focus on the legislative process was indeed phenomenal. As Doris Kearns writes: "He began and ended each day by reading a substantial amount of material related to Congress. The *Congressional Record*, clipped and summarized, appeared by his bed at 7:15 A.M. Placed at his bedside at 11 P.M. each night were memos from the staff, which described in detail each of the legislative contacts they had made that day, reported noteworthy conversations with particular members, and called attention to special problems."[91] Under Johnson's leadership, an extraordinary amount of landmark domestic legislation was passed. This includes the historic Civil Rights Act of 1964, the Voting Rights Act of 1965, the Medicare Act of 1965, the Elementary and Secondary Education Act of 1965, and the Fair Housing Act of 1968. Johnson's "war on poverty" reduced poverty in America by approximately one-third. Johnson's philosophy of presidential leadership is best expressed in his own words: "The president of this country, more than any other single man in the world, must grapple with the course of events and the directions of history. What he must try to do always, is to build for tomorrow in the immediacy of today."[92]

Political parties and party leadership were relevant to both Presidents Kennedy and Johnson, although, as scholars note, it is during the Kennedy-Johnson era that the presidency began its transformation into a more personal and less partisan organ of government. The Kennedy campaign, with an emphasis on media skills, charisma and image, marks the beginning of this development. Kennedy's presidential campaign was not by any means divorced from the Democractic Party organization, nor while in office did Kennedy circumvent the Democratic congressional leadership. However, it was during the Kennedy campaign and the Kennedy presidency that a "personalized" presidency emerged.[93]

Johnson, like Kennedy, also appreciated the relationship of political parties to the governing process. As Kearns notes: "To Johnson, the merits of the party system were tested not by its forthright advocacy of virtuous ideals but by its actual contribution to the creation of tangible and beneficial conditions—by results and consequences. And, he claimed, by this test the American party system had proven itself not only valuable but indispensable"[94] However, like Kennedy, Johnson significantly contributed to the development of a personalized presidential office. By the end of the Johnson era, the independent and personal nature of presidential decision-making had become almost institutionalized. Great Society programs were often formulated by presidential task forces that operated quite independent of the Democratic Party's congressional and organizational leadership.[95] The events of 1968, described in a preceeding chapter, further accelerated the decline of political parties in the governing process. Presidents operating within the context of a strong party system would no longer characterize the governing process. It was the end of an era.

A Strong Presidency and the National Interest

The previous review of American presidents was intended to accentuate the positive contributions of strong presidencies.[96] It was not an exercise in hero worship, nor was it a naive oversight of the dangers associated with "energy in the executive." Indeed, some of the country's best presidents have abused their power and, in doing so, directly violated the federal constitution. President Lincoln, for example, so severely violated the civil liberties of the American people during the Civil War that his conduct as president has at times been compared to that of a dictator. As noted, Lincoln's use of military tribunals to try civilians and his controversial decision to suspend the writ of habeus corpus were declared unconstitutional in federal court.

President Truman was also charged with overstepping the bounds of presidential authority. At the outbreak of the Korean War, Truman ordered a federal seizure of steel plants that were facing closure due to a nationwide steel strike. Truman's executive order was ruled unconstitutional by the United States Supreme Court.[97]

President Kennedy's decision to send military advisors to Vietnam and President Johnson's tremendous escalation of the war effort will forever remain the most blatant example of the dangers inherent in broad and unconstrained presidential authority. Indeed, the names of 58,000 servicemen etched into a black granite wall in Washington, D.C. are a haunting and somber reminder that broad grants of presidential power can have disastrous and extremely tragic consequences.

Yet this is a risk the American people must take if the presidency is once again to serve as a creative and energizing force for the American people. On balance, the evidence suggests that the nation is best served by powerful American presidents. Territorial expansion and international diplomacy; political power for the common people; preservation of the Union; environmental protection; regulation of monopolies; the spread of democracy around the globe; a world forum committed to resolving international conflicts; the defeat of Hitler and fascist aggression; containment of communism; crisis management; great strides towards economic and social justice; and even men walking on the moon are among the many positive developments in American history that can be directly attributed to the actions of powerful presidents. The historical record supports Hamilton's contention that "energy in the executive" is a prerequisite to good government.

Those who express opposition or skepticism to calls for a restored presidency note the current absence of a cataclysmic crisis that demands impressive executive action. Why is it necessary, these critics ask, to restore the power of the American presidency when the specters of civil war, fascism, communist aggression or economic depression are now behind us. This point of view, which at first glance seems valid, ignores the fact that current domestic and foreign policy crises are as threatening to the welfare and security of the United States as those that confronted the country in previous decades. What follows is a brief discussion of policy dilemmas that pose threats equal to those of war or economic depression—and which require, for the purpose of resolution, an empowered presidency.

The National Debt and Deficit Reduction

The 1992 presidential campaign catapulted the issue of national debt and deficit reduction to the forefront of national politics. Independent candidate H. Ross Perot heavily criticized the federal government's spending and borrowing policies. Perot's television infomercials demonstrated to the American people how serious this issue had become. In the tradition of American politics, both major parties, recognizing the political value of the debt issue, were quick to acknowledge and address Perot's concerns. Resolution of the national debt and balancing the federal budget have now become central concerns of both parties. These issues are paramount in the minds of the American people and no president or presidential candidate can avoid dealing with them.

How serious is the debt and how great is the budget deficit? Projected figures supplied by the Congressional Budget Office document a condition of critical proportions. The gross national debt in 1994 was 4.6 trillion dollars. This rose to 4.9 trillion in 1995. Current federal debt projections show 5.2 trillion for 1996, 5.6 trillion in 1997, 6.0 trillion in 1998, 6.4 trillion for 1999, and 6.8 trillion in the year 2000. CBO figures regarding the budget deficit indicate an increase from $175 billion in 1995 to $299 billion in the year 2000. By the year 2005, the deficit is projected to be 472 billion dollars.[98] As New York Governor Mario Cuomo stated in his classic keynote address at the Democratic National Convention in 1984, the debt incurred by the United States Government constitutes a "mortgage on our children's future." Such figures beg for stronger presidential leadership.

The Crime Wave

Crime has reached alarming proportions in the United States. Statistical data gathered by the Department of Justice reveal that in 1993 over 43 million crimes against persons and private property were committed in the United States. Eleven million were violent acts against individuals, while 32 million were committed against property. In 1993, the "victimization rate," which is based on the number of crimes per 1,000 people, reveal "52 violent victimizations per 1,000 persons and 322 property crimes per 1,000 households."[99] Particularly distressing is the fact that American teenagers face the greatest risk of becoming crime victims. One in eight persons 12–15 years of age reported being the victim of a violent crime. Although Justice Department data indicate only a modest increase in the number of crimes, from 42.9 million in 1992 to 43.6 million in 1993 (1.7 percent), the figures are nevertheless staggering. Although the American federal system inherently constrains presidential power in the area of law enforcement, crime in America has reached such epidemic proportions that a more concerted effort on the part of the federal government—spearheaded by an empowered presidency—is now justified.

Poverty

As part of his quest for the Great Society, President Lyndon Johnson declared war on poverty. To Johnson's credit, poverty was markedly reduced. In 1959, 20.8 percent of all families were living below the poverty level. By 1969, this figure had declined to 10.4 percent. For the next decade, poverty levels in America remained basically the same, with no discernible movement in percentages.[100] From 1980 to 1993, however, a slow but generally steady rise in the percentage of American families living in poverty can be observed. Table 6 presents the evidence.

Table 6
Percentage of American Families Living In Poverty
1980–1993

Year	1980	1982	1984	1986	1988	1990	1992	1993
Percent	11.5	13.6	13.1	12.0	11.6	12.0	13.3	13.6

Source: U.S. Census Bureau, Housing and Household Statistics Division

The poverty problem is especially acute for African-American and Hispanic families. 1993 census data broken down by race reveal 10.5 percent of white families, 32.9 percent of African-American families, and 29.3 percent of Hispanic families living in poverty.[101] One of the more recently evolved roles of the modern American presidency, as identified by Clinton Rossiter, is the Manager of Prosperity.[102] While there are limits to what presidents can do to promote economic prosperity (particularly within the framework of a capitalist economy), it is fair to expect the president to take the lead in establishing public policies which reduce poverty and create job opportunities. The extent to which the president can effectively address the poverty problem depends heavily on the power of the presidential office.

Global and Domestic Terrorism

Terrorist acts throughout the world, as well as within the United States, will require constant attention and decisive action on the part of future presidents. Cecil V. Crab and Kevin Mulcahy note that the United States "is the wealthiest and most powerful nation known to history, and this fact inevitably creates resentment and hostility toward it."[103] Terrorist acts waged against American citizens and property are perpetrated by a variety of organizations and sects. The common denominator, if one exists, is that each is motivated by a rigid ideological or religious doctrine combined with a fanatical devotion to their cause.

For the last two decades, the fundamentalist, anti-western religious sects of the Middle East presented the most direct threat to the lives of American civilians, diplomats, and military personnel. To citizens of the United States, terrorism and Middle East religious fundamentalism seemed synonymous. At the same time, terrorism against Americans appeared to be an activity that occured in airports and cities in countries far from the shores of the United States.

Perceptions of terrorism changed with the decade of the nineties. The bombing of the World Trade Center in New York City in 1993 by Islamic extremists demonstrated in no uncertain terms that terrorism within the borders of the United States was more than possible. This was further confirmed by the brutal bombing of a federal building in Oklahoma City in 1995 which claimed 169 lives, many of whom were pre-schoolers enrolled in the building's day care center. The Oklahoma bombing also brought to an end the terrorist stereotype, as the intensive manhunt which ensued resulted in the arrest of three American citizens with links to right wing militia groups. Although it is difficult to assess the strength and potential danger of the heavily armed militias due to their confederative structure, it is reasonable to surmise that the next wave of terrorist acts directed against American citizens and federal property will emanate from radical militia groups based on American soil.

Terrorism takes many forms, including assassination, indiscriminate bombings of men, women, and children, bank robberies, liberation of imprisoned comrades, kidnapping for ransom, and hijacking.[104] Whether they involve bullets, a bomb, or garrote, acts of terrorism directed against the United States government and the American people will undoubtedly remain a pressing issue for future presidents. Only a strong presidency employing the force of federal power will ensure that the American people will be safe against the terrorist threat. A president's control over the federal bureaucracy, particularly the Department of Justice and the attorney general, is especially relevant.

Ethnic Separatism and Civil Strife

The collapse of the Soviet Union, the dismantling of the Berlin Wall, and the subsequent end of the Cold War was heralded by many as the beginning of a world free from the threat of a massive military confrontation and nuclear holocaust. President George Bush, whose term of office coincided with the final disintegration of the Soviet empire, spoke of a "New World Order," in which world peace would be maintained through the laws of the United Nations and extensive international cooperation. Peace finally appeared to be within the reach of humankind. Unfortunately, the Soviet dissolution appears to have given rise to yet another and even more volatile problem: separatist movements and civil war.

For over forty years, the world political framework was condi-

tioned and determined by the foreign policies of two super powers—
the United States and its rival the Soviet Union. Alliances in Europe,
Africa, the Mid-East and Latin America were structured according to
U.S. and Soviet military, economic and political interests. It was a
bipolar world in which allies and enemies were distinguishable and
global coalitions predictable.

Although few bemoan the collapse of a political system as oppressive and fundamentally corrupt as that of the Soviet Union, there
was clearly an element of political stability that was present during
the bipolar political framework. A constant yet predictable tension
characterized Cold War politics. With the end of the Cold War, however, the predictable dimension of international politics appears to
have vanished. In the words of Arthur M. Schlesinger, Jr.:

> Lifting the lid of ideological repression in eastern Europe releases
> ethnic antagonisms deeply rooted in experience and in memory. The
> disappearance of ideological competition in the third world removes
> superpower restraints on national and tribal confrontations. As the
> era of ideological conflict subsides, humanity enters—or, more pre-
> cisely, reenters—a possibly more dangerous era of ethnic and racial
> animosity.[105]

The question that needs to be asked is whether the modern presidency is strategically positioned within the framework of American
government to deal decisively with civil strife in the post-Cold War
era. A presidency constrained by bureaucracy, subject to incessant
congressional hearings, and hounded by journalists obsessed with
sensationalist reporting is unlikely to be able to respond to international disorder in the tradition of Franklin Roosevelt or Harry
Truman.

As this work was progressing, a brutal civil war raged in a land
once known as Yugoslavia. Bosnian Serbs, in the interest of establishing a Serbian nation, instituted a policy of ethnic cleansing and
genocide. Concentration camps were established, Bosnian Muslims
were systematically slaughtered, mass graves were uncovered, and
hospitals were routinely targeted by Serb artillery. Close to two hundred United Nations peacekeeping troops were captured and held
hostage by the Serbian army. Yet despite the atrocities, which to
some extent paralleled those of Hitler's Third Reich, the American
president for several years seemed incapable of preventing bloodshed
and forging a lasting peace. A peace settlement, spearheaded by
President Clinton, was eventually reached. NATO troops, including

a contingent of 30,000 American soldiers, were deployed to Bosnia for the purpose of enforcing the provisions of the peace plan. While the president's actions certainly need to be applauded, as peace appears to have been restored, the question which surfaces is why it took so long for the president of the United States to take such decisive action.

Racial Division

Although racial tension in the United States does not approach the deep ethnic animosity found in other parts of the world, there is, nevertheless, a growing division between white and black Americans that requires concern. The O.J. Simpson murder trial in 1995, labeled as "the trial of the century," brought to light the existence of a severe racial chasm in American society. In the immediate aftermath of the Simpson verdict of not guilty, talk show hosts, media commentators, and political pundits focused their attention on the vast differences in opinions that currently separate whites from blacks. Indeed, the extent to which race currently divides Americans is perhaps the most telling story of the O.J. Simpson trial.

Polls conducted during and after the Simpson trial discovered extremely different perceptions between whites and blacks towards the American judicial system and American society. One *U.S. News and World Report* survey conducted immediately after the verdict, which found the former football legend and media celebrity not guilty of double murder (of Simpson's former wife and a friend), discovered 62 percent of whites were convinced Simpson was guilty, while 55 percent of blacks believed Simpson was not guilty.[106] Interviews and media coverage suggested that whites were distressed over the verdict, while blacks were elated. According to the report: "That blacks felt they had gained something and whites felt they had lost says more about our national divide than it does about O.J. Simpson. The Simpson trial moved beyond murder, domestic abuse, or interracial marriage. It came to represent not just different perceptions of justice by black and white Americans but different perceptions of America itself."[107] Seventy percent of blacks believed Simpson (who is African-American) was acquitted on the basis of the facts, while 53 percent of whites believed "other factors" were responsible for the trial's outcome.[108] Following the trial, sixty-six percent of blacks expressed the view that the police often frame innocent people, while only 28 percent of whites agreed.[109] Black and white attitudes beyond the issue of justice also reveal a deep racial divide. One NBC poll discovered that 84 percent of blacks blame racial discrimination for their economic condition, while 30 percent of whites share this view.

Race has been a source of political tension within the fabric of American politics for several decades. The movement of white ethnic groups and white southerners towards the Republican Party over the course of the past twenty-five years is very much tied to the Democratic Party's support for social and economic policies that are perceived as advancing the status of African-Americans. The very same issues have resulted in firm support among blacks for the Democratic Party. The deep racial divide, which captured the attention of commentators during the Simpson trial has, in other words, been a feature of American politics and society for a long time.

A system characterized by deep racial tension has serious implications for social unrest, particularly in urban areas. The violent riot in Los Angeles following the verdict in the first "Rodney King trial" in 1992 demonstrates in no uncertain terms the current volatility of the racial divide.[110] Was the riot unique to the conditions of Los Angeles? Are other American cities, such as Chicago, Philadephia, and New York also vulnerable to such violent eruptions? As we approach the twenty-first century, it is clear that the need to establish common ground between blacks and whites is one of the most pressing concerns in America.

While it might seem unrealistic to expect presidents to bridge the racial divide, it does seem reasonable to assign a share of this responsibility to the occupant of the Oval Office. The presidency, like no other arm of American government, is strategically positioned to effectively bridge the widening gap between the races. The ability of the president to help create meaningful jobs for racial minorities is obviously one step towards healing racial tension. With one-third of African-Americans living below the poverty level, meaningful job creation within the nation's inner cities must be on the presidential agenda.

In addition to job creation, future presidents can serve as a productive force for racial tolerance and harmony. How effective a president is in this respect will heavily depend on moral authority and communicative skills. Moreover, only the occupant of the presidency, not members of the Senate or House of Representatives, can unite the American public. As Pendleton Herring puts it: "We can symbolize our national unity in the presidency, our sectional interests in the Senate, and our localisms in the House."[111] Thus, capacity to forge national unity is clearly one of the most pressing challenges for future presidents. The American people, regardless of race or creed either subconsciously or consciously look to the presidency as a source of national healing. The words of Avery Leiserson are especially pertinent as we approach the twenty-first century:

> Diversity and division, not consensus or solidarity, underlie and reinforce the mass-psychological dependence, reliance and yearning for a trusted respected, and admired figure like the president, to show us the way out of the clamor of conflicting voices, to help us discern the direction of public national interest, and to persuade us to do what what the common good requires. The presidency serves the nation as a vital, unifying center; a focal point for rallying the moral strength and confidence of the people when they are disturbed, at a loss for direction among the clash of contending views and interests.[112]

The national debt and deficit reduction, crime, poverty, terrorism, civil strife, and the racial divide are policy areas which demand creative presidential leadership. To this list, one could also add environmental protection, improvements in infrastructure and welfare reform. While this is not to suggest that Congress or state governments are totally incapable of policy problem solving, the historical record does indicate that the most serious dilemmas that have faced the American people over the course of two centuries have been resolved most effectively through presidential leadership.

However, to effectively legislate presidential agendas and to harness the power of government for the common good, the presidency requires power. Presidents cannot lead in a creative fashion when their agenda are routinely undermined by special interest dollars and lobbyists. Presidents cannot have power or moral authority when the media relentlessly search for flaws in personal character or conduct. Presidents cannot unite the branches of government towards a national goal when Congress is consumed with hearings, when iron triangles and issue networks thwart presidential initiatives, or when federal bureaucrats feel little political loyalty to the occupant of the Oval Office.

Reform is clearly required if the presidency is to once again serve as a dynamic force for national leadership. A number of reforms have been advocated in the preceding pages of this work which have the potential to restore and expand presidential power. One set focuses on strengthening political parties and connecting the presidency to the party system in a more direct fashion. The second set of reform proposals is designed to provide the president with legal leverage over the legislative process and the executive branch. Taken together, these reforms, if implemented, should provide the president with the political and legal authority necessary for bold and energetic leadership during what promises to be a challenging twenty-first century.

Afterword

Several developments pertinent to the study of presidential power have transpired between the opening and closing chapters of this particular volume. The line item veto, described in a previous chapter, was passed into law. The new law, which should enhance presidential leverage in the policy making process, becomes effective in January of 1997. Extended lobbying regulation, also discussed in a previous chapter, was passed into law during the writing of this work. Lobbying activity will now be more closely monitored within the context of federal decision making, yet another development favorable to presidential leadership. Additionally, the Clinton administration relaxed restrictions on the political activity of federal employees, the size of the federal bureaucracy was trimmed, and political parties continue to show signs of new vitality. For those concerned with the resurrection of presidential authority, such developments are encouraging.

On the political front, two historic developments occurred during the writing of this work. In the mid-term congressional election of 1994, voters elected a majority of Republicans to both houses of Congress. Forty years have passed since the Republican Party has controlled the national legislature. A referendum on President Clinton's first two years was the explanation offered by political pundits to account for the so-called political earthquake. Indecisive presidential leadership and a leftward drift in policy priorities on the part of the president resulted in a historic transfer of legislative authority.

However, despite a serious electoral setback for the Democratic Party, the president proved once again that he was indeed the "comeback kid." In the 1996 presidential contest, the president was reelected in convincing fashion. Such a development seemed unthinkable in the aftermath of the 1994 election. The 1996 election, like that of 1994, was also historic, as President Clinton was the first Democratic president since Franklin D. Roosevelt to win reelection.

Several variables were related to the president's reelection. First, and perhaps foremost, was the healthy state of the American economy. Unemployment figures were the lowest in seven years, inflation was under control, and the stock market was exceptionally strong. Exit polls generated by Voter News Service and published in the *New York Times* revealed that fifty-three percent of voters rated the economy as "good," while four percent rated the economy as "excellent." Perceptions of the economy were clearly related to the election outcome.

In addition to a strong economy, the policy positions articulated by President Clinton throughout the course of the campaign effectively connected the president to the center of the American electorate—that critical bloc of voters which routinely determines the outcome of presidential elections. As part of his "New Democrat" strategy, accelerated no doubt by the results of the 1994 congressional election, President Clinton strongly embraced an array of issues which in years prior were most effectively communicated by the Republican Party. This included welfare reform, crime control, antiterrorism, and family values. Indeed, just prior to the Democratic National Convention, the president signed into law a sweeping welfare reform bill. The new law transferred a substantial amount of control over welfare policy from the federal to state governments—one of the most far-reaching developments in the area of social welfare policy since the New Deal.

In 1996, it was impossible for the Republican Party to hang the so-called L Word on President Clinton, as the president's rhetoric and actions were hardly those of a liberal Democrat. Exit polls discovered that six out of ten voters who described themselves as "moderate" voted for President Clinton. Clinton's strategic appeal to middle class, centrist values was handsomely rewarded on election day with 379 electoral votes, a landslide in the electoral college.

There was a foreign policy dimension to Clinton's reelection as well. Election year 1996, like that of 1992, was a post-Cold War presidential contest. During the Cold War, which spanned several decades, Republican presidential candidates, despite the minority status of their party, could win the support of voters based on the perception that the Republican Party could most effectively contain communism and thwart the ambitions of the Soviet Union. The specter of communist aggression often worked to the advantage of Republican presidential candidates. The elections of Eisenhower in 1952 and 1956,

Nixon in 1968 and 1972, Reagan in 1980 and 1984, and Bush in 1988—seven out of ten presidential contests in the Cold War era—reflected American fears of the Soviets and the potential of communist expansionism. Political scientists have often attributed Republican presidential victories to the issue of communism and the "red menace."

However, with the almost overnight disintegration of the Soviet Union, the Republican Party was severely deprived of one of its most important and strategic campaign issues. President Clinton could not be accused of being "soft" on communism, a charge frequently leveled at previous Democratic presidential candidates, nor could Republicans present their candidate as the one most capable of containing communism—because communism, for all intents and purposes, was no longer a presidential campaign issue. Thus, the 1996 election results need to be examined in light of this important development.

The style and poor telegenic skills of Bob Dole, especially when contrasted with those of Bill Clinton, were also relevant to the 1996 presidential election outcome. Dole, a veteran and highly talented legislator, lacked the dynamism, image, and vigor required for a modern media-based presidential campaign. At seventy-three years of age, a monotone voice, and often stern appearance, the Republican nominee simply could not inspire or capture the imagination of the American people. While few could challenge Dole's integrity, patriotism, and sense of ethics, his campaign nevertheless failed to excite the American electorate. The 1996 presidential election underscored what political scientists have been suggesting for many years: media skills and personal image are critical in the modern age of campaigning.

Another factor relevant to the presidential election result involved the advantage of incumbency. Unlike Bob Dole, President Clinton could enjoy the luxury of highly publicized policy-related visits to states of strategic electoral significance. Moreover, the president could direct federal aid in a fashion which enhanced his own reelection efforts. Federal largesse distributed to states rich in electoral votes, California in particular, was reported to be quite extensive.

President Clinton's harmonious and uncontested nomination, a nation at peace, as well as a constant flow of spot ads were also instrumental in the election outcome. Clinton's ads portrayed the president as a man of vision and the protector of American families. At the same time, Clinton's spot-ads diminished the credibility of Bob Dole and raised questions regarding the senator's commitment to Medicare. Like most presidential campaigns in the modern era, it was apparent that a sizeable share of Clinton's campaign budget was directed towards the production of persuasive campaign commercials and attack advertising.

President Clinton's reelection, won with relative ease, raises a question regarding presidential governance. Is President Clinton, the first Democrat since Franklin D. Roosevelt to win reelection, positioned for a successful second term of office? Will the president be able to lead?

It is clear that doubts regarding Clinton's personal character will continue to cloud his presidency throughout the next four years. At the same time, the president, much to his chagrin, will continue to face a Republican Congress inclined towards oversight-related activity. There is still a distinct possibility of more Whitewater hearings.

Equally troubling for the president is the ongoing activity of a tenacious special prosecutor by the name of Kenneth Starr. Starr's independent investigation might unearth new evidence related to Whitewater which could prove not only detrimental to the president, but also the president's wife. Rumors continue to circulate that Starr's investigation will result in more federal indictments.

In addition to the Whitewater investigation, a fund-raising scandal involving the Demoratic National Committee could lead to additional hearings and investigations. The committee has been accused of conducting an illegal fund-raising operation involving Asian foreign interests. Democratic Party fund-raising activity during the 1996 election will be the subject of much discussion and inquiry in the months ahead.

In addition to congressional hearings and investigations, there is little doubt that interest group money and lobbyists will routinely challenge the Clinton agenda, the media will continue to probe for sensational stories regarding presidential malfeasance, and a bloated federal bureaucracy will inevitably slow the pace of creative national leadership. Such impediments to bold executive leadership are bound to surface throughout the president's second term because the Clinton presidency, like most presidencies of the post-Watergate era, is not a party-centered presidency.

Indeed, there is little to suggest that President Clinton's second term of office will be much different from that of his first with respect to the place of parties in the governing process. The "New Democrat," from most indications, is still detached from the Democratic Party. With respect to the 1996 presidential contest, the president's campaign, like that of 1992, was more candidate than party-centered. Some commentators even went so far as to suggest that Clinton, in his effort to appear moderate, purposely distanced himself from the

Democratic congressional candidates. In light of this strategy, there is reason to question the future working relationship between the president and fellow Democrats in Congress. Following the election, several commentators predicted that Clinton would be forced to pursue a bipartisan approach to governing. Such predictions proved to be insightful. Only one month after the election, former Senator William Cohen, a moderate Republican from Maine, was nominated by President Clinton for the post of Defense Secretary.

President Clinton's partisan coattails were not very long in light of the 1996 congressional elections results. The percentage of votes received by the president in house districts across the country and, more specifically, the percentage of votes received by the president vis-à-vis the winners of the various congressional races, is, of course, the more precise gauge of presidential coattails. However, even in the absence of hard evidence, a general observation does not suggest lengthy presidential coattails.

Prior to the election, the Republican Party occupied 235 seats in the House of Representatives, while the Democrats controlled 197 seats. There was one Independent and two vacancies. Following the election, the partisan configuration had changed, but only minimally. For the 105th Congress, Republicans will occupy 227 seats, and the Democrats 206 seats. There is still one Independent and, at the time of this writing, one undecided seat. A net gain of only 9 seats in the House of Representatives for congressional Democrats, along with the fact that the Democrats will remain the minority party in Congress, is quite telling regarding President Clinton's coattails, and, more generally, the current strength of coattails in American politics. As the head of the Democratic Party, President Clinton failed to carry a majority of Democrats into Congress. Moreover, among those Democrats who were elected or reelected, it is doubtful if many feel beholden to the president for their seat in Congress. President Clinton received only 49 percent of the national popular vote.

In senate elections, the Democrats lost, rather than gained, seats. Prior to the election, the partisan configuration of the Senate was 53 Republicans to 47 Democrats. For the 105th Congress, 55 seats will belong to Republicans and 45 seats to Democrats. Presidential coattails in senatorial races were nonexistent.

As this work goes to print, President Clinton's second term is about to commence. A second Clinton term will, no doubt, be fascinating and intriguing. The president, like most presidents, will want to be remembered as one of the country's most creative and dynamic chief executives. He will govern with history in mind. He will be con-

cerned how presidential scholars and historians will evaluate the
Clinton presidency. One can only speculate where the forty-second
president of the United States will be ranked, as so much can tran-
spire during a second term.

It is clear, however, that in most instances presidents who have
been evaluated favorably have been those who governed in a strong
and decisive fashion. Such presidents not only interpreted the powers
of the presidency in broad terms, but, at the same time, occupied an
office which afforded the opportunity for bold and creative leadership. This is why it is important for congressmen, federal judges,
teachers of government, college students, and, more generally, the
American people, to think long and hard about the present condition
of the presidency. The United States is in need of strong presidential
leadership, and the American people are often served by strong presidents. To pursue measures, or to allow conditions to persist,that inherently weaken the presidential office is to put the republic at risk.

Appendix

A Suggestion for Classroom Participation

A thematic supplement concerning the restoration of presidential power provides a rich opportunity for undergraduate students to engage in classroom discussion and organized debate. After two decades of college teaching and many years as a college debate coach, I can state with great confidence that students in political science courses deeply appreciate the opportunity to argue over clearly defined and debatable issues.

One format that I have found to be especially stimulating and useful for learning purposes is to allow opposing teams consisting of two students to formally debate the merits of a current and pressing political topic. My typical classroom debates last for approximately twenty to thirty minutes. A debatable issue is assigned to two teams approximately one week in advance. Students are encouraged to build their case from the content of the text and from the suggested bibliography. This, of course, requires one or two trips to the library. During the debate, each student is allotted five minutes to present his or her argument. I require all debaters to speak from the podium. This lends itself to a more formal atmosphere and serves as a useful exercise in public speaking. Following the deliveries, any student in the class who wishes to rise and briefly speak from the floor on behalf of the affirmative or negative position is allowed to do so. The leaders of the affirmative and negative are then allowed to summarize and close their case within the space of two minutes. A three judge panel, consisting of students, will then cast anonymous ballots that determine the outcome of the contest. I serve as the moderator throughout the debate and provide each debater with a brief written critique. *The American Presidency Under Siege*, along with the many other works regarding the current state of presidential leadership, provides students with an array of interesting and debatable issues. Ten of my favorite issues are as follows:

1. Is the United States currently in need of a stronger presidency?
2. Should the mass media expose the private lives of presidential candidates and presidents?
3. Are special interest groups and lobbyists harmful to presidential leadership?
4. Should congressional investigations into presidential conduct be curtailed?
5. Is a party-centered presidency desirable in this day and age?
6. Should party leaders have more control over the presidential nominating process?
7. Would abolishing the electoral college result in better presidential leadership?
8. Should a president's cabinet consist of senators and congressmen (the legislative cabinet)?
9. Should the Twenty-Second Amendment be repealed?
10. Should the president have line-item veto?

These are some of the debatable issues that I have experienced considerable success with in terms of stimulating classroom debate and discussion. Organized and structured argumentation, particularly when the quality of the argumentation is judged by one's peers, facilitates learning and brings to life the subject of presidential politics. It is a motivational device and effective teaching tool which I highly recommend.

Notes

Chapter One

1. A reprint of President Clinton's inaugural address can be found in William Crotty, editor, *America's Choice: The Election of 1992* (Guilford, Connecticut: Dushkin, 1993), pp. 171–173.

2. This is a personal observation by the author who has attended the inaugurations of Presidents Reagan, Bush, and Clinton.

3. The most romantic of all presidential honeymoons appears to have been that of President Franklin D. Roosevelt. According to James MacGregor Burns, during the early days of the Roosevelt administration, "everybody, it seemed, loved the president." Republicans in Congress seemed willing to put "country before party," while farm leaders, labor leaders, businessmen, publishers, and the print press all expressed support for the newly elected president. Even Adolf Hitler, according to Burns, "had a good word for him." James MacGregor Burns, *Roosevelt: The Lion and the Fox* (New York: Harcourt Brace and Co., 1956), p. 184.

4. *Time*, June 7, 1993, p. 25.

5. *Time*, May 3, 1993, p. 46.

6. Ibid.

7. Examples include the National Voter Registration Act (the federal motor voter bill), the Brady Bill, NAFTA, deficit reduction, and anti-crime legislation.

8. *Congressional Record*, August 6, 1993.

9. *Business Week*, June 7, 1993, p. 29.

10. *U.S. News and World Report*, November 15, 1993, p. 13.

11. *The Public Perspective*, vol. 6 (February/March 1995): 9, figure 1.

12. Michael Barone and Grant Ujifusa, *Almanac of American Politics* (Washington, D.C.: National Journal, Inc., 1992), pp. 71–83.

13. See John Kenneth White, *The New Politics of Old Values* (Hanover: University Press of New England, 1988), passim, and John L. Palmer and Isabel V. Sawhill, "Perspectives on the Reagan Experiment" in John L. Palmer and Isabel V. Sawhill, editors, *The Reagan Experiment* (Washington, D.C.: The Urban Institute Press, 1982), pp. 2–4.

14. Louis W. Koenig, *The Chief Executive*, 5th edition (New York: Harcourt Brace Jovonavich, 1986), p. 2.

15. Leon Halpert, "Presidential Leadership of Congress: Evaluating President Reagan's Success in the House of Representatives," *Presidential Studies Quarterly*, vol. XXI (fall 1991): 723.

16. David Stockman, *The Triumph of Politics: Why The Reagan Revolution Failed* (New York: Harper and Row Publishers, 1986).

17. Bruce Oppenheimer, "Declining Presidential Success With Congress" in Richard W. Waterman, editor, *The Presidency Reconsidered* (Itasca: F.E. Peacock Publishers, Inc., 1993), p. 75.

18. Arthur Schlesinger, Jr., *The Imperial Presidency* (Boston: Houghton Mifflin Co., 1973).

19. Forrest McDonald, Foreword in Martin L. Fausold and Alan Shank, editors, *The Constitution and the American Presidency* (Albany: SUNY Press, 1991), p. xi.

20. Theodore C. Sorensen, *A Different Kind of Presidency: A Proposal for Breaking the Political Deadlock* (New York: Harper and Row Publishers, 1984), pp. 5–6.

21. Richard E. Neustadt, *Presidential Power and the Modern Presidents* (New York: The Free Press, 1990), p. ix.

22. Robert Shogan, *None of the Above* (New York: Nal Books, 1982), p. 4.

23. Michael A. Genovese, *The Presidential Dilemma* (New York: Harper and Row Publishers, 1995), p. 27. In this volume, Genovese explores the failure of modern presidents over the course of the past twenty-five years. Such failure is attributed by Genovese to nine systemic variables: the intent of the Founding Fathers, the constitutional design of American government, the decline of leadership skills, the American political culture, the cyclical nature of politics and national leadership, political party decline, the dynamics of the presidential selection process, a capitalist economy, and the decline of the United States as an international superpower. This is one of the most multi-dimensional treatments regarding the subject of modern presidential leadership.

24. For a review of President Johnson's legislative skills, see George C. Edwards III, *Presidential Influence in Congress* (San Francisco: W.H. Freeman and Co., 1980), chapters 5–6.

25. James P. Pfiffner, *The Modern Presidency* (New York: St. Martin's Press), p. 225.

26. Richard Rose, *The Postmodern President: The White House Meets the World* (New Jersey: Chatham House Publishers, Inc., 1988), p. 270.

Chapter Two

1. Discussions of various American presidents can be found in Clinton Rossiter, *The American Presidency*, Revised Edition (New York: The New American Library, 1962), chapters 2–4, and Marcus Cunliffe, *American Presidents and the Presidency* (New York: American Heritage Press, 1972), passim.

2. A number of works on the American presidency contain excellent discussions regarding constraints and obstacles to presidential leadership. See, for example, Rossiter, *The American Presidency*, ch. 2, Louis W. Koenig, *The Chief Executive*, 5th edition (New York: Harcourt Brace Jovanovich, Publishers, 1986), p. 3–6, and Benjamin I. Page and Mark P. Petracca, *The American Presidency* (New York: McGraw-Hill, 1983), chapters 8–9.

3. Fred Harris, *Deadlock or Decision* (New York: Oxford University Press, 1993), p. 64.

4. Data obtained by author from Office of Records and Information, Office of Clerk of House of Representatives, May 11, 1994.

5. This is the result of the Supreme Court decision of U.S. v. Harriss (1954). In this case the court upheld the constitutionality of the Federal Regulation of Lobbying Act of 1946 against the claim that the law violated the First Amendment. At the same time, however, the Court narrowly construed the meaning of the law thereby allowing many forms of lobbying to go completely unregulated. A concise discussion of the Lobbying Act, the Harriss ruling, and existing loopholes can be found in Norman J. Ornstein and Shirley Elder, *Interest Groups, Lobbying and Policymaking* (Washington, D.C.: Congressional Quarterly Press, 1978), pp. 101–104. At the time of this writing, Congress is considering a proposed bill that will regulate lobbying activity in all three branches of government.

6. Hedrick Smith, *The Power Game* (New York: Random House, 1988), p. 31.

7. Ibid.

8. Edward Schneir and Bertram Gross, *Legislative Strategy: Shaping Public Policy* (New York: St. Martin's Press, 1993), p. 22.

9. Smith, *The Power Game*, p. 31.

10. Extensive description of interest group activity in the nation's capital can be found in Ornstein and Elder, *Interest Groups, Lobbying and Policymaking*, Allan J. Cigler and Burdett A. Loomis, editors, *Interest Group Politics* (Washington, D.C. Congressional Quarterly Press, 1983) and Ronald J. Hrebenar and Ruth K. Scott, *Interest Group Politics in America* (Englewood Cliffs: Prentice-Hall, 1982).

11. Data obtained by author from the Registration Unit, U.S. Justice Department, May 11, 1994.

12. Ornstein and Elder, *Interest Groups, Lobbying and Policymaking*, p. 51.

13. Pat Choate, *Agents of Influence* (New York: Knopf, 1990).

14. Larry Makinson, *The Price of Admission* (Washington, D.C.: Center for Responsive Politics, 1993), p. 15.

15. Ibid., p. 14.

16. Ibid.

17. Ibid., p. 17.

18. Discussion of iron triangles, or subgovernments, can be found in many works. See, for example, Joel D. Aberbach, *Keeping a Watchful Eye: The Politics of Congressional Oversight* (Washington, D.C.: The Brookings Institution, 1990), pp. 83–86, and Hugh Heclo, *A Government of Strangers: Executive Politics in Washington* (Washington, D.C.: The Brookings Institution, 1977), pp. 224–225.

19. Smith, *The Power Game*, p. 174.

20. Ibid., pp. 173–179.

21. Heclo, *A Government of Strangers*, p. 13.

22. Harold Seidman, *Politics, Position and Power* (New York: Oxford University Press, 1970), p. 35.

23. For a review of the literature regarding the changing character of iron triangles, see John R. Wright, *Interest Groups and Congress: Lobbying, Contributions, and Influence* (Boston: Allyn and Bacon, 1996), pp. 168–171. Also, Robert Salisbury, et al., "Triangles, Networks, and Hollow Cores: The Complex Geometry of Washington Interest Representation" in Mark P. Petracca, ed., *The Politics of Interests: Interest Groups Transformed* (Boulder: Westview Press, 1992), pp. 130–149.

24. Hugh Heclo, "Issue Networks and the Executive Establishment" in Anthony King, ed., *The New American Political System* (Washington, D.C.: American Enterprise Institute for Public Policy Research, 1978), p. 102.

25. Wright, *Interest Groups and Congress*, p. 171.

26. Richard Rose, *The Postmodern President* (New Jersey: Chatham House Publishers, Inc., 1988), p. 162.

27. Ibid.

28. Data obtained by author from Office of Personnel Management, May 19, 1994.

29. Seidman, *Politics, Position and Power*, p. 26.

30. Rossiter, *The American Presidency*, pp. 55–56.

31. Heclo, *A Government of Strangers*, p. 3.

32. Rose, *The Postmodern President*, p. 173.

33. Harry S. Truman, *Memoirs*, volume I (New York: Doubleday, 1955), p. 226.

34. Ibid., pp. 226–227.

35. Lyndon Baines Johnson, *The Vantage Point: Perspectives of the Presidency* (New York: Holt, Rinehart and Winston, 1971), p. 21.

36. Richard M. Nixon, *In The Arena: A Memoir of Victory, Defeat and Renewal* (New York: Simon and Schuster, 1990), p. 270.

37. Ronald Reagan, *An American Life* (New York: Simon and Schuster, 1990), p. 597.

38. Harold M. Barger, *The Impossible Presidency: Illusions and Realities of Presidential Power* (Glenview: Scott, Foresman and Co., 1984), p. 188.

39. Ibid.

40. Benjamin I. Page and Mark P. Petracca, *The American Presidency*, pp. 203–207.

41. Ibid.

42. Barger, *The Impossible Presidency*, p. 163.

43. Larry J. Sabato, *Feeding Frenzy: How Attack Journalism Has Transformed American Politics* (New York: The Free Press, 1991), p. 1.

44. Herbert Schmertz, "The Media and the Presidency," *Presidential Studies Quarterly*, vol. XVI (winter, 1986): 13.

45. Doris A. Graber, *Mass Media and American Politics*, 3rd edition (Washington, D.C.: Congressional Quarterly Press, 1989), p. 237. Study also

cited in Lyn Ragsdale, *Presidential Politics* (Boston: Houghton Mifflin Co., 1992), p. 158. According to Ragsdale: "Even when other politicians are mentioned—members of Congress, executive branch officials, governors, heads of state—they are depicted as supporting characters to the president in the lead role."

46. For commentary of press coverage regarding the 1968 Tet Offensive and the Vietnam War, see Michael Maclear, *The Ten Thousand Day War* (New York: St. Martin's Press, 1981), pp. 220–221. Also, Michael Baruch Grossman and Martha Joynt Kumar, *Portraying the President: The White House and the News Media* (Baltimore: Johns Hopkins University Press, 1981), pp. 318–319.

47. Michael Baruch Grossman and Martha Joynt Kumar, *Portraying the President*, p. 9.

48. Richard Pious, *The American Presidency* (New York: Basic Books, 1979), p. 417. Also cited in Austin Ranney, *Channels of Power* (New York: Basic Books, 1983), p. 142.

49. Ranney, *Channels of Power*, p. 141.

50. Grossman and Kumar, *Portraying the President*, p. 12.

51. Ibid., p. 12.

52. Quoted in Grossman and Kumar, *Portraying the President*, p. 12.

53. Smith, *The Power Game*, p. 429.

54. Ibid.

55. Stephen Ansolabehere, Roy Behr, and Shanto Iyengar, *The Media Game: American Politics in the Media Age* (New York: MacMillan Publishing Co., 1993), p. 27.

56. Thomas E. Patterson, *Out of Order* (New York: Vintage Books, 1994), p. 21. See figure 1.1.

57. James Madison, "Federalist 51," Clinton Rossiter, editor, *The Federalist Papers* (New York: New American Library, 1961), pp. 321–322.

58. Two cases are of paramount importance: Nixon v. Sirica (1973) and United States v. Nixon (1974). A federal appeals court, and subsequently the United States Supreme Court, ruled against the President's claim of executive privilege, thereby requiring President Nixon to comply with a subpoena to release tape recordings of White House conversations. The Supreme Court decision is more commonly known as "the Watergate tapes case."

59. C. Herman Pritchett, "The President's Constitutional Position" in Thomas E. Cronin and Rexford G. Tugwell, editors, *The Presidency Reappraised* (New York: Praeger, 1977), p. 14.

60. Thomas E. Cronin, *The State of the Presidency*, 2nd edition (Boston: Little, Brown and Co., 1980), p. 190.

61. Nixon, *In The Arena*, pp. 205–206.

62. Gerald R. Ford, Foreword in Robert Turner, *Repealing the War Powers Resolution* (New York: Maxmillan Publishing Co., 1991), p. ix.

63. Louis Fisher, *Presidential War Power* (Lawrence: University of Kansas Press, 1995), p. 13.

64. Ibid., p. 185.

65. Christopher J. Deering, "Congress, the President, and Military Policy," in Roger H. Davidson, ed., *Congress and the Presidency: Invitation to Struggle* (Beverly Hills: Sage Publications, 1988), pp. 146–147.

66. L. Gordon Crovitz, "Micromanaging Foreign Policy," *The Public Interest*, Issue 100 (summer, 1990): 112.

67. The seminal article is Aaron Wildavsky, "The Two Presidencies," *Trans-Action* 4 (December 1966): 7–14. Wildavsky discovered that between the years 1948–1964, Congress supported the president's domestic initiatives roughly forty percent of the time, while on foreign policy measures the Congress supported the president approximately seventy percent of the time—hence "two presidencies." A plethora of scholars have since reexamined the two presidencies thesis. Some argue that it still applies, while others argue that it has become obsolete. An excellent collection of articles specifically concerned with the two presidencies thesis, including a reprint of the original study, can be found in Steven A. Shull, ed., *The Two Presidencies: A Quarter Century Assessment* (Chicago: Nelson-Hall Publishers, 1991).

68. Conference Committee Report cited in Margaret N. Davis, "The Congressional Budget Mess," in Gordon S. Jones and John A. Marini, editors, *The Imperial Congress: Crisis in the Separation of Powers* (New York: Pharos Books, 1988), p. 159.

69. Allen Schick, "The Battle of the Budget" in Harvey C. Mansfield, Sr., editor, *Congress Against The President* (New York: The Academy of Political Science, 1975), p. 51.

70. James A. Thurber, "The Consequences of Budget Reform for Congressional-Presidential Relations," in Roger H. Davidson, ed., *Congress and the Presidency: Invitation to Struggle* (Beverly Hills: Sage Publications, 1988), p. 101.

71. Davis, "The Congressional Budget Mess," Jones and Marini, editors, p. 159.

72. Aberbach, *Keeping A Watchful Eye*, p. 41.

73. Herman A. Mellor, "Congressional Micromanagement: National Defense," in Jones and Marini, editors, p. 111. (The author of this article is identifed as a Defense Department Official and former aide on Capitol Hill who is writing under a pseudonym.)

74. See Jones and Marini, editors, *The Imperial Congress*, chapters 4–5.

75. Robert A. Diamond, editor, *Powers of Congress* (Washington, D.C.: Congressional Quarterly Press, 1976), p. xiii.

76. Allen Schick, "Politics through Law: Congressional Limitations on Executive Discretion," in Anthony King, editor, *Both Ends of the Avenue* (Washington, D.C.: American Enterprise Institute, 1983), pp. 170–179.

77. James Sundquist, *Constitutional Reform and Effective Government* (Washington, D.C.: The Brookings Institution, 1986).

78. Schick, "Politics through Law," in King, editor, *Both Ends of the Avenue*, p. 171.

79. Ibid., p. 174.

80. Ibid., p. 176.

81. Sundquist, *Constitutional Reform and Effective Government*, p. 218.

82. Ibid., pp. 220–222.

83. Schick, "Politics through Law," in King, editor, *Both Ends of the Avenue*, p. 154.

84. Steven A, Shull, *Domestic Policy Formation* (Westport: Greenwood Press, 1983), p. 174.

Chapter Three

1. Robert Harmel, "The Roots of President-Party Relations: Intellectual, Conceptual, and Contextual," in Robert Harmel, ed., *Presidents and Their Parties: Leadership or Neglect?* (New York; Praeger Publishers, 1984), p. 255.

2. William Nisbet Chambers, "Party Development and the American Mainstream," in William Nisbet Chambers and Walter Dean Burnham, editors, *The American Party Systems: Stages of Development*, 2nd edition (London: Oxford University Press, 1979), p. 10.

3. Everett Carll Ladd, Jr., "Political Parties and Governance in the 1980s" in Arnold J. Meltsner, editor, *Politics and the Oval Office: Towards Presidential Governance* (San Francisco: Institute for Contemporary Studies, 1981), pp. 63–78. Also, David E. Price, *Bringing Back the Parties* (Washington, D.C.: Congressional Quarterly Press, 1984), pp. 69–82.

4. Godfrey Hodgson, *All Things to All Men: The False Promise of the American Presidency* (New York: Simon and Schuster, 1980), p. 166.

5. This argument is based on the literature that advocates a more responsible political party system. See Committee on Political Parties of the American Political Science Association, *Toward a More Responsible Two Party System* (New York: Rinehart and Company, Inc., 1950) and Austin Ranney, *The Doctrine of Responsible Party Government* (Urbana: The University of Illinois Press, 1954). For a thorough review of obstacles to party responsibility in American politics, see John Kenneth White and Jerome M. Mileur, editors, *Challenges to Party Government* (Carbondale, Illinois: Southern Illinois University Press, 1992).

6. Hodgson, *All Things to All Men*, p. 164.

7. Discussions of political parties as vital linkage mechanisms between the people and the polity are found in many scholarly works. See, for example, V.O. Key, Jr., *Politics, Parties, and Pressure Groups*, 5th edition (New York: Thomas Y. Crowell Company, 1964), p. 9. In democracies, according to Key, political parties "perform an essential function in the management of succession to power, as well as the process of obtaining popular consent to the course of public policy."

8. Harmel, "The Roots of President-Party Relations," p. 254.

9. James MacGregor Burns, *The Power to Lead: The Crisis of the American Presidency* (New York: Simon and Schuster, 1984), p. 214.

10. John H. Aldrich, *Why Parties? The Origin and Transformation of Political Parties in America* (Chicago: University of Chicago Press, 1995), p. 18.

11. Jimmy Carter, *Keeping Faith: Memoirs of a President* (New York: Bantam Books, 1982), p. 80.

12. The notion of party decline contributing to a more porous political process is discussed in several works. See, for example, Allan J. Cigler and Burdett A. Loomis, "Introduction: The Changing Nature of Interest Group Politics," in Allan J. Cigler and Burdett A. Loomis, *Interest Group Politics* (Washington, D.C.: Congressional Quarterly Press, 1983), pp. 17–20.

13. A. James Reichley, *The Life of the Parties* (New York: The Free Press, 1992), p. 314.

14. Three classic works regarding the dynamics of machine politics include Mike Royko, *Boss: Richard J. Daley of Chicago* (New York: E. P. Dutton, Inc, 1971), Milton Rakove, *Don't Make No Waves, Don't Back No Losers* (Bloomington: Indiana University Press, 1975) and Harold F. Gosnell, *Machine Politics: Chicago Model*, 2nd edition (Chicago: University of Chicago Press, 1968). An excellent discussion of the Pendergast machine, the organization

through which Harry Truman emerged, can be found in David McCullough, *Truman* (New York: Simon and Schuster, 1992), chapters 5–6.

15. Consider demographic data regarding Irish males—a core constituency of urban political machines. In 1950, 4.2 percent of first generation Irish males were classified as professional, while 9.5 percent of second generation Irish males were classified as professional. In 1969, 14.1 percent of males of Irish decent were in the professional category. This was slightly higher than the national figure of 13.6 percent. In 1950, 7.6 percent of first generation Irish males were classified as managers, while 11.6 percent of second generation Irish males were classified as managers. In 1969, 19.1 percent of Irish males were in the managerial class compared to 17.0 percent of the nation as a whole. Stephan Thernstrom, editor, *Harvard Encyclopedia of American Ethnic Groups* (Cambridge: Harvard University Press, 1980), p. 541.

16. Colorful commentary regarding political parties as social insurance agencies appears in the classic work by William L. Riordan, *Plunkitt of Tammany Hall* (New York: E.P. Dutton and Co.,Inc. 1963), pp. 27–28. One of the classic statements in this work pertains to the party's role in helping families left destitute as a result of a fire. As ward boss Plunkitt states: "It's philanthropy, but it's politics too—mighty good politics. Who can tell how many votes one of these fires bring me."

17. G. Calvin MacKenzie, "Partisan Leadership Through Presidential Appointments," in L. Sandy Maisel, editor, *The Parties Respond* (Boulder: Westview Press, 1994), p. 342.

18. V.O. Key, Jr., *Politics, Parties and Pressure Groups*, 5th edition (New York: Thomas Y. Crowell, 1964), pp. 355–356.

19. Figures cited in MacKenzie, "Partisan Leadership Through Presidential Appointments," p. 347, Table 14.1.

20. Martin and Susan Tolchin, *To the Victor: Political Patronage from the Clubhouse to the White House* (New York: Vintage Books, 1971), p. 98.

21. Frank J. Sorauf, *Party Politics in America*, 3rd. edition (Boston: Little, Brown and Co., 1976), p. 81.

22. Ann O'M. Bowman and Richard C. Kearney, *State and Local Government*, 2nd edition (Boston: Houghton Mifflin Company, 1993), pp. 218–220.

23. Sidney M. Milkis, *The President and the Parties* (New York: Oxford University Press, 1993), p. 137.

24. Ibid.

25. Key, *Politics, Parties and Pressure Groups*, 5th edition, pp. 356–359.

26. Malcolm E. Jewell and David M. Olson, *American State Political Parties and Elections*, Revised edition (Homewood, Illinois: The Dorsey Press, 1982), p. 95.

27. Gary L. Rose, *Connecticut Politics At The Crossroads* (Lanham: University Press of America, 1992), p. 75.

28. For a discussion of incentives related to political activism see James Q. Wilson, *Political Organizations* (New York: Basic Books, 1973), pp. 36–51. Also, Frank J. Sorauf and Paul Allen Beck, *Party Politics in America*, 6th edition (Glenview, Illinois: Scott, Foresman and Co., 1988), pp. 102–113.

29. In addition to the classic works on machine politics, two recent essays capture this tradition. Arthur Schlesinger, Jr., "Faded Glory," *New York Times Magazine*, July 12, 1992, and Tom Wicker, "Let Some Smoke In," *New York Times Magazine*, June 14, 1992.

30. Theodore H. White, *The Making of the President 1972* (New York: Bantam Books, 1973), p. 90.

31. Sorauf and Beck, *Party Politics in America*, passim; Key, *Politics, Parties and Pressure Groups*, p. 179.

32. Theodore Roosevelt received 4,216,020 popular votes and 88 electoral votes; Robert LaFollette received 4,822,856 popular votes and 13 electoral votes; and Henry Wallace received 1,157,172 popular votes and 0 electoral votes. Source: *The World Almanac and Book of Facts* (Mahwah: Funk and Wagnalls, 1993).

33. Nelson W. Polsby and Aaron Wildavsky, *Presidential Elections* 8th edition (New York: Free Press, 1991), p. 122.

34. For example, in the 1968 Democratic nominating process, Senator Eugene McCarthy won 72 percent of the primary vote in Pennsylvania, yet Hubert Humphrey received 80 percent of the Pennsylvania delegation's vote at the Democratic National Convention. In Illinois, Robert Kennedy and McCarthy collectively received two-thirds of the primary vote. At the convention however, Humphrey received 95 percent of the votes from the Illinois delegation. Information obtained from William Crotty, *Party Reform* (New York: Longman, 1983), pp. 26–27.

35. Several works regarding the 1968 Democratic Convention and the reforms that followed are readily available. See Crotty, *Party Reform*, chapters 3–4, Lester G. Seligman and Carry R. Covington, *The Coalitional Presidency* (Chicago: The Dorsey Press, 1989), pp. 54–57. My discussion of the 1968 Convention is based primarily on my own recollections of the event, which I watched on television, and Crotty's concise description.

36. An excellent study of the Wallace phenomenon is Jody Carlson, *George C. Wallace and the Politics of Powerlessness: The Wallace Campaigns for the Presidency, 1964–1976* (New Brunswick, N.J.: Transaction Books, 1981), chapters 7–9 pertain to the 1968 election.

37. Crotty, *Party Reform*, p. 21.

38. The first reform commission was the Commission on Party Structure and Delegate Selection, known as the McGovern-Fraser Commission. This commission, in operation from 1969–1972, was responsible for extremely broad and sweeping nominating reforms. This was followed by several other Democratic reform commissions through 1984 which essentially made modifications to McGovern-Fraser guidelines. A chronological chart of Democratic reform commissions through 1980 is found in Crotty, *Party Reform*, pp. 40–43.

39. Everett Carll Ladd, Jr., *Where Have All the Voters Gone?* 2nd edition (New York: W.W. Norton, 1982), p. 56. A full review of Republican Party reform efforts can be found in Crotty, *Party Reform*, pp. 205–232. Although the Republican Party has been affected by Democratic reform efforts (most notably by the proliferation of presidential primary laws), this is not to suggest that reforms within the Republican Party have proceeded at the same pace or have had the same democratizing impact as that of the Democrats. As Crotty states, Republican reforms "lack the bite of the Democratic proposals," p. 217.

40. Crotty, *Party Reform*, pp. 138–152.

41. Among the many works that discuss candidate-centered presidential campaigns is Robert Agranoff, editor, *The New Style In Election Campaigns*, 2nd edition (Boston: Holbrook Press, Inc., 1976).

42. Jimmy Carter is a good example of a self-starting candidate who essentially circumvented the formal party organization. In the early stages of the presidential nominating contest, Carter was referred to by the party establishment and the media as "Jimmy Who?".

43. Lester G. Seligman and Carry R. Covington, *The Coalitional Presidency* (Chicago: The Dorsey Press, 1989), p. 33. This book is especially relevant for understanding the interrelationship between party decline and the crisis in presidential leadership. The unpredictable and shifting nature of governing coalitions underscores the importance of strong political parties as stabilizing forces in the governing process. This is one of the very best books on the subject.

44. Examples from the 1992 presidential nominating contest include the South Dakota primary with 26 percent of registered voters voting, 25 percent in the Colorado primary, 20 percent in South Carolina, 21 percent in Mississippi, 18 percent in Michigan, and 16 percent in Connecticut. Source: *New York Times*, March 26, 1992, A18. The average primary turnout during the 1988 presidential nominating contest was 24 percent. Source: *ABC News, The 88 Vote* (New York: Capital Cities/ABC, 1988), xix.

45. Consider some recent evidence from the 1992 nominating campaign. In 10 of the 32 primaries in which Clinton was declared the winner, he received a plurality rather than a majority of the votes. *1992 Presidential*

Primary Election Results (Washington, D.C.: Federal Election Commission, 1992). In 1976, Jimmy Carter won the New Hampshire primary with 28 percent of the vote, thereby establishing himself as the Democratic frontrunner. See Gary R. Orren and Nelson W. Polsby, editors, *Media and Momentum: The New Hampshire Primary and Nomination Politics* (New Jersey: Chatham House Publishers, 1987), p. 191.

46. See Jeanne Kirkpatrick, *The New Presidential Elite* (New York: Russell Sage Foundation, 1976), chapter 9. As Kirkpatrick notes: "The dynamics of preconvention competition make it extremely likely that factions will coalesce around the candidacies of persons competing for the presidential nomination," p. 262. Another very thorough work which raises serious questions regarding the representative quality of primary contests is James I. Lengle, *Representation and Presidential Primaries: The Democratic Party in the Post–Reform Era* (Westport, Connecticut: Greenwood Press, 1981). In Lengle's view, primary elections resulting in unrepresentative outcomes will inevitably yield weaker, one-term presidents and "stronger bureaucratic or Congressional leadership." p. 117.

47. John H. Kessel, *Presidential Campaign Politics*, 4th edition (Pacific Grove, California: Brooks/Cole Publishing Company, 1992), p. 123.

48. Stephen E. Frantzich, *Political Parties in the Technological Age* (New York: Longman, 1989), p. 208.

49. Ibid., p. 209

50. Kessel, *Presidential Campaign Politics*, 4th edition. p. 139.

51. In 1984, the Reagan/Bush campaign spent $27 million on campaign ads, while the Mondale/Ferraro campaign spent $23 million. Stephen J. Wayne, *The Road to the White House*, 3rd edition (New York: St. Martin's Press, 1992), p. 209. In 1988, the Bush/Quayle campaign spent $31.5 million for television ads, while the Dukakis/Bentsen campaign budgeted $30 million. Wayne, *The Road to the White House 1992*, 4th edition, pp. 212–213.

52. Larry Sabato, *The Rise of Media Consultants* (New York: Basic Books, Inc., 1981), p. 3.

53. Larry Sabato, *The Party's Just Begun: Shaping Political Parties for America's Future* (Glenview, Illinois: Scott, Foresman and Company, 1988), pp. 77–86. For a comprehensive review of recent party organizational developments at the state level, see Cornelius P. Cotter, James L. Gibson, John F. Bibby and Robert J. Huckshorn, *Party Organizations in American Politics* (Pittsburgh: University of Pittsburgh Press, 1989).

54. Rose, *Connecticut Politics At The Crossroads*, p. 77.

55. Jack Dennis, "Trends in Public Support for the Two Party System," *British Journal of Political Science* 5 (1975), pp. 187–230.

56. Ibid., p. 230.

57. ABC News/Washington Post, June 24–28, 1992. Population size = 1,007 adults. Telephone poll. Data obtained from the Roper Center at the University of Connecticut, Storrs.

58. Louis Harris and Associates, July 17–19, 1992. Population size = 1,256 adults. Telephone poll. Data obtained from the Roper Center at the University of Connecticut, Storrs.

59. Ibid.

60. Census Bureau through 1984, Voter Research and Surveys for 1988 and 1992. Figures cited in the *New York Times*, November 5, 1992, p. B4.

61. Norman H. Nie, Sidney Verba and John Petrocik, *The Changing American Voter*, enlarged edition (Cambridge: Harvard University Press, 1979.

62. John F. Bibby, *Politics, Parties and Elections in America*, 2nd edition (Chicago: Nelson-Hall Publishers, 1992), p. 269.

63. Nelson W. Polsby and Aaron Wildavsky, *Presidential Elections*, 8th edition (New York: The Free Press, 1991), pp. 35–36.

64. Herbert E. Alexander, *Financing Politics: Money, Elections and Political Reform* (Washington, D.C.: Congressional Quarterly Press, 1976), p. 73.

65. Ibid., p. 102.

66. This is a very broad treatment of federal campaign finance laws. For detailed description, see Alexander, *Financing Politics* and Frank J. Sorauf, *Money In American Elections* (Glenview, Illinois: Scott, Foresman and Company, 1988).

67. Jeanne Jordan Kirkpatrick, *Dismantling the Parties* (Washington, D.C.: American Enterprise Institute for Public Policy Research, 1978), p. 14.

Chapter Four

1. Richard Rose, *The Postmodern President* (New Jersey: Chatham House, 1988), p. 270, table 13.1.

2. The Chicago Tribune Poll (1982) ranks Carter among the ten worst presidents, while the Murray Poll (1982) ranks Carter twenty-fifth among thirty-six presidents. Polls presented in Larry Berman, *The New American Presidency* (Boston: Little, Brown and Co., 1987), p. 125, table 4.2.

3. Gerald Pomper, "The Nominating Contests and Conventions" in Gerald Pomper, editor, *The Election of 1976* (New York: David McKay Co., Inc.), p. 10.

4. Burton I. Kaufman, *The Presidency of James Earl Carter, Jr.* (Lawrence: University of Kansas Press, 1993), p. 15.

5. Victor Lasky, *Jimmy Carter: The Man and the Myth* (New York: Richard Marek Publishers, 1979), p. 55.

6. Ibid.

7. Gerald Pomper, "The Nominating Contests and Conventions," p. 11.

8. Hamilton Jordan, *Crisis: The Last Year of the Carter Presidency* (New York: G.P. Putnam's Sons, 1982), p. 328.

9. Lasky, *Jimmy Carter: The Man and the Myth*, p. 190.

10. Edwin Diamond and Stephen Bates, *The Spot: The Rise of Political Advertising on Television*, 3rd. edition (Cambridge: MIT Press, 1992), p. 213.

11. Ibid., p. 224.

12. Ibid., p. 225.

13. Ibid., p. 214.

14. Jules Witcover, *Marathon: The Pursuit of the Presidency 1972–1976* (New York: The Viking Press, 1977), p. 645.

15. Kaufman, *The Presidency of James Earl Carter, Jr.*, p. 20.

16. Quoted in Berman, *The New American Presidency*, p. 314. The problems of the Carter presidency as they relate to party decline and personalized campaigning are concisely treated in pp. 309–322.

17. Jimmy Carter, *Keeping Faith: Memoirs of a President* (New York: Bantam Books, 1982), pp. 69, 80.

18. Robert Shogan, *None of the Above: Why Presidents Fail and What Can Be Done About It* (New York: Nal Books, 1982), p. 12.

19. Lester G. Seligman and Cary R. Covington, *The Coalitional Presidency* (Chicago: The Dorsey Press, 1989), p. 68.

20. Martin Shaffer, "An Aerial Photograph of Presidential Leadership: President Carter's Energy Plan Revisted," *Presidential Studies Quarterly*, vol. XXV (spring 1995), p. 291.

21. Ibid.

22. Ibid., pp. 291–292.

23. Berman, *The New American Presidency* , p. 316.

24. Shaffer, "An Aerial Photograph of Presidential Leadership," p. 292.

25. Ibid., pp. 293–294.

26. Ibid., p. 292.

27. Carter, *Keeping Faith*, p. 80.

Chapter Five

1. A cumulative account of the percentage of delegates secured by the major Democratic and Republican candidates during the 1992 presidential primary elections can be found in Charles D. Hadley and Harold W. Stanley, "Surviving the 1992 Presidential Nominating Process" in William Crotty, editor, *America's Choice: The Election of 1992* (Guilford, Connecticut: Dushkin Publishing Group, 1993), p. 36, Table 3.1.

2. Thomas E. Patterson, *Out of Order* (New York: Vintage Books, 1994), p. 2.

3. David S. Broder, *The Party's Over: The Failure of Politics in America* (New York: Harper and Row Publishers, 1971), p. 239.

4. Wilson Carey McWilliams, *The Politics of Disappointment: American Elections, 1976–1994* (New Jersey: Chatham House Publishers, Inc., 1995), pp. 155–156.

5. Kathleen A. Frankovic, "Public Opinion in the 1992 Campaign" in Gerald Pomper, editor, *The Election of 1992* (New Jersey: Chatham House Publishers, Inc., 1993), p. 123.

6. Ross K. Baker, "Sorting Out and Suiting Up: The Presidential Nominations" in Gerald Pomper, editor, *The Election of 1992*, p. 63.

7. Patterson, *Out of Order*, p. 195.

8. Charles D. Hadley and Harold W. Stanley, "Surviving the 1992 Presidential Nomination Process" in William Crotty, editor, *America's Choice*, p. 37.

9. Ross K. Baker, "Sorting Out and Suiting Up: The Presidential Nominations" in Gerald Pomper, editor, *The Election of 1992*, p. 60.

10. Benjamin Ginsberg, Walter R. Mebane Jr., and Martin Shefter, "The Presidency and Interest Groups: Why Presidents Cannot Govern" in Michael Nelson, editor, *The Presidency and the Political System*, 4th edition (Washington, D.C.: Congressional Quarterly Press, 1995), p. 345.

11. Kathleen A. Frankovic, "Public Opinion in the 1992 Campaign" in Gerald Pomper, editor, *The Election of 1992*, p. 118. Following the Democratic Convention, Clinton obtained a 23 point lead over George Bush.

12. Peter V. Miller, "The 1992 Horse Race in the Polls," in William Crotty, ed., *America's Choice: the Election of 1992*, p. 142.

13. John H. Aldrich and Thomas Weko, "The Presidency and the Election Campaign: Framing the Choice in 1992," in Michael Nelson, editor, *The Presidency and the Political System*, 4th edition, p. 266.

14. Ibid.

15. A copy of President Clinton's address appears in William Crotty, ed., *America's Choice*, pp. 174–179.

16. Charles O. Jones, "Campaigning to Govern: The Clinton Style" in Colin Campbell and Bert A. Rockman, editors, *The Clinton Presidency: First Appraisals* (New Jersey: Chatham House Publishers, 1996), p. 33.

17. My overview of the president's health care reform effort has drawn from three very helpful articles: Barbara Sinclair, "Trying to Govern Positively in a Negative Era: Clinton and the 103rd Congress" in Colin Campbell and Bert A. Rockman, *The Clinton Presidency: First Appraisals*, pp. 111–118; Graham K. Wilson, "The Clinton Administration and Interest Groups" in Campbell and Rockman, editors, pp. 225–230; Paul J. Quirk and Joseph Hinchliffe, "Domestic Policy: The Trials of a Centrist Democrat" in Campbell and Rockman, editors, pp. 274–277.

18. Paul J. Quirk and Joseph Hinchliffe, "Domestic Policy: The Trials of a Centrist Democrat," p. 275.

19. Ibid.

20. Barbara Sinclair, "Trying to Govern Positively in a Negative Era: Clinton and the 103rd Congress," p. 114.

21. Charles Lewis, *Well Healed* (Washington, D.C.: Center for Public Integrity, 1994) p. 1.

22. Ibid.

23. quoted in *Well Healed*, p. 2.

24. Ibid., p. 3.

Chapter Six

1. Theodore J. Lowi, *The Personal President: Power Invested, Promise Unfulfilled* (Ithaca: Cornell University Press, 1985), p. 192.

2. This reform proposal represents the work of Thomas E. Cronin and Robert D. Loevy, "The Case for a National Pre-Primary Convention," *Public Opinion* (December/January 1983): 5–53.

3. An excellent critique of primary elections can be found in James I. Lengle, *Representation And Presidential Primaries: The Democratic Party in the Post-Reform Era* (Westport: Greenwood Press, 1981).

4. See Martin P. Wattenberg, "When You Can't Beat Them, Join Them: Shaping the Presidential Nominating Process to the Television Age," *Polity* 21 (spring 1989): 587–597.

5. For a discussion regarding the failure of the Direct Plan in Congress and the politics which contributed to its defeat, see Lawrence D. Longley, "Electoral College Reform: Problems and Prospects," in *Paths to Political Reform*, William J. Crotty, ed. (Lexington, MA: D.C. Heath and Co., 1980), pp. 140–148.

6. See John K. White, "Reviving the Political Parties: What is to be Done?" in *Improving the Electoral Process*, Michael S. Dukakis and Gerald M. Pomper, editors (New York: Twentieth Century Fund, forthcoming).

7. Larry J. Sabato, *The Party's Just Begun: Shaping Political Parties for America's Future* (Glenview, Il.: Scott, Foresman and Co., 1988), p. 239.

8. Ibid., p. 217.

9. Information based on phone conversation with Republican Party Central Committee staff worker in Iowa.

10. Ibid.

11. Sabato, *The Party's Just Begun*, p. 217.

12. Information based on phone conversation with FEC Information Specialist, December 21, 1994.

13. The Senate bill was S–3, while the House bill was HR 3750. The two bills were passed by both chambers and sent to conference committee for consideration. Neither of the two versions were enacted into law.

14. A copy of the position paper can be obtained from the author who served on the Legal Subcommittee of the Committee for Party Renewal during this reform effort. A previous position paper on campaign finance reform was also issued and filed as testimony before Congress by members of the Committee for Party Renewal in 1979. The Committee has been an active advocate of federal campaign finance reform for close to twenty years.

15. Position paper, March 25, 1990.

16. Alex N. Dragnich and Jorgen S. Rasmussen, *Major European Governments*, 7th edition (Chicago: The Dorsey Press, 1986), p. 75.

17. "Campaign Finance Reform: A Report to the Majority Leader and Minority Leader United States Senate," issued by the Campaign Finance Reform Panel, March 6, 1990.

18. Ibid., pp. 15–16.

19. "Position Paper on Presidential Debates," Committee for Party Renewal, *Party Line* (fall 1986), pp. 4–5.

20. My thanks to the staff of Senator Mitch McConnell for forwarding a copy of the proposed bill. Particular thanks to Melissa B. Patack, counsel to Senator McConnell, for discussing the finer details of the bill.

21. Figure cited in the *Hartford Courant*, September 30, 1994.

22. Stephen J. Wayne, et al., *The Politics of American Government* (N.Y.: St. Martin's Press, 1995), p. 269.

23. Ibid., p. 274.

24. James Pfiffner, "Political Appointees and Career Executives: The Democracy-Bureaucracy Nexus," in Patricia W. Ingraham and Donald F. Kettl, editors, *Agenda for Excellence* (New Jersey: Chatham House, 1992), p. 48.

25. Patricia W. Ingraham and David H. Rosenbloom, "The State of Merit in the Federal Government" in Ingraham and Kettl, *Agenda for Excellence*, p. 287. My discussion is based on the review of court cases in this chapter. It should be noted that on October 6, 1993, President Clinton signed into law amendments to the Hatch Act which allow for more partisan activity on the part of federal civil servants. While such a development is positive from the perspective of party vitality, reform efforts to more effectively connect the president to his party must extend to the reclassification of civil service jobs as well. Extending the appointment power of the president throughout the executive branch, rather than simply relaxing restrictions on partisan activity for career civil servants, is the more direct and politically useful course of action.

26. Sabato, *The Party's Just Begun*, p. 230.

27. A thorough review of leading cases can be found in Jerome M. Mileur, "Legislating Responsibility: American Political Parties and the Law" in *Challenges to Party Government*, John Kenneth White and Jerome M. Mileur, editors (Carbondale: Southern Illinois University Press, 1992), pp. 167–189.

28. For a detailed discussion of the Eu case, see the report by Professor Kay Lawson in a special issue of *Party Line* (1989), published by the Committee for Party Renewal.

29. Sabato, *The Party's Just Begun*, p. 203.

30. The literature containing proposals to strengthen political parties is extensive. See, for example, the American Political Science Association's Committee on Political Parties, "Toward a More Responsible Two-Party System," *American Political Science Review* 44 (September, 1950), pp. 1–14, William J. Crotty, ed. *Paths to Political reform*, A. James Reichley, ed., *Elections American Style* (Washington, D.C.: The Brookings Institution, 1987), Sabato, *The Party's Just Begun*, James W. Davis, *The President as Party Leader* (New York: Praeger Publishers, 1992), A. James Reichley, *The Life of the Parties: A History of American Political Parties* (New York: The Free Press, 1992), Gary L. Rose, ed., *Controversial Issues in Presidential Selection*,

Second Edition (Albany: State University of New York Press, 1994), Robert D. Loevy, *The Flawed Path to the Presidency 1992* (Albany: State University of New York Press, 1995).

31. Nelson W. Polsby and Aaron Wildavsky, *Presidential Elections: Strategies and Structures of American Politics*, 9th edition (New Jersey: Chatham House Publishers, Inc., 1996), p. 53.

32. Paul S. Herrnson, "The Revitalization of National Party Organizations," in L. Sandy Maisel, ed., *The Parties Respond: Changes in American Parties and Campaigns* (Boulder: Westview Press, 1994), pp. 52–56.

33. Ibid., p. 60.

34. Sidney M. Milkis, "The Presidency and the Political Parties" in Michael Nelson, ed., *The Presidency and the Political System*, 4th edition (Washington, D.C.: Congressional Quarterly Press, 1995), p. 361.

35. Quoted in Milkis, "The Presidency and the Political Parties," p. 362.

36. Barbara Sinclair, "Trying to Govern Positively in a Negative Era: Clinton and the 103rd Congress," in Colin Campbell and Bert A. Rockman, editors, *The Clinton Presidency: First Appraisals* (New Jersey: Chatham House Publishers, 1996), p. 93.

37. Ibid.

38. Ibid., p. 94.

39. *New York Times Magazine*, January 28, 1996, pp. 40–41.

40. Ibid.

41. Barbara Sinclair, "Parties in Congress: New Roles and Leadership Trends" in L. Sandy Maisel, ed., *The Parties Respond*, pp. 303–304.

42. Nicol C. Rae, *Southern Democrats* (New York: Oxford University Press, 1994), p. 74, Table 4.2. The decline of sectionalism within Congress is also thoroughly discussed in David W. Rhode, "Electoral Forces, Political Agendas, and Partisanship in the House and Senate," in Roger H. Davidson, ed., *The Post Reform Congress* (New York: St. Martin's Press, 1992), pp. 27–47.

43. Ibid., p. 79.

44. A treatment of Republican realignment in the South can be found in the work of Jack Bass and Walter DeVries, *The Transformation of Southern Politics: Social Change and Political Consequences Since 1945* (New York: New American Library, 1977); also, Nicol C. Rae, *Southern Democrats*, pp. 40–64.

45. The conservatism of the Republican Party was glaringly apparent in the contest for the Republican Party's presidential nomination in 1996. The

first two candidates to withdraw from the nominating contest due to lack of funds and popularity within the party were California Governor Pete Wilson and Pennsylvania Senator Arlen Specter—the only Republican candidates who could legitimately be considered moderate centrists.

46. Charles O. Jones, *Separate But Equal Branches: Congress and the Presidency* (New Jersey: Chatham House Publishers, 1995), p. 250.

47. Ibid., pp. 250–251.

Chapter Seven

1. Alexander Hamilton, "Federalist 70" in Clinton Rossiter, ed., *The Federalist Papers* (New York: New American Library, 1961), p. 423.

2. Ibid.

3. Ibid., p. 424

4. See, for example, Lyn Ragsdale, *Presidential Politics* (Boston: Houghton Mifflin Co., 1993).

5. Terry Eastland, *Energy in the Executive: The Case for the Strong Presidency* (New York: The Free Press, 1992), p. 279.

6. Thomas E. Cronin, *The State of the Presidency*, 2nd edition (Boston: Little, Brown and Co., 1980), p. 244.

7. Erwin C. Hargrove, *The Power of the Modern Presidency* (New York: Alfred Knopf, Inc., 1974), p. 79.

8. Hugh Heclo, "The Changing Presidential Office" in Arnold J. Meltsner, ed., *Politics in the Oval Office: Towards Presidential Governance* (San Francisco: Institute for Contemporary Studies, 1981), p. 162.

9. Ibid., p. 166.

10. James MacGregor Burns, *Presidential Government* (Boston: Houghton Mifflin Co., 1966), p. 130.

11. Peter L. Szanton, Reconstructing the Presidency," in Meltsner, ed., *Politics in the Oval Office*, p. 191.

12. Cronin, *The State of the Presidency*, 2nd ed., pp. 257–260.

13. Henry Kissinger, *The White House Years* (Boston: Little, Brown and Co., 1979), p. 39.

14. Hugh Heclo and Lester S. Salamon, editors, *The Illusion of Presidential Government* (Boulder, Co.: Westview Press, 1981), Appendix A, p. 334.

15. Heclo, "The Changing Presidential Office," in Meltsner, *Politics in the Oval Office*, p. 183.

16. Bradley Nash, et al., *Organizing and Staffing the Presidency* (New York: Center for the Study of the Presidency, 1980), pp. 150–151.

17. Szanton, "Reconstructing the Presidency" in Meltsner, *Politics in the Oval Office*, p. 203.

18. Nash, et al., *Organizing and Staffing the Presidency*, p. 156.

19. Ibid., p. 157.

20. Ibid., p. 1.

21. Ibid., p. 163.

22. Cronin, *The State of the Presidency*, p. 289.

23. James MacGregor Burns, *The Deadlock of Democracy* (Englewood Cliffs: Prentice-Hall, 1963), p. 331.

24. Ibid., p. 331.

25. James P. Pfiffner, *The Modern Presidency* (New York: St. Martin's Press, 1994), p. 146. Figures represent bills on which the president took a position.

26. Quoted in Marcus Cunliffe, *American Presidents and the Presidency* (New York: American Heritage Press, 1968), p. 342.

27. Ibid., p. 342.

28. Andrew Taylor, "House Passes Line-Item Veto; Long Road Ahead in Senate," *Congressional Quarterly* (February 11, 1995): 441.

29. Russell M. Ross and Fred Schwengel, "An Item Veto for the President?" *Presidential Studies Quarterly*, vol. XII (winter 1982): 70.

30. HRC *Legislative Digest*, vol. 24, no. 4 (January 28, 1995).

31. Louis Fisher, "Should Congress Grant the President Line Item Veto or Expanded Recision Authority?" *Congressional Digest* (February 1993): 45.

32. Taylor, "House Passes Line Item Veto," p. 442.

33. Judith A. Best, "The Item Veto: Would the Founders Approve?" *Presidential Studies Quarterly*, vol. XIV (spring 1984): 188.

34. Fisher, "Should Congress Grant the President Line Item Veto or Expanded Recission Authority?", p. 49.

35. George F. Will, "The Presidency In The American Political System," *Presidential Studies Quarterly*, vol. XIV (summer 1984): 327.

36. Ibid.

37. Robert Dornan, "Should Congress Grant the President Line Item Veto or Expanded Recission Authority?" *Congressional Digest* (February 1993): 52.

Chapter Eight

1. Wilfred E. Binkley, *President and Congress*, Revised 3rd edition (New York: Vintage Books, 1962), p. 11.

2. Richard Pious, *The American Presidency* (New York: Basic Books, Inc., 1979), p. 19.

3. Forrest McDonald, *The American Presidency* (Lawrence: University Press of Kansas, 1994), pp. 147–149.

4. Henry Steele Commager, *The Defeat of America: Presidential Power and the National Character* (New York: Simon and Schuster, 1974), p. 126.

5. Donald Robinson, "The Inventors of the Presidency," *Presidential Studies Quarterly*, vol. XIII (winter 1983): 8.

6. Ibid. p. 13.

7. Ibid. p. 10.

8. Sidney M. Milkis and Michael Nelson, *The American Presidency: Origins and Development 1776–1993*, 2nd edition (Washington, D.C.: Congressional Quarterly Press, 1994), p. 30.

9. Arthur Schlesinger, Jr., *The Cycles of American History* (Boston: Houghton Mifflin Co., 1986), p. 285.

10. Adlai Stevenson, III, "The Presidency—1984," *Presidential Studies Quarterly*, vol. XIV (winter 1984): 18.

11. George McGovern, "Considerations on Our Political Process," *Presidential Studies Quarterly*, vol. XIV (summer 1984): 341.

12. Milkis and Nelson, *The American Presidency*, p. 82.

13. Ibid.

14. James Thomas Flexner, *George Washington and the New Nation, 1783–1793*, vol. III (Boston: Little, Brown and Co., 1969), pp. 370–371.

15. Milkis and Nelson, *The American Presidency*, pp. 84–85.

16. Glen A. Phelps, "George Washington and the Paradox of Party," *Presidential Studies Quarterly*, vol. XIX (fall 1989): 734.

17. James W. Davis, *The President as Party Leader* (New York: Praeger, 1992), p. 2.

18. Noble E. Cunningham, Jr., *In Pursuit of Reason: The Life of Thomas Jefferson* (Baton Rouge: Louisiana State University Press, 1987), p. 268.

19. Morton Borden, "Jefferson," in *America's Ten Greatest Presidents*, Morton Borden, ed. (Chicago: Rand McNally Co., 1961), p. 63.

20. Alf J. Mapp, Jr., *Thomas Jefferson* (Lanham: Madison Books, 1991) p. 21.

21. James MacGregor Burns, *The Deadlock of Democracy* (Englewood Cliffs: Prentice-Hall, 1963), p. 36.

22. George Fort Milton, *Presidential Power 1789–1943* (New York: Octagon Books, 1980), p. 72.

23. Burns, *The Deadlock of Democracy*, p. 39.

24. Edward S. Corwin, *The President: Office and Powers 1787–1984*, revised 5th edition (New York: New York University Press, 1984), p. 21.

25. Robert Remini, *The Legacy of Andrew Jackson* (Baton Rouge: Louisiana State University Press, 1988), pp. 8–43.

26. William N. Chambers, "Jackson" in *America's Ten Greatest Presidents*, Morton Borden, ed. (Chicago: Rand McNally Co., 1961), p. 83.

27. Corwin, *The President: Office and Powers 1787–1984*, p. 21.

28. Remini, *The Legacy of Andrew Jackson*, p. 8.

29. Remini, *The Life of Andrew Jackson* (New York: Harper and Row, 1988), p. 307.

30. Marquis James, *The Life of Andrew Jackson* (Indianapolis: The Bobbs-Merill Co., 1938), p. 610.

31. Remini, *The Legacy of Andrew Jackson*, p. 2.

32. Clinton Rossiter, *The American Presidency*, 2nd edition (New York: The New American Library, 1960), p. 100.

33. Charles A. McCoy, *Polk and the Presidency* (Austin: University of Texas Press, 1960), p. 81.

34. Ibid.

35. Norman A. Graebner, "James Polk" in *America's Ten Greatest Presidents*, Morton Borden, ed. (Chicago: Rand McNally Co., 1961), p. 115.

36. McCoy, *Polk and the Presidency*, p. 225.

37. Paul H. Bergeron, "President Polk and Economic Legislation," *Presidential Studies Quarterly*, vol. XV (fall 1985): 783.

38. Quoted in Bergeron, "President Polk and Economic Legislation," p. 783.

39. McCoy, *Polk and the Presidency*, p. 82.

40. Davis, *The President as Party Leader*, p. 8.

41. This includes the Schlesinger Poll (1948), the Schlesinger Poll (1962), the Maranell Accomplishment Poll (1970), the U.S. Historical Society Poll (1977), the Chicago Tribune Poll (1982), and the Murray Poll (1982). See Larry Berman, *The New American Presidency* (Boston: Little, Brown and Co., 1987), pp. 124–125.

42. Alexander Groth, "Lincoln and the Standards of Presidential Conduct," *Presidential Studies Quarterly*, vol. XXII (fall, 1992): 765.

43. Ex Parte Merryman, (1861).

44. Ex Parte Milligan, (1866).

45. Groth, "Lincoln and the Standards of Presidential Conduct," p. 767.

46. Eric L. McKitrick, "Party Politics and the Union and Confederate War Efforts" in William Nisbet Chambers and Walter Dean Burnham, editors, *The American Party Systems: Stages of Development* 2nd edition (London: Oxford University Press, 1979), pp. 117–151.

47. Davis, *The President as Party Leader*, p. 9.

48. McKitrick, "Party Politics and the Union and Confederate War Efforts," p. 123.

49. Ibid., p. 131.

50. Ibid., pp. 134–139.

51. Ibid., p. 145.

52. James MacGregor Burns, *The Workshop of Democracy* (New York: Alfred A. Knopf, 1985), p. 213.

53. Ibid., pp. 213–214.

54. Ibid., p. 217.

55. Nathan Miller, *Theodore Roosevelt: A Life* (New York: William Morrow and Co., Inc., 1992), p. 356.

56. Ibid., p. 357.

57. Willard Gatewood, Jr., *Theodore Roosevelt and the Art of Controversy* (Baton Rouge: Louisiana State University Press, 1970), p. 11.

58. Lewis Gould, *The Presidency of Theodore Roosevelt* (Lawrence: University Press of Kansas, 1991), pp. 10–12.

59. Gatewood, *Theodore Roosevelt and the Art of Controversy*, p. 13.

60. Nicholas Roosevelt, *Theodore Roosevelt; The Man As I Knew Him* (New York: Dodd, Mead and Co., 1967), pp. 107–108.

61. Gould, *The Presidency of Theodore Roosevelt*, p. 11.

62. Miller, *Theodore Roosevelt: A Life*, p. 358.

63. Theodore Roosevelt, *Theodore Roosevelt: An Autobiography* (New York: MacMillan, 1913), p. 438. Reprinted by DeCapo Press, 1985.

64. Ibid., p. 439.

65. John Morton Blum, *The Progressive Presidents* (New York: W.W. Norton and Co., 1982), p. 10.

66. Arthur S. Link, *Wilson: The New Freedom*, vol. 2 (Princeton: Princeton University Press, 1956), pp. 146–147.

67. Quoted in Link, *Wilson: The New Freedom*, vol. 2, p. 147.

68. A text of this historic speech can be found in Robert I. Vexler, editor, *Woodrow Wilson: 1856–1924* (Dobbs Ferry, New York: Oceana Publications, 1969), pp. 35–37.

69. Link, *Wilson: The New Freedom*, vol. 2, p. 153.

70. Ibid., p. 154.

71. John Morton Blum, *The Progressive Presidents*, pp. 61–106.

72. James MacGregor Burns, *Deadlock of Democracy*, p. 132.

73. Kendrick A. Clements, *The Presidency of Woodrow Wilson* (Lawrence: University Press of Kansas, 1992) p. xii.

74. James MacGregor Burns, *Roosevelt: The Lion and the Fox* (New York: Harcourt Brace and Co., 1956), p. 146.

75. William E. Leuchtenburg, *Franklin D. Roosevelt and the New Deal 1932–1940* (New York: Harper and Row, 1963), p. 2.

76. Ibid., p. 327.

77. James MacGregor Burns, *Roosevelt: The Soldier of Freedom* (New York: Harcourt Brace Jovanovich, Inc., 1970), p. 546.

78. Rossiter, *The American Presidency*, p. 141.

79. Burns, *Roosevelt: The Lion and the Fox*, pp. 375–380.

80. Rossiter, *The American Presidency*, p. 31.

81. Donald R. McCoy, *The Presidency of Harry S. Truman* (Lawrence: University Press of Kansas, 1989), p. 320.

82. David McCullough, *Truman* (New York: Simon and Schuster, 1992), p. 633.

83. McCoy, *The Presidency of Harry S. Truman*, p. 315.

84. Rossiter, *The American Presidency*, p. 154.

85. Godfrey Hodgson, *All Things to All Men: The False Promise of the Modern American Presidency* (New York: Simon and Schuster, 1980), p. 164.

86. Theodore C. Sorensen, *Kennedy* (New York: Harper and Row Publishers, 1965), p. 390.

87. James N. Giglio, *The Presidency of John F. Kennedy* (Lawrence: University Press of Kansas, 1991), p. 29.

88. Sorensen, *Kennedy*, p. 390.

89. Giglio, *The Presidency of John F. Kennedy*, p. 29.

90. Milkis and Nelson, *The American Presidency*, p. 325.

91. Doris Kearns, *Lyndon Johnson and the American Dream* (New York: Harper and Row, 1976), p. 233.

92. Lyndon Johnson, "Comments on the Presidency," in *The Power of the Presidency: Concepts and Controversy*, 2nd ed., Robert S. Hirschfield, editor (Chicago: Aldine Publishing Co., 1973), p. 149.

93. The personalized nature of presidential politics and governance is a pervasive theme in the current literature regarding the American presidency. See, for example, Theodore, J. Lowi, *The Personal President: Power Invested, Promises Unfulfilled* (Ithaca: Cornell University Press, 1985), chapters 4, 5.

94. Kearns, *Lyndon Johnson and the American Dream*, p. 156.

95. Milkis and Nelson, *The American Presidency*, p. 329.

96. The various presidents selected for review in this particular chapter do not reflect any particular bias on the part of the author. Such presidents were selected primarily because presidential scholars routinely identify such individuals as among our best national leaders. Admittedly, the inclusion of Kennedy reflects more of a personal and perhaps generational attachment, rather than an objective assessment of presidential performance. For a review of presidential rankings see Larry Berman, *The New American Presidency* (Boston: Little, Brown and Co., 1987), pp. 124–125.

97. Youngstown Sheet and Tube Company v. Sawyer (1952).

98. Congressional Budget Office, The Projections Unit Budget Analysis Division.

99. Department of Justice, Bureau of Justice Statistics Data.

100. Bureau of the Census, Housing and Household Economic Statistics Division.

101. Ibid.

102. Clinton Rossiter, *The American Presidency*, Revised edition (New York: New American Library, 1962), p. 34.

103. Cecil V. Crab and Kevin Mulcahy, *American National Security: A Presidential Perspective* (Pacific Grove, California: Brooks/Cole, 1991), p. 33.

104. Walter Laquer, *Terrorism* (Boston: Little, Brown and Co., 1977), pp. 104–108.

105. Arthur M. Schlesinger, Jr., *The Disuniting of America: Reflections on a Multicultural Society* (New York: W.W. Norton and Co., 1992), pp. 9–10.

106. *U.S. New and World Report*, October 16, 1995, p.33

107. Ibid.

108. Ibid.

109. Ibid.

110. In this trial, several white Los Angeles police officers were found not guilty of using excessive force against Mr. King, who is black. The trial attracted national attention because the brutal beating of Mr. King was videotaped by a civilian who happened to observe the incident from his apartment's balcony. In a second trial, conducted in federal court, the police officers were found guilty of violating Mr. King's civil rights. The trials are known as the "Rodney King trials" even though Mr. King was the plaintiff, not the defendant in both trials.

111. Pendleton Herring, *Presidential Leadership* (New York: Rinehard and Co., Inc., 1940), p. 14.

112. Avery Leiserson, "Social Unrest and the Presidency," in Charles W. Dunn, ed., *The Future of the American Presidency* (Morristown, New Jersey: General Learning Press, 1975), p. 289.

Bibliography

Aberbach, Joel D. *Keeping a Watchful Eye: The Politics of Congressional Oversight*. Washington, D.C.: The Brookings Institution, 1990.

Agranoff, Robert, ed. *The New Style in Election Campaigns*, 2nd ed. Boston: Holbrook Press, Inc., 1976.

Aldrich, John H. *Why Parties? The Origin and Transformation of Political Parties in America*. Chicago: University of Chicago Press, 1995.

Alexander, Herbert E. *Financing Politics: Money, Elections and Political Reform*. Washington, D.C.: Congressional Quarterly Press, 1976.

Ansolabehere, Stephen, Behr, Roy and Iyengar, Shanto. *The Media Game: American Politics in the Media Age*. New York: MacMillan Publishing Co., 1990.

Barger, Harold M. *The Impossible Presidency: Illusions and Realities of Presidential Power*. Glenview: Scott Foresman and Co., 1984.

Bergeron, Paul H. "President Polk and Economic Legislation," *Presidential Studies Quarterly* 15 (fall 1985): 782–795.

Berman, Larry. *The New American Presidency*. Boston: Little, Brown and Co., 1987.

Best, Judith A. "The Item Veto: Would the Founders Approve?" *Presidential Studies Quarterly*, 14 (spring 1984): 183–188.

Blum, John Morton. *The Progressive Presidents*. New York: W.W. Norton, 1980.

Borden, Morton, ed. *America's Ten Greatest Presidents*. Chicago: Rand McNally Co., 1961.

Broder, David S. *The Party's Over: The Failure of Politics in America*. New York: Harper and Row Publishers, 1972.

Burns, James MacGregor. *Roosevelt: The Lion and the Fox*. New York: Harcourt Brace and Co., 1956.

———. *The Deadlock of Democracy*. Englewood Cliffs: Prentice-Hall, 1963.

———. *Presidential Government*. Boston: Houghton Mifflin Co., 1966.

———. *Roosevelt: The Soldier of Freedom*. New York: Harcourt Brace Jovanovich Inc., 1970.

———. *The Power to Lead: The Crisis of the American Presidency*. New York: Simon and Schuster, 1984.

———. *The Workshop of Democracy*. New York: Alfred A. Knopf, 1985.

Campbell, Colin and Rockman, Bert A. eds. *The Clinton Presidency: First Appraisals*. New Jersey: Chatham House Publishers, 1996.

Carter, Jimmy. *Keeping Faith: Memoirs of a President*. New York: Bantam Books, 1982.

Chambers, William Nisbet. "Party Development and the American Mainstream," in William Nisbet Chambers and Walter Dean Burnham, eds. *The American Party Systems; Stages of Development*, 2nd ed. London: Oxford University Press, 1979.

Choate, Pat. *Agents of Influence*. New York: Knopf, 1990.

Cigler, Allan J. and Loomis, Burdett A. eds. *Interest Group Politics*. Washington, D.C.: Congressional Quarterly Press, 1983.

Clements, Kendrick A. *The Presidency of Woodrow Wilson*. Lawrence: University Press of Kansas, 1992.

Commager, Henry Steel. *The Defeat of America: Presidential Power and the National Character*. New York: Simon and Schuster, 1974.

Committee on Political Parties of the American Political Science Association. "Toward a More Responsible Two-Party System." *American Political Science Review*, 44 (September 1950): 1–14.

Corwin, Edward S. *The President: Office and Powers 1787–1984*, Revised 5th ed. New York: New York University Press, 1984.

Cotter, Cornelius P., et al. *Party Organization in American Politics*. Pittsburgh: University Press of America, 1992.

Cronin, Thomas E. *The State of the Presidency*, 2nd ed. Boston: Little, Brown and Co., 1980.

——— and Loevy, Robert D. "The Case for a National Pre- Primary Convention." *Public Opinion*, (December/January 1983): 50–53.

Crotty, William, ed. *Paths to Political Reform*. Lexington, MA: D.C. Heath and Co., 1980

————. *Party Reform*. New York: Longman, 1983.

————. *America's Choice: The Election of 1992*. Guilford: Dushkin Publishing Co., 1993.

Crovitz, Gordon L. "Micromanaging Foreign Policy." *The Public Interest*, 100 (summer 1990).

Cunliffe, Marcus. *American Presidents and the Presidency*. New York: American Heritage Press, 1972.

Davis, James W. *The President as Party Leader*. New York: Praeger, 1992.

Davis, Margaret N. "The Congressional Budget Mess" in Gordon S. Jones and John A. Marini, eds. *The Imperial Congress: Crisis in the Separation of Powers*. New York: Pharos Books, 1988.

Dennis, Jack. "Trends in Public Support for the Two Party System." *British Journal of Political Science*, 5 (1975): 187–230.

Diamond, Edwin and Bates, Stephen. *The Spot: The Rise of Political Advertising on Television*, 3rd ed. Cambridge: MIT Press, 1992.

Eastland, Terry. *Energy in the Executive: The Case for a Strong Presidency*. New York: The Free Press, 1992.

Edwards, George C. III. *Presidential Influence in Congress*. San Francisco: W.H. Freeman and Co., 1980.

Fisher, Louis. *The Politics of Shared Power: Congress and the Executive*, 3rd ed. Washington, D.C.: Congressional Quarterly Press, 1993.

————. *Presidential War Power*. Lawrence: University Press of Kansas, 1995.

Frantzich, Stephen E. *Political Parties in the Technological Age*. New York: Longman, 1989.

Genovese, Michael A. *The Presidential Dilemma: Leadership in the American System*. New York: Harper Collins, 1995.

Giglio, Games N. *The Presidency of John F. Kennedy*. Lawrence: University Press of Kansas, 1991.

Gosnell, Harold F. *Machine Politics: Chicago Model*, 2nd ed. Chicago: University of Chicago Press, 1968.

Gould, Lewis. *The Presidency of Theodore Roosevelt*. Lawrence: University Press of Kansas, 1991.

Graber, Doris A. *Mass Media and American Politics*, 3rd ed. Washington, D.C.: Congressional Quarterly Press, 1989.

Grossman, Michael Baruch and Kumar, Martha Joynt. *Portraying the President: The White House and the News Media*. Baltimore: Johns Hopkins University Press, 1981.

Groth, Alexander. "Lincoln and the Standards of Presidential Conduct." *Presidential Studies Quarterly*, 22 (fall 1992): 765–777.

Halpert, Leon. "Presidential Leadership of Congress: Evaluating President Reagan's Success in the House of Representatives." *Presidential Studies Quarterly*, 21 (fall 1991): 717–735.

Hargrove, Erwin C. *The Power of the Modern Presidency*. New York: Alfred Knopf, Inc., 1974.

Heclo, Hugh. *A Government of Strangers: Executive Politics in Washington*. Washington, D.C.: The Brookings Institution, 1977.

———. "Issue Networks and the Executive Establishment" in Anthony King, ed., *The New American Political System*. Washington, D.C.: American Enterprise Institute for Public Policy Research, 1978.

———. "The Changing Presidential Office" in Arnold J. Meltsner, ed., *Politics in the Oval Office: Towards Presidential Governance*. San Francisco: Institute for Contemporary Studies, 1981.

——— and Salamon, Lester S. eds. *The Illusion of Presidential Government*. Boulder, Co.: Westview Press, 1981.

Herring, Pendleton. *Presidential Leadership*. New York: Rinehart and Co. Inc., 1940.

Hodgson, Godfrey. *All Things to All Men: The False Promise of the Modern American Presidency*. New York: Simon and Schuster, 1980.

Hrebenar, Ronald J. and Scott, Ruth K. *Interest Groups Politics in America*. Englewood Cliffs: Prentice-Hall, 1982.

Ingraham, Patricia W. and Rosenbloom, David H. "The State of Merit in the Federal Government" in Patricia W. Ingraham and Donald F. Kettl, eds. *Agenda for Excellence*. New Jersey: Chatham House Publishers, 1992.

Johnson, Lyndon Baines. *The Vantage Point: Perspectives on the Presidency*. New York: Holt, Rinehart and Winston, 1971.

Jones, Charles O. *Separate But Equal Branches: Congress and the Presidency*. New Jersey: Chatham House Publishers, 1995.

Kaufman, Burton I. *The Presidency of James Earl Carter, Jr.* Lawrence: University Press of Kansas, 1993.

Kearns, Doris. *Lyndon Johnson and the American Dream.* New York: Harper and Row, 1976.

Key, V.O. Jr. *Politics, Parties and Pressure Groups,* 5th ed. New York: Thomas Y. Crowell Co., 1964.

Kirkpatrick, Jeanne Jordan. *The New Presidential Elite.* New York: Russell Sage Foundation, 1976.

———. *Dismantling the Parties.* Washington, D.C.: American Enterprise Institute for Public Policy Research, 1978.

Koenig, Louis W. *The Chief Executive,* 5th ed. New York: Harcourt Brace Jovonavich, 1986.

Ladd, Everett Carll, Jr. "Political Parties and Governance in the 1980s" in Arnold J. Meltsner, ed. *Politics and the Oval Office: Towards Presidential Governance.* San Francisco: Institute for Contemporary Studies, 1981.

———. *Where Have All the Voters Gone?,* 2nd ed. New York: W.W. Norton, 1982.

Lasky, Victor. *Jimmy Carter: The Man and the Myth.* New York: Richard Marek Publishers, 1979.

Lengle, James I. *Representation and Presidential Primaries: The Democratic Party in the Post-Reform Era.* Westport: Greenwood Press, 1981.

Leuchtenburg, William E. *Franklin D. Roosevelt and the New Deal 1932– 1940.* New York: Harper and Row, 1963.

Link, Arthur S. *Wilson: The New Freedom.* Vol 2. Princeton: Princeton University Press, 1956.

Loevy, Robert D. *The Flawed Path to the Presidency 1992.* Albany: SUNY Press, 1995.

Lowi, Theodore J. *The Personal President: Power Invested, Promises Unfulfilled.* Ithaca: Cornell University Press, 1985.

MacKenzie, Calvin G. "Partisan Leadership Through Presidential Appointments" in Sandy Maisel, ed. *The Parties Respond.* Boulder: Westview Press, 1994.

Maisel, Sandy L. ed. *The Parties Respond: Changes in American Parties and Campaigns,* 2nd ed. Boulder: Westview Press, 1994.

Makinson, Larry. *The Price of Admission.* Washington, D.C.: Center for Responsive Politics, 1993.

McCoy, Charles A. *Polk and the Presidency.* Austin: University of Texas Press, 1960.

McCoy, Donald R. *The Presidency of Harry S. Truman*. Lawrence: University Press of Kansas, 1989.

McCullough, David. *Truman*. New York: Simon and Schuster, 1992.

McDonald, Forrest. *The American Presidency*. Lawrence: University Press of Kansas, 1994.

McGovern, George. "Considerations On Our Political Process." *Presidential Studies Quarterly*, 14 (summer 1984): 341–347.

McWilliams, Wilson Carey. *The Politics of Disappointment: American Elections 1976–94*. New Jersey: Chatham House Publishers, 1995.

Milkis, Sidney M. *The President and the Parties*. New York: Oxford University Press, 1993.

——— and Nelson, Michael. *The American Presidency: Origins and Development 1776–1993*, 2nd ed. Washington, D.C: Congressional Quarterly Press, 1994.

Milton, George Fort. *Presidential Power 1789–1943*. New York: Octagon Books, 1980.

Nash, Bradley, et al. *Organizing and Staffing the Presidency*. New York: Center for the Study of the Presidency, 1980.

Nelson, Michael, ed. *The Presidency and the Political System*, 4th ed. Washington, D.C.: Congressional Quarterly Press, 1995.

Neustadt, Richard E. *Presidential Power and the Modern Presidents*. New York: The Free Press, 1990.

Nixon, Richard M. *In the Arena: A Memoir of Victory, Defeat, and Renewal*. New York: Simon and Schuster, 1990.

Oppenheimer, Bruce. "Declining Presidential Success With Congress" in Richard W. Waterman, ed. *The Presidency Reconsidered*. Itasca: E.E. Peacock Publishers, Inc., 1993.

Orren, Gary R. and Polsby, Nelson W. eds. *Media and Momentum: The New Hampshire Primary and Nomination Politics*. New Jersey: Chatham House Publishers, 1987.

Ornstein, Norman J. and Elder, Shirley. *Interest Groups, Lobbying and Policymaking*. Washington, D.C.: Congressional Quarterly Press, 1978.

Page, Benjamin I. and Petracca, Mark P. *The American Presidency*. New York: McGraw-Hill, 1983.

Patterson, Thomas E. *Out of Order*. New York: Vintage Books, 1994.

Pfiffner, James. "Political Appointees and Career Executives: The Democracy-Bureaucracy Nexus" in Patricia W. Ingraham and Donald F. Kettl, eds., *Agenda for Excellence*. New Jersey: Chatham House Publishers, 1992.

————. *The Modern Presidency*. New York: St. Martin's Press, 1994.

Pious, Richard. *The American Presidency*. New York: Basic Books, 1979.

Price, David E. *Bringing Back the Parties*. Washington, D.C.: Congressional Quarterly Press, 1984.

Ragsdale, Lyn. *Presidential Politics*. Boston: Houghton Mifflin Co., 1993.

Rakove, Milton. *Don't Make No Waves, Don't Back No Losers*. Bloomington: Indiana University Press, 1975.

Ranney, Austin. *The Doctrine of Responsible Party Government*. Urbana: The University of Illinois Press, 1954.

————. *Channels of Power*. New York: Basic Books, 1983.

Reichley, James A., ed. *Elections American Style*. Washington, D.C.: The Brookings Institution, 1987.

————. *The Life of the Parties*. New York: The Free Press, 1992.

Remini, Robert. *The Legacy of Andrew Jackson*. Baton Rouge: Louisiana State University, 1988.

Riordan, William L. *Plunkitt of Tammany Hall*. New York: E.P. Dutton and Co., Inc. 1963.

Robinson, Donald. "The Inventors of the Presidency." *Presidential Studies Quarterly*, 13 (winter 1983): 8–25.

Rose, Gary L., ed. *Controversial Issues in Presidential Selection*, 2nd ed. Albany: SUNY Press, 1994.

Rose, Richard. *The Postmodern President*. New Jersey: Chatham House Publishers, 1988.

Ross, Russell M. and Schwengel, Fred. "An Item Veto for the President?" *Presidential Studies Quarterly*, 12 (winter 1982): 66–79.

Rossiter, Clinton, ed. *The Federalist Papers*. New York: The New American Library, 1961.

————. *The American Presidency*, revised ed. New York: The New American Library, 1962.

Royko, Mike. *Boss: Richard Daley of Chicago*. New York: E.P. Dutton, Inc., 1971.

Sabato, Larry. *The Rise of Media Consultants*. New York: Basic Books, Inc., 1981.

———. *The Party's Just Begun: Shaping Political Parties for America's Future*. Glenville: Scott, Foresman and Co., 1988.

———. *Feeding Frenzy: How Attack Journalism Has Transformed American Politics*. New York: The Free Press, 1991.

Schick, Allen. "The Battle of the Budget" in Harvey C. Mansfield, Sr., ed. *Congress Against the President*. New York: The Academy of Political Science, 1975.

———. "Politics Through Law: Congressional Limitations on Executive Discretion" in Anthony King, ed. *Both Ends of the Avenue*. Washington, D.C.: American Enterprise Institute, 1983.

Schlesinger, Arthur J. Jr. *The Imperial Presidency*. Boston: Houghton Mifflin Co., 1973.

———. *The Cycles of American History*. Boston: Houghton Mifflin Co., 1986.

———. "Faded Glory." *New York Times Magazine*, June 14, 1992.

———. *The Disuniting of America: Reflections on a Multicultural Society*. New York: W.W. Norton and Co, 1992.

Schmertz, Herbert. "The Media and the Presidency." *Presidential Studies Quarterly*, 16 (winter 1986): 11–21.

Schneir, Edward and Gross, Bertram. *Legislative Strategy: Shaping Public Policy*. New York: St. Martin's Press, 1993.

Seidman, Harold. *Politics, Position and Power*. New York: Oxford University Press, 1970.

Seligman, Lester G. and Covington, Carry R. *The Coalitional Presidency*. Chicago: The Dorsey Press, 1989.

Shaffer, Martin. "An Aerial Photograph of Presidential Leadership: President Carter's Energy Plan Revisited." *Presidential Studies Quarterly*, 25 (spring 1995): 287–299.

Shogan, Robert. *None of the Above*. New York: Nal Books, 1982.

Shull, Steven A. ed. *The Two Presidencies: A Quarter Century Assessment*. Chicago: Nelson-Hall Publishers, 1991.

Smith, Hedrick. *The Power Game*. New York: Random House, 1988.

Sorauf, Frank J. *Money in American Elections*. Glenview: Scott, Foresman and Co., 1988.

Sorenson, Theodore C. *A Different Kind of Presidency: A Proposal for Breaking the Political Deadlock*. New York: Harper and Row, 1984.

Stevenson, Adlai III. "The Presidency—1984." *Presidential Studies Quarterly*, 14 (winter 1984): 18–21.

Stockman, David. *The Triumph of Politics: Why the Reagan Revolution Failed*. New York: Harper and Row Publishers, 1986.

Sundquist, James. *Constitutional Reform and Effective Government*. Washington, D.C.: The Brookins Institution, 1986.

Szanton, Peter L. "Reconstructing the Presidency" in Arnold J. Meltsner, ed. *Politics in the Oval Office: Towards Presidential Governance*. San Francisco: Institute for Contemporary Studies, 1981.

Tolchin, Martin and Tolchin, Sandy. *To the Victor: Political Patronage from the Clubhouse to the White House*. New York: Vintage Books, 1971.

Truman, Harry S. *Memoirs*, Vol I. New York: Doubleday, 1955.

Vexler, Robert I., ed. *Woodrow Wilson: 1856–1924*. Dobbs Ferry: Oceana Publications, 1969.

Wattenberg, Martin P. "When You Can't Beat Them, Join Them: Shaping the Presidential Nominating Process to the Television Age." *Polity*, 21 (spring 1989): 587–597.

Wayne, Stephen J. *The Road to the White House*, 3rd ed. New York: St. Martin's Press, 1992.

White, John Kenneth. *The New Politics of Old Values*. Hanover: University Press of New England, 1988.

——— and Mileur, Jerome M., eds. *Challenges to Party Government*. Carbondale: Southern Illinois University Press, 1992.

White, Theodore H. *The Making of the President 1972*. New York: Bantam Books, 1973.

Wicker, Tom. "Let Some Smoke In." *New York Times Magazine*, June 14, 1992.

Will, George F. "The Presidency in the American Political System." *Presidential Studies Quarterly*, 14 (summer 1984): 324–334.

Wilson, James Q. *Political Organizations*. New York: Basic Books, 1973.

Index